D0437927

Patterns of Interracial Politics

Conflict and Cooperation in the City

Institute for Research on Poverty
Monograph Series

Vernon L. Allen, Editor, *Psychological Factors in Poverty*

Frederick Williams, Editor, *Language and Poverty: Perspectives on a Theme*

Murray Edelman, *Politics as Symbolic Action: Mass Arousal and Quiescence*

Joel F. Handler and Ellen Jane Hollingsworth, *"The Deserving Poor": A Study of Welfare Administration*

Robert J. Lampman, *Ends and Means of Reducing Income Poverty*

Larry L. Orr, Robinson G. Hollister, and Myron J. Lefcowitz, Editors, with the assistance of Karen Hester, *Income Maintenance: Interdisciplinary Approaches to Research*

Charles E. Metcalf, *An Econometric Model of the Income Distribution*

Glen G. Cain and Harold W. Watts, Editors, *Income Maintenance and Labor Supply: Econometric Studies*

Joel F. Handler, *The Coercive Social Worker: British Lessons for American Social Services*

Larry L. Orr, *Income, Employment, and Urban Residential Location*

Stanley H. Masters, *Black–White Income Differentials: Empirical Studies and Policy Implications*

Irene Lurie, Editor, *Integrating Income Maintenance Programs*

Peter K. Eisinger, *Patterns of Interracial Politics: Conflict and Cooperation in the City*

In Preparation

David Kershaw and Jerilyn Fair, *The New Jersey Income-Maintenance Experiment, Volume I: Operations, Surveys, and Administration*

Patterns of Interracial Politics

Conflict and Cooperation in the City

Peter K. Eisinger

University of Wisconsin—Madison

ACADEMIC PRESS   New York   San Francisco   London
A subsidiary of Harcourt Brace Jovanovich, Publishers

JS
1112
.E57

This book is one of a series sponsored by the Institute for
Research on Poverty of the University of Wisconsin pursuant
to the provisions of the Economic Opportunity Act of 1964.

Copyright © 1976 by the Regents of the University of Wisconsin
System on behalf of the Institute for Research on Poverty.
All rights reserved.
No part of this publication on may be reproduced or transmitted
in any form or by any means, electronic or mechanical, including
photocopy, recording, or any information storage and retrieval
system, without permission in writing from the publisher.

ACADEMIC PRESS, INC.
111 Fifth Avenue, New York, New York 10003

United Kingdom Edition published by
ACADEMIC PRESS, INC. (LONDON) LTD.
24/28 Oval Road, London NW1

Library of Congress Cataloging in Publication Data

Eisinger, Peter K.
    The patterns of interracial politics.

    (Institute for Research on Poverty monograph
series)
    Bibliography: p.
    Includes index.
    1.   Milwaukee-Politics and government.   2.   Mu-
nicipal government–United States.   3.   Political
participation–United States.   4.   United States– Race
question.   I.   Title.   II.   Series; Wisconsin.
University–Madison. Institute for Research on Poverty.
Monograph series.
JS1112.E57   320.9'775'9503   75-13094
ISBN 0–12–235550–4

PRINTED IN THE UNITED STATES OF AMERICA

For my family

79820

The Institute for Research on Poverty is a national center for research established at the University of Wisconsin in 1966 by a grant from the Office of Economic Opportunity. Its primary objective is to foster basic, multidisciplinary research into the nature and causes of poverty and means to combat it.

In addition to increasing the basic knowledge from which policies aimed at the elimination of poverty can be shaped, the Institute strives to carry analysis beyond the formulation and testing of fundamental generalizations to the development and assessment of relevant policy alternatives.

The Institute endeavors to bring together scholars of the highest caliber whose primary research efforts are focused on the problem of poverty, the distribution of income, and the analysis and evaluation of social policy, offering staff members wide opportunity for interchange of ideas, maximum freedom for research into basic questions about poverty and social policy, and dissemination of their findings.

Contents

LIST OF TABLES   xi
FOREWORD   xv
ACKNOWLEDGMENTS   xvii

1 A Framework for the Study of Interracial Politics   1

The Significance of Blacks in Urban Politics   5
The Existence of Racial Elites   10
Elites and Masses   11
The Elements of Racial Conflict and Cooperation   17
Alternative Relationships in the Politics of Race   20

2 The Survey and the City   31

Basic Methods of the Survey   32

3 Political Integration in the City   51

The Meaning of Political Integration   53
The Measurement of Integrative Elements   59
Conclusions   72

4 Political Goals: The Quest for Community   75

The Nature of Community   76
Conclusion   98

5 Patterns of Conventional Political Participation   101

    An Analysis of Conventional Participation Data   103
    Distinguishing Participatory Styles   105
    Indices of Conventional Political Participation   108
    National and Local Orientation   116
    Racial Cohesion in Electoral Politics: Voting Patterns in Milwaukee   117
    Individual Contacts with Public Officials   119
    Conclusions   123

6 Protest in Milwaukee   125

    Attitudes toward Protest as a Political Tactic   126
    The Uses and Organization of Protest among Blacks and Whites   138
    Some Conclusions   144

7 Conclusions and Implications   147

    A Summary of the Prevailing Patterns   148
    Varieties of Elite Opportunity   160
    Conflict and Cooperation between the Races   165
    Conclusion   166

Appendix A   Derivation of Conventional Political
Participation Indices   169

Appendix B   Questionnaire Used in the Survey   175

INDEX   193

List of Tables

1.1   Four Types of Interracial Political Relationships, Defined in Terms of
Agreement on Integrative Norms, Political Goals, and Political Behavior   22

2.1   Characteristics of the Milwaukee Population (1970 Census) and the Sample
Population (1970 Survey), by Race   34

2.2   Demographic Comparisons among the Second Ten Largest Cities in the
United States   42

2.3   Selected Socioeconomic Comparisons among Populations of the Second Ten
Largest Cities, 1970   44

2.4   Ratio of Black Officeholders to Black Population in the Second Ten
Largest Cities. 1970   49

3.1   Survey Responses Indicating Different Evaluative Orientations toward
Government, by Race   60

3.2   Responses, by Race, to Questionnaire Item 37   65

3.3   Responses, by Race, to Questionnaire Item 39   65

3.4   Responses, by Race, to Questionnaire Item 41   66

3.5   Responses, by Race, to Questionnaire Item 61   66

3.6   Responses, by Race, to Questionnaire Item 64   67

3.7   Responses, by Race, to Questionnaire Item 46   68

3.8   Responses, by Race, to Questionnaire Item 50   69

3.9   Correlations (Gamma) between Respondents' Status and Agreement on
Integrative Norms, by Race   69

3.10   Political Integration Index: Distribution of Response Scores Indicating
Commitment to Integrative Norms, by Race   70

3.11   Correlations (Gamma) between High Integration Scores and Status Variables,
by Race   71

3.12   Responses, by Race to Statements Concerning Attitudes toward
Conventional Political Efficacy   73

3.13 Responses, by Race, to Questionnaire Item 49   74
4.1   Respondents' Identification of Problems Facing the City of Milwaukee, by
      Race   80
4.2   Correlations (Gamma) between Status Variables and Identification of Urban
      Problems in Conventional Terms, by Race   82
4.3   Frequency of Mention of Conventional Types of Urban Problems, by Race   83
4.4   Percentage and Number of Respondents, by Race, Who Had Heard of
      Selected Control-Sharing Programs   86
4.5   Correlations (Gamma) between Status Variables and Having Information
      about Control-Sharing Programs, by Race   87
4.6   Levels of Conceptualization Indicated by Responses Defining "Community
      Control," by Race   88
4.7   Levels of Conceptualization Indicated by Responses Defining "Citizen
      Participation," by Race   89
4.8   Responses, by Race, to Statements Indicating Attitudes toward Local
      Community versus City Government   91
4.9   Respondents' Attitudes toward "Community Control" and the Communitarian
      Perspective, by Race   93
4.10 Responses, by Race, to Questionnaire Item 48   95
4.11 Responses, by Race, Indicating Preferences for the Main Locus of Control
      over Local Public Schools   95
5.1   Political Participation Index Scores, by Race   109
5.2   Voting Turnout in Milwaukee, by Race, 1968   110
5.3   Correlations (Gamma) between Types of Political Participation and Status
      Variables, by Race   113
5.4   Distribution of Respondents' Scores on National and Local Indices of
      Political Participation, by Race   117
5.5   Correlations (Gamma) between Status Variables and National and Local
      Political Participation, by Race   118
5.6   Types of Individual Political Contacts Made by Respondents, by Race   121
5.7   Targets of Individual Political Contacts Made by Respondents, by Race   122
6.1   Types of Reasons Given by Respondents, by Race, for Protest and
      Demonstration by Others   128
6.2   Percentage and Number of Respondents Wanting to See More, Fewer, or No
      Demonstrations, Controlling for Race and for Protest Participation   129
6.3   Responses, by Race, to Statements Indicating Attitudes toward Protest   130
6.4   Socioeconomic Differences between Protesters and Nonprotesters, by Race   134
6.5   Correlations (Pearson's r) between Frequency of Protest and Status Variables
      for Protesters Only, by Race   136
6.6   Percentage and Number of Respondents Owning, Buying, or Renting Homes,
      Controlling for Race and for Protest Participation   137
6.7   Targets of Protest Activity Engaged in by Respondents, by Race   140
6.8   Protester Respondents Who Belonged to Groups Responsible for
      Stimulating Instances of Protest, by Type of Group and by Race   142
7.1   Status of Respondents and Protest Experience, Controlling for Level of
      Conventional Political Activity, by Race   154
7.2   Occupation of Respondents and Protest Experience, Controlling for Level of
      Conventional Political Activity, by Race   155
7.3   Distribution, by Race, of Level of Conventional Activity Combined with
      Participation in Protest   157

7.4   Distribution of Respondents, by Race, According to Category of Score on
      Political Integration Index and Level of Conventional Activity Combined
      with Participation in Protest   162
7.5   Distribution of Major Pockets of Opportunity as Indicated by Mass
      Participation and Integration Patterns, by Race   163
A.1   Correlation (Pearson's *r*) Matrices among Types of Respondents' Conventional
      Political Participation, by Race   170

Foreword

The concentration of the low-income population within both geographic areas and racial groups is now widely recognized. This phenomenon is, perhaps, nowhere more clearly seen than in the central-city ghettos of most major American cities. In large measure a result of the rural–urban migration of the 1950s and 1960s, the populations of these densely populated areas are predominantly poor and largely black. It was the existence of these ghettos and their potential for social tension and violence that was one of the forces motivating the announcement of the "War on Poverty" and the subsequent passage of the Economic Opportunity Act of 1964.

Federal poverty policy, with its focus on local community action involving the participation of the poor, has contributed to the cohesion of ghetto blacks and to an awareness of their potential political power. Moreover, because of the mandated and subsidized participation of local people in the policymaking and resource-allocation functions of these organizations, a group of political leaders endogenous to the community was created. Although representing their community, these leaders—often called "elites" by political scientists—interacted with elected city officials and the city executive bureaucracy. Through this participation and often through their participation in political protests, these leaders became widely known within the city. They, in effect, used their racial and community political base to gain recognition and—to varying degrees—political power within the city.

This development was, in part, a direct legacy of the War on Poverty. Through it, low-income blacks gained a cohesion and a political voice which they, in the absence of federal support, would not have had. Aside from the gains that have accrued to ghetto blacks, this development has had a powerful impact on the structure of urban politics. Increasingly the politics of these large urban areas has become interracial politics.

In this volume, Professor Peter Eisinger explores the implications of this phenomenon on the nature of political relationships in large cities. Has the effect been to stabilize political relationships or to create political instability? Under what conditions will racial groups cooperate or engage in open conflict? In the context of interracial politics, what forces will encourage political leaders to be hardliners as opposed to negotiators, or to engage in flamboyant and dramatic as opposed to low-key behavior? What circumstances must exist to enable either black or white leaders—ultimately dependent upon and loyal to their racial political base—to achieve statesman-like status with the ability to transcend racial lines? It is such questions, basic to understanding contemporary big-city politics, that Professor Eisinger analyzes both theoretically and empirically in this study. Relying on survey data from Milwaukee, he tests hypotheses that emerge from his theoretical propositions and then attempts to draw the implications of these results for urban interracial politics nationally, and for Milwaukee. The importance of these issues to low-income urban blacks in particular, and to urban residents in general, is clear.

Professor Eisinger is an Associate Professor of Political Science at the University of Wisconsin—Madison. Since his appointment to the university faculty, he also has been a Senior Staff Member of the Institute for Research on Poverty, and has served on the Research Advisory Committee of the Institute. His study is a welcome addition to the Institute's Research Monograph Series.

Robert H. Haveman
Director, Institute for Research on Poverty

Acknowledgments

I am grateful to a number of people who have helped me in one way or another to complete this project, and I wish to thank them here. Many colleagues read all or portions of this book in its various stages, including Murray Edelman, Richard Merelman, Booth Fowler, Joel Grossman, Michael Lipsky, Ira Sharkansky, Allan Rosenbaum, and Paul Schumacher. Several project assistants—Will Sullivan, Floyd Stoner, and Bob Neis—provided unfailing help and have followed the progress of this book with an interest beyond the call of duty. I am thankful in addition for the aid and interest of the members of the Wisconsin Survey Research Laboratory, including Harry P. Sharp, Tracy Noble, and Charles Palit. The book could not have been written without the support of the Institute for Research on Poverty, which provided me with the time and assistance to think about this material over the years. I would like to thank Robert Haveman for his encouragement and Marjean Jondrow, Elizabeth Evanson, and Camille Smith for their fine editorial assistance. I also wish to acknowledge the typing done by the secretarial staff at the University of Essex, whose members responded most generously to a visitor's needs, and the secretaries at the Institute for Research on Poverty for their skilled work. Finally, I must thank the Government and Legal Processes Committee of the Social Science Research Council for the grant that made this survey possible. No responsibility for anything that appears here lies with the Institute for Research on Poverty or the SSRC or any of the many persons who gave aid and advice: The buck stops with me.

A Framework for the Study of Interracial Politics

1

Scarcely more than a dozen years ago, few observers of the American metropolis would have assigned urban blacks a central role in the political life of big cities. For Michael Harrington, writing in the early 1960s, black ghetto dwellers were prominent among those who could be classified as "politically invisible."[1] Few blacks held elective political office in local governments, and, as Edward Banfield and James Q. Wilson noted in their classic text on big-city politics, those who did generally found it necessary to be "politicians first and Negroes second."[2]

Matters have changed substantially in the few years since these and similar assessments were made. In part, this has been a function of a remarkable increase in the urban black population. From 1960 to 1970, the number of blacks in the central cities of the nation's sixty-seven largest metropolitan areas increased by 2.8 million, a leap of 58 percent during the decade. The significance of this massive growth in black population in these cities is enhanced by the simultaneous exodus to the suburbs of nearly 2 million whites.[3]

Mere population growth is scarcely sufficient, of course, to account for the present crucial position of blacks in city politics. Accompanying these population changes, feeding upon the manpower strength they provided but also res-

---

[1] Michael Harrington, *The Other America* (Baltimore, Md.: Penguin, 1963), p. 13.
[2] Edward Banfield and James Q. Wilson, *City Politics* (Cambridge, Mass.: Harvard University Press, 1963), p. 293.
[3] U.S. Government, Department of Commerce News Release, February 10, 1971.

ponding to them, came a host of electoral, ideological, strategic, legislative, and psychological developments of such profound significance for black political capabilities and expectations that the decade of the 1960s justifiably could be characterized, without exaggeration, as one of the single most important 10-year periods in the 300-year political history of American blacks. By the end of the decade, racial considerations probably had become the most important and pervasive criteria in structuring urban political conflict over a range of issues, from housing to education and from crime to health care. Toward the latter part of the 1960s, black population gains had begun to be translated into voting strength with the election of black mayors in Cleveland, Gary, and Newark; and, by 1973, this little group of pioneer black mayors had been augmented by black mayoral victories in Los Angeles, Detroit, Atlanta, Dayton, Grand Rapids, Raleigh, and nearly 100 other towns and cities across the country.

The increasing acceptability, among both races, of the notion of racial autonomy and the heightened visibility of racially defined interests have set a stage on which open political conflict between the races in the city is frequent and intense. But, at the same time, the new and potential strength of the black urban dwellers and their newly racially self-conscious leaders have made them, under certain conditions, desirable allies for some white groups in politics.

Given the increasing extent to which urban political conflict and coalitions are structured by racial interests and racial blocs, it seems important to explore the conditions that are likely to shape these interracial political relationships. At its most general substantive level, then, the purpose of this present inquiry is to contribute to an understanding of some of these factors.

To speak in broad terms of the conditions that shape interracial political relationships, however, is to consider a problem of enormous dimensions. It is immediately apparent that such conditions must embrace ideological considerations, political and social structure, historical and situational factors, group and elite psychology, demographic constraints, and questions of strategy. As a means of reducing the task before us to a practical scope, I have chosen to explore one theme that not only cuts across all of these factors in one way or another but has more general theoretical interest for those concerned with the composition and nature of intergroup political relationships. This theme is the importance of the mass population as a contributing element to the context within which intergroup political relationships are formed and worked out. *Specifically, this book is an attempt to explore from a theoretical standpoint the implications for interracial political relationships of particular empirical configurations of mass behavior and beliefs.*

The argument of the book rests on the following premises, upon which the remainder of this chapter will elaborate.

Premise 1. Blacks have come to represent an increasingly significant, often autonomous, and cohesive political force in American cities.

Premise 2. Leaders or elites (the terms are used here interchangeably) who arise and endeavor to maintain their leadership status in both the black and the white communities seek to lead, and do lead, groups that are defined on a deliberate or a de facto racial basis. These groups come into contact with one another in politics that cut across racial lines in the natural course of events.

Premise 3. In general, those who seek to acquire and maintain leadership positions are dependent on mass followings, in the sense that they are unlikely to gain such positions or persist in them without some degree of mass support or acquiescence. Elites arise and operate, then, in a context in which certain patterns of mass behavior preferences and beliefs contribute to the structure of costs and opportunities that leaders and would-be leaders must confront.

Premise 4. One way in which the dependence of elites on masses is expressed is that elites and elite aspirants, to the extent that they wish to gain or maintain legitimacy as leaders, will take account of central tendencies in mass behavior and belief in their respective racial communities in making strategic choices.[4] These mass patterns also will encourage elites who hold certain strategic predispositions and will discourage others.

Premise 5. The nature of interracial relationships in politics—relationships both of conflict and of cooperation—is, in turn, partly dependent on the strategic predispositions and choices made by the elites who lead racially defined groups.

Before discussing in greater detail the substance of these premises, it is necessary to offer some preliminary definitions and clarifications.

I assume that, in general, the relationships among groups, both organized and unorganized, in political enterprises are forged ultimately by elites or leaders. When I speak of elites, I mean to include those leaders or spokesmen of actual or potential groups who attain positions of preeminence through formal appointment, hiring, drafting, succession, election, or self-appointment. Thus, elected officials, interest-group leaders, those who acquire that vague status of "community spokesmen," bureaucrats, and leaders of political movements, stable and ad hoc, may be included in the notion of "elites" as it is used here.

The incumbents of these positions and those who aspire to them are of theoretical interest for us only insofar as they seek to speak for, lead, or mobilize a group in politics. Like the notion of elite, that of "group" covers a broad

---

[4]This assumption of rationality on the part of elites is essentially based on the Downsian model. It seems reasonable to suppose that, in general, leaders wish to maintain their status and aspirants wish to achieve such status. The most rational policy, therefore, is to maximize the support that enables a leader to achieve his objectives. This he can do by pursuing strategies that converge with majority predispositions. For an application of this rationalistic model to various aspects of politics, see Anthony Downs, *An Economic Theory of Democracy* (New York: Harper and Row, 1957).

territory. Groups may be organized in a formal sense. Civil rights organizations, churches, neighborhood associations, and political parties and movements are all examples of organized groups. Groups also may be unorganized, quasi-organized, or potential, as, for example, the black "community," electoral blocs, or the unaffiliated sympathizers of a cause or movement.

In postulating the dependence of elites on mass groupings, I should make it clear that I do not mean to imply that elites have no influence over mass behavior and belief; they are not puppets. We know that elites can mold mass opinion and provide cues and opportunities for political action.[5] We also know, from a large body of research, that the low degree of convergence between mass and elite commitments to democratic norms often means that elites operate without the active support or scrutiny of the mass. What is important to stress, however, is that, under certain conditions, especially where questions of strategic choice requiring a mass response are concerned, influence and constraint work in both directions, from elites to masses and from masses to elites. Furthermore, it is important to point out that mass preferences, expressed through behavior or opinion, are not always malleable; they often remain unyielding to elite manipulation, forcing would-be leaders to work within the limits imposed on them by the tolerance and capabilities of their followers. In addition, many elites do not find it in their interests to seek to influence and change mass patterns of behavior and belief. A more common elite pattern, particularly among those who seek leadership status and especially in the era of opinion polling, is to ride the opportunities provided by *existing* mass predilections. I shall argue that, theoretically, these mass patterns may be seen as important factors in helping to structure the context of opportunities, constraints, and costs that bear on elites in forging interracial political relationships of conflict and cooperation.

The mass patterns found in one American city form the central empirical element of the book. The study is based on an examination of mass-level survey data collected in the black and white communities of Milwaukee. The question of which mass patterns in particular are important for this inquiry is discussed later in the chapter. It should be noted at the outset that I do not present systematic data on how elites actually respond to the patterns of mass behavior and belief. What I have sought to do is to present a careful empirical description of the pressures on elites generated at the mass level and to set these mass-level data into a theoretical framework that suggests their importance. Where possible, I have illustrated with examples of elite response the validity of the theoretical argument I construct.

Finally, I have considered the nature, or forms, of interracial political relationships. Basically, I argue that intergroup political relationships can be arrayed

[5] Robert Dahl, *Who Governs?* (New Haven, Conn.: Yale University Press, 1961), p. 164.

across a continuum of varieties of conflict and cooperation. Elites lead their respective groups in different forms of political conflict or into different types of coalitions (cooperation) in the pursuit of electoral office or in quest of favorable governmental or private institutional decisions. The nature of the conflict–cooperation continuum is discussed in the last section of this chapter.

The Significance of Blacks in Urban Politics

Much of the analysis in this book is based on the premise that it often is appropriate to view urban racial communities as relatively distinctive, occasionally cohesive political groups, at least insofar as they establish a basic set of elite opportunities and constraints. These opportunities and constraints create a particular mood by which elites in the respective racial communities must assess their strategic options. In this section, I shall attempt to justify an analytical strategy that employs mass racial comparisons by showing that, with modest qualifications, it is perfectly accurate to speak of the *black* political community in a city, by which we necessarily imply attributes of relative cohesion, assertiveness, and self-conscious integrity.[6] (It should be said by way of reassurance that, at various stages of the analysis, controls are introduced into the comparisons to take account of the obvious and sometimes important dimensions of heterogeneity in both black and white racial communities.)

To speak of distinctive racial political communities and to elevate the racial cleavage to a position of prime importance in urban politics is to imply, first, that the two racial communities establish contexts for leadership that differ from one another in certain respects. This is true in part, to give only one example, because members of the different races frequently hold markedly different attitudes with regard to the range of appropriate and permissible modes of political action. (We shall see later, for example, how racial attitudes toward political protest and violence differ.) But it is also true, in a more general sense, to the degree to which black thinking about politics, at the mass as well as at the elite level, is centrally dominated by the problem of how to deal with whites and white supremacy.[7] In contrast, it is clear that the difficulties and strategies involved in coping with the other race scarcely can be said to be a primary defining feature of the context of white politics. Thus, the context within which black leaders arise and operate is different in certain ways from the one in which their white counterparts work.

---

[6] Such a perspective finds much justification in the literature. In one of the most recent examples, Holden speaks of the two races in America as constituting two "nations," especially insofar as blacks and whites regard each other as different and exclusive moral communities. Matthew Holden, *The Politics of the Black "Nation"* (New York: Chandler, 1973), p. 1.

[7] Ibid., p. 42.

The black political community, in particular, functions as an identifiable and relatively cohesive entity in more ways than simply as a distinctive setting for political leadership. It can, and does, frequently act to differentiate itself from the white community by taking independent and internally cohesive political action. This is especially (but not exclusively) true at the mass level, where the intricacies of elite factional disputes are obscured by the necessities of the greater clash between the races. A good example of racial solidarity can be seen in the runoff election for mayor of Atlanta in 1973, when the black population, after a frequently bitter intraracial primary battle, united to defeat the white incumbent, Sam Massell.

In short, there is justification for viewing black urban populations as constituting racial political communities, distinctive from white political communities and capable of independent and cohesive action. In order to understand the implications of this view, however, one must, first, break away from the conventional historical interpretation of the black role in urban politics, and second, overcome the resistance of those who insist on stressing the heterogeneity of the black community and its inability to resolve internal tensions in order to present a united racial front.

The historical interpretation holds that blacks traditionally have gained whatever minor influence they had in city politics as auxiliaries or adjuncts of white political machines and power structures. As recently as the end of the decade of the 1950s, blacks still were generally subordinate and dependent participants in the competition among white ethnics or in the clash between political machines and reformers. James Q. Wilson, reporting on his study of Negro politics in Chicago, could write, with some degree of confidence in the general applicability of his observation, that the extent of black political organization was dependent upon the extent of white political organization, and that the fortunes of the former were wedded to those of the latter.[8] The situation was similar in other parts of the country. Hanes Walton wrote, for example:

> In New York blacks were involved in Tammany Hall. . . . In Memphis blacks were part of the Crump machine. In Richmond blacks were a part of the Byrd dynasty, and in Kansas City they were part of the Pendergast machine. . . . Each white machine had its black "submachine." A black boss was picked to secure black votes to support the white machine. The black electorate was in every instance subordinate to and manipulated by the white machine.[9]

Other students of black politics provided a host of substantiating evidence to this effect for other cities.[10] Under such circumstances, the likelihood of overt

---

[8] James Q. Wilson, *Negro Politics* (New York: Free Press, 1960), p. 23.

[9] Hanes Walton, *Black Politics* (Philadelphia: J. P. Lippincott, 1972), pp. 57-58.

[10] Daniel Thompson, for example, writes of New Orleans circa 1960: "Because whites, in the biracial New Orleans social system, have a near monopoly of social power, it would be

competition between the races for the prizes of city politics or the voluntary interracial coalescence of independent forces was problematic at best. The patterns of interracial political relationships took their form in a hierarchical context in which position and influence were functions of race.

A variant of the view of blacks as urban auxiliaries that focuses on their role outside of or beyond the machine context finds expression even now in the colonial analogy. From this perspective, the function of the ghetto is to serve the needs of the imperial white society. Two proponents of this view, Stokely Carmichael and Charles Hamilton, interpret black politics in terms of a process of co-optation, involving the development of "an entire class of 'captive leaders' in the black communities . . . beholden to the white power structure."[11]

Although there was much accuracy in these observations in the past, there are powerful reasons to reject them now in favor of a perspective that emphasizes the growing independence and differentiation of blacks from whites in the pursuit of urban politics. Roland Warren cites at least four factors that have contributed to these developments: the organization of poor blacks, the ghetto riots, black power ideologies, and the move toward decentralization.[12] All of this ferment, we may add, has come at a time when the growth of black population in the central cities has made the achievement of certain black political goals a genuine possibility.[13]

Some observers argue, in spite of these developments, that the social and ideological heterogeneity of the black community provides sufficient reason for resisting an interpretation of urban politics that emphasizes the centrality of the racial cleavage and the growing independence, if not autonomy, of the black

---

meaningless to discuss Negro leadership as though it were isolated from white influence. Actually, in any biracial system composed of a relatively powerless minority and a powerful majority, the patterns of intergroup leadership are determined very largely by the majority group." *The Negro Leadership Class* (Englewood Cliffs, N.J.: Prentice-Hall, 1963), pp. 58-59. Donald R. Matthews and James W. Prothro saw the influence of Negro leaders throughout the South restricted to the black subcommunity, without power in the community at large. *Negroes and the New Southern Politics* (New York: Harcourt, Brace, and World, 1966), p. 178. Edward Banfield, in studies done in the early 1960s, saw blacks and black problems relegated to a position of secondary influence and concern in northern cities like Boston and Los Angeles. *Big City Politics* (New York: Random House, 1965), pp. 49, 90.

[11] Stokely Carmichael and Charles V. Hamilton, *Black Power* (New York: Vintage, 1967), p. 13.

[12] Roland Warren, "Politics and the Ghetto System," in *Politics and the Ghettos*, ed. Roland Warren (New York: Atherton, 1969), p. 28.

[13] To give one example, the number of black elected officials in cities has increased rapidly in the last few years. According to the annual reports entitled *National Roster of Black Elected Officials*, compiled by the Joint Center for Political Studies (Atlanta, 1970, 1971, 1972 and 1973), the number of black mayors, city councilmen, and other municipal officials nationwide increased from 623 in 1970 to 1053 in 1973. The number of black elected school board members rose from 362 in 1970 to 744 in 1973.

political community. To focus on black cohesion and racial independence is, these writers argue, an oversimplification of the matter. Bayard Rustin, for example, writes: "The notion of the undifferentiated black community is the intellectual creation of both whites—liberals as well as racists to whom all Negroes are the same—and of certain small groups of blacks who illegitimately claim to speak for the majority."[14] This position is exaggerated and rigidified by the argument that what in the cities appears, at first glance, to be racial conflict is, on closer inspection, *class* conflict; that the cleavage we observe is economic in character and has little to do with race. After all, the argument goes, middle-class blacks wish to have as little association with poor blacks as do middle-class whites.[15]

Even an impressionistic survey of contemporary intellectual and ideological currents in the black community, which range from the most militant revolutionary doctrines to the standard pleas for maintenance of the old liberal–labor–black coalition, yields sufficiently convincing evidence of political diversity. Furthermore, the class tensions that exist within the black population result in diversity of interests, many of which overlap with white concerns. But it would be naive to ignore both the persistence of the racial cleavage in the city and the demonstrated capacity of racial blocs (white as well as black, it should be said) to achieve coherence. The natural tension among the social classes of the black "nation," as Matthew Holden observes, "has not prevented a substantial measure of collective action."[16] In a variety of circumstances, issues arise in the city that divide the races into relatively cohesive and exclusive groups; differences within these groups—that is, within the black community as well as within the white community—are put aside in deference to generally perceived racial interests.

No better illustration of this can be found than the voting patterns in cities in which blacks have won the mayoralty. In Cleveland in 1967, black wards gave Carl Stokes 95 percent of their vote while all-white wards went over 80 percent for his white opponent, Seth Taft. An estimated 90 percent of those who had voted for Stokes's white opponents in the Democratic primary switched to the Republican Taft in the mayoral election.[17] In Gary, Richard Hatcher received

---

[14] Bayard Rustin, "The Failure of Black Separatism," *Harper's*, January 1970, p. 27.

[15] For an articulation of this point of view, see Edward Banfield, *The Unheavenly City* (Boston: Little, Brown, 1970), pp. 67-87. As Verba and Nie point out, however, even if controlling for class eliminates the effects of race, we still have not eliminated race as a significant social distinction. It is the coexistence of lower social status and race that creates some of the most severe racial tensions in American society. Sidney Verba and Norman Nie, *Participation in America* (New York: Harper and Row, 1972), p. 157.

[16] Matthew Holden, "The Internal Politics of Black Communities: Centrifugalism in the North" (Paper presented at the National Conference of Black Political Scientists, Morehouse College, Atlanta, Georgia, May 7, 1970), p. 48.

[17] Jeffery K. Hadden, Louis H. Masotti, and Victor Thiessen, "The Making of the Negro Mayors, 1967," reprinted in *Big City Mayors*, ed. Leonard I. Ruchelman (Bloomington, Ind.: Indiana University Press, 1969), pp. 128-135.

93 percent of the vote in black wards and 10 percent in white areas.[18]

Michael Parenti's study of the efforts of poor blacks in Newark to gain quite limited goals through political action is particularly instructive concerning the capacity of the white community to achieve cohesion in the face of perceived racial threat. The urban blacks of Newark, Parenti concludes, inhabit the world of the ruled. What especially impresses Parenti is that the *"plurality of actors and interests"* of the (white) ruling world "displayed a remarkable capacity to move in the same direction against some rather modest lower-class claims."[19]

Mutually exclusive racial cohesion of these dimensions is not, perhaps, a condition of daily political life in most cities. Nevertheless, many segments of the black population are coming to emphasize their differences to a decreasing extent. There exist both pragmatic and cultural sources of pressure for black political cohesion. Holden points out, for example, that

> *within the black world, those who want the approval of their audience and constituencies are more likely to get that approval,* and more likely to retain it, *if they maintain that black–white associations in common activity are neither very practical nor (often) desirable instruments to satisfy the hope for deliverance.*[20]

And:

> Once it started to become fashionable to be "black," being black meant something more than admission of one's genotype. *It meant the elevation of the cultural styles of the lower-middle and lower-class black people to places of premier esteem, and the increasing payment of deference to those styles by black people whose ordinary cultural styles would be somewhat different.*[21]

In their study of racial ideology in Detroit, two Michigan scholars find evidence that makes it possible to speak of a black political community, *which crosses class lines,* held together by a common ideology whose elements are race pride, militancy, and distrust of government.[22] Not only are blacks in Detroit developing a sense of racial solidarity in politics, but, Joel Aberbach and Jack Walker find, this solidarity is matched by increasingly bitter resentment by whites. What emerges from their analysis, they conclude, is "the outlines of an ominous confrontation between the races."[23]

[18] Ibid., p. 135.

[19] Michael Parenti, "Power and Pluralism: A View from the Bottom," *Journal of Politics* 32 (1970): 519 (italics added).

[20] Holden, *Black "Nation,"* p. 68 (italics in original).

[21] Ibid., p. 72 (italics in original).

[22] Joel Aberbach and Jack Walker, "Political Trust and Racial Ideology," *American Political Science Review* 64 (December 1970): 1212.

[23] Ibid., p. 1215.

Without question, even in the most tolerant cities, significant parts of both racial communities are antipathetic to one another and express these hostilities in politics. Thus, after making the necessary and proper qualifications, it is possible to employ as a useful focus of analysis the notion of an emergent black politics of major proportions, informed by racial interests that transcend the natural cleavages in the black community. The same may be said for the white community, much of which demonstrates a willingness to coalesce, in politics, simply on racial grounds. To speak, in this context, of the patterns of interracial conflict and cooperation, then, is neither oversimplified nor inaccurate.

The Existence of Racial Elites

A second premise of this inquiry involves the assertion, which we may take almost as a given, that, in large American cities today, there exist leaders in both racial communities who in fact lead or seek to lead groups defined at least in part on a deliberate or a de facto racial basis.[24] For black communities, certainly, this is a statement virtually beyond challenge. Every big city, including Milwaukee, has a host of formal voluntary organizations designed to articulate and foster particularly black interests. Traditional civil rights groups fall into this category. In addition, there is inevitably, especially in this era of federal involvement in the cities, a multitude of public programs that either are designed for clients who happen to be largely black or are located in geographical areas that are predominantly black. These programs give rise to new interest aggregations, provide a basis for new leaders to arise, and provide formal opportunities in the bureaucracy for the development of racial elites. Model Cities, manpower training, welfare, and community action agencies all are examples of such programs. Then too, within many cities, including Milwaukee, there are racially homogeneous electoral districts that send to city councils blacks who become identified as spokesmen for the black community. Finally, there are black political movements of various types, organized around racial ideologies or racial interests, that catapult elites into public view. As these people gain visibility, they come to be seen, and often see themselves, as "black spokesmen." In all of these cases, such black leaders and spokesmen come into contact with white leaders in the political arena and forge relationships based on mutual or conflicting needs.

White communities are not so frequently organized on such a self-consciously racial basis, although whites have organized in Milwaukee to fight open housing and school integration. But many politically relevant organizations (businessmen's, union, and homeowners' groups, for example) and electoral districts are

---

[24] For confirmation of this statement in regard to the present research setting of Milwaukee, see Henry Schmandt, John C. Goldbach, and Donald B. Vogel, *Milwaukee: A Contemporary Profile* (New York: Praeger, 1971), Chapter 6.

de facto racially homogeneous. It should be said that, even when these black and white elites do not enter the political arena to promote interests defined specifically in terms of race, they nevertheless generally must bring together, in conflict or coalition, racially differentiated groups of followers.

Elites and Masses

In order to understand how patterns of mass behavior and belief provide opportunities for and impose constraints on leaders, we must understand the nature of the mutual dependence of elites and masses and the sorts of functions each performs in the process leading up to the establishment of intergroup political relationships.

When we speak of political conflict or cooperation, we usually imply a relationship between or among groups. In general, each group is comprised of elites and followers in a tandem, mutually dependent relationship. There are, of course, exceptions to the dual structure of political groups. Political relationships on occasion may be established by elites *or* masses acting without one another and not needing one another. Elites may compete with other elites, for example, through the judicial process. Litigation generally does not require mass support. Many early civil rights victories were won by elites in the courts long before a mass following had been established and even before the issues were subjects of mass discourse. Likewise, masses without leaders may come into conflict. As Peter Lupsha has pointed out, the race riots after World War I and during World War II in places like Chicago, East St. Louis, and Detroit are examples of political conflict pursued by leaderless masses.[25]

In general, however, the establishment of political relationships among groups involves interchanges among elites acting in conjunction with mass constituencies. Elites and masses in such a relationship are mutually dependent. Mass populations, as organized or potentially organizable political followings, offer elites an important resource. The value of this resource varies: It increases with the willingness of the masses to be mobilized and with their degree of discipline in response to elite directives. But, whatever the value, elites generally are bound to seek the resources masses can offer to support their initiatives and claims.

As we shall see, elites need masses because the latter, as followers, lend credibility to the leadership claims of the former. Mass followings also make credible the threats and promises elites are wont to make. To the extent that elites capitalize on mass responses for these purposes, they will in all likelihood be taken seriously by other elites with whom they seek to establish political relationships of conflict or cooperation.

[25] Peter Lupsha, "On Theories of Urban Violence," *Urban Affairs Quarterly* 4 (March 1969): 275.

The relationship between elites and masses is not of value to elites only. Unorganized masses of people generally have little chance to influence the course of public affairs in a self-conscious way. In order to wield influence, organization—or at least some sense of collective identity—is necessary, and, in either case, leadership normally is required. Elites, then, may help masses not only to mobilize and develop cohesion but also to foster a sense of identity by pointing out commonality of interests and characteristics among members of the mass.

Once elites have performed these basic functions for the masses, the elites continue to be essential in the pursuit of intergroup conflict or cooperation. Strategy must be determined, and decisions about the distribution and application of resources must be made. Communication must occur with the elites of other groups in regard to mutual objectives or disagreements; then negotiation or other bargaining tactics may ensue. At each step of the way, the elites function as mass spokesmen and representatives.

Since masses and elites are clearly dependent upon one another in politics, it would be logically incorrect to suppose that we could understand the behavior and beliefs of one without knowing much about those of the other. As Murray Edelman has written in regard to elite behavior,

> The emphasis in modern leadership theory is . . . upon the willingness of the followers to follow. The implication is that the leader's choices are quite narrowly prescribed by followers' demands. . . . Leadership is a complex thing and we are learning to look for its dynamics in mass responses.[26]

Even when mass demands are not explicitly communicated, elites are sufficiently dependent upon followers, as Dahl argues, to seek to *imagine* what mass preferences might be in order to establish criteria for making policy decisions.[27]

Since our interest here is in the ways in which mass behavior and belief help to structure the possibilities for elite interaction in democratic politics, it is necessary to spell out precisely the nature of elite dependence on the masses. It must be understood, first, that dependence has both positive and negative aspects. Mass resources that may be put at the disposal of elites have an enabling function, a positive aspect of a dependent relationship. But those same resources also may be withheld, constraining elites or forcing them into inaction. Dependence, then, also has its negative side.

Elites may be dependent on masses for the following basic reasons:

1. Masses are crucial for the selection and survival of elites.
2. Masses provide support for elite initiatives.

[26] Murray Edelman, *The Symbolic Uses of Politics* (Urbana, Ill.: University of Illinois Press, 1964), p. 73.
[27] Dahl, *Who Governs?*, p. 164.

3. Masses also impose constraints on elite initiatives.
4. Masses help to structure the context of opportunities within which elites arise and act.

Elite Selection and Legitimation

Since members of the masses need spokesmen to articulate their needs and demands and to represent them in the political arena, the masses (or segments of the mass) must identify or select elites.

Perhaps most commonly, a number of self-identified candidates present themselves as possibilities for leadership status. In order to establish their claim to leadership, elites either must be selected in a process involving formal decisions of choice or must demonstrate the capacity to mobilize followings whose willingness to be led legitimizes their self-identification as leaders. Selection through formal decision may take the form of election, appointment, or hiring. When the selection of leaders is not accomplished through a process of formal decision, the acquiescence of a mass following, organized or unorganized, to the demands, cues, and initiatives of a particular spokesman is sufficient to legitimize his claims to leadership, at least initially.

At other times, the selection of elites occurs without the prior self-identification of leaders or candidates for leadership—without, indeed, overt competition for leadership status. Organized or quasi-organized segments of the mass must seek out and select a spokesman, sometimes from among their number and sometimes from outside the group. Protesters at city hall, for example, may suddenly need to select a spokesman or a delegation to confer with the mayor. Here, the mass identifies, selects, and legitimizes a leader through impromptu election, appointment, or acclamation.

Regardless of how elites are selected by the masses, they are likely to sustain their positions of leadership only as long as some significant proportion of their particular mass following is willing to be led by them. Hence, it is important for elites and their mass constituents to share to some degree certain values and assumptions about the political process. The types of elites who are likely to rise to power and to survive are important considerations in the exploration of the nature of interracial politics.

Mass Support for Elite Initiatives

Once members of the mass have chosen leaders, through either formal or tacit processes, the masses can do much to support elite initiatives. For example, by demonstrating a willingness to be mobilized and by deferring to the leaders' strategies, the masses provide support in political relationships. Discussing protest organization, Michael Lipsky writes that the "leaders' ability to control protest constituents and guarantee their behavior represents a bargaining strength."[28] To the extent that masses allow leaders to control their behavior— say, through their willingness to vote as a bloc or to turn out for a demonstra- tion—they provide support. Masses provide support not only through their overt backing of leadership initiatives and strategy but also by providing skills to help in the mobilization effort. Hence, the organizational capabilities and degree of attentiveness to leadership cues and to public issues found among the masses also provide support for elites. Support for leaders, then, is a function of cohesion within the relevant mass following, the degree to which the elite can control mass behavior, and the cooperation provided by the masses.

Mass Constraint of Elite Initiatives

Elites may be seriously handicapped in pursuing what they believe to be collective interests by the unwillingness of their constituents to follow. In part, they are constrained by the anxieties and the limited capabilities and resources of their followers. Gary Marx found, for example, that, during the peak of the civil rights movement (1964), over one-quarter of his sample of urban blacks were afraid to take part in civil rights demonstrations.[29] Some evidence is avail- able to indicate that, in 1961, black voter registration rates were substantially lower in southern counties, where there existed a long history of lynching and racial violence, than in counties where such acts of intimidation, though present, were less common.[30] Some nonvoting blacks did not go to the polls out of fear of white reprisals.

At other times, leadership initiatives and pleas will fail to elicit a mass re- sponse, owing to a lack of interest, thus undercutting elite efforts. Apathy may exercise as significant a constraint on elites as outright mass opposition, for in political competition, to make claims on behalf of a constituency unwilling to demonstrate its support may be fatal not only to the disposition of the claim but also to the credibility of the leader.

Mass Impact on the Structure of Opportunities

To view the pursuit of intergroup political conflict and cooperation as a process involving simply the interplay between elite initiatives and mass response is to see only part of the picture. The masses, too, have certain pacesetting roles, providing opportunities for elites to follow.

In the sense in which I use the phrase, the structure of opportunities here is a

[28] Michael Lipsky, "Protest as a Political Resource," *American Political Science Review* 62 (December 1968): 1149.

[29] Gary Marx, *Protest and Prejudice* (New York: Harper and Row, 1967), p. 20.

[30] Matthews and Prothro, *New Southern Politics*, pp. 166-168.

function of mass initiatives, attitudes, demands, and behavior preferences. Where any one of these is firmly established among a particular segment of the mass, it offers opportunities to certain types of elites who find the given pattern of behavior or belief congenial. To other would-be leaders, however, such patterns may serve to warn them off infertile ground, where their claims to leadership would not be heeded.

On the one hand, members of the mass may initiate political campaigns, upon whose bandwagon elites may climb. In such a case, the elites are drawn into a political situation by opportunities provided by the masses. The elites may lend support to the effort, they may seize the reins of the campaign, or they may subvert or quell it in some instances, thus gaining stature in the eyes of those antagonistic to the masses.

One example of mass initiative is the spontaneous letter-writing campaign. This may offer legislators an opportunity to hold hearings or to introduce legislation in response. By so doing, they gain recognition as leaders and perhaps solidify their position as leaders by appearing responsive to mass concerns. Another example is the outbreak of rent strikes, which offers some officially situated elites (such as city councilmen) an opportunity to press for housing-code reform, and others, perhaps from among the striking tenants, an opportunity to rise to prominence.[31]

These are examples of unorganized or quasi-organized masses pressing claims through action. When such action is intense and sustained, it gives notice of such deeply felt expectations that action on the part of the relevant established elites becomes almost imperative for their survival as leaders. And whether or not action on their part is forthcoming, it provides opportunities for new elites, emergent "leaders of the people."

The structure of opportunities is not only a function of those mass initiatives that draw elites into a particular political conflict. It is also a product of mass attitudes and mass predilections for styles of political expression. These may not draw elites into the conflict so much as provide a congenial mood or climate for some elites and a hostile environment for others.

We shall find later, for example, that antipathy toward protest behavior is widespread among the white community in Milwaukee, but that sympathy for it, as well as willingness to engage in it, is common among blacks. These attitudes are generalized, in the sense that they do not appear to be focused on any particular protest incident or event. Clearly, then, elites bent on mobilizing broad-based white protest organizations will discover great obstacles in their path. These obstacles may in fact be so great that would-be leaders attracted to protest modes may never choose this route to leadership recognition in the white community or even seek leadership status at all. In the black community, how-

---

[31] See, for example, Michael Lipsky, *Protest in City Politics: Rent Strikes, Housing, and the Power of the Poor* (Chicago: Rand McNally, 1970), pp. 59-62.

ever, opportunities to gain positions of leadership by mobilizing protest groups are much greater, for the climate is responsive to such initiatives. In short, the attitudinal climate, as well as the general state of willingness among the masses to engage in particular forms of political action, provides clear opportunities for predisposed or opportunistic elites and discourages others whose sympathies run counter to those of the bulk of the potential reservoir of followers.

Styles of political expression are not simply a function of modes of popular participation. Different groups may respond to different sorts of leadership rhetoric, and they may pursue different goals. Catchphrases like "law and order" or "community control" appear to have become code words, the meaning of which varies, depending on the race of the user. To the extent that different groups respond differently to such elements of rhetoric, we may say that different climates for elite opportunities exist. Clearly, elites who wish to exploit the tensions or hopes that lie beneath these phrases must choose carefully the communities in which they seek to lead.

In a similar way, different groups may seek different sorts of goals through politics or construct their policy priorities in different ways. The goals of a group are produced by a combination of elite suggestion and projection and the upward communication of spontaneously felt needs of people in the mass. As much as any other process, the articulation of political goals may serve forcefully to winnow aspirants to leadership positions, providing opportunities for some and closing opportunities to others. An obvious illustration is the rise of antiwar spokesmen to positions of power in the national Democratic party; not only did articulation of antiwar sentiments by elites elicit a heavy supportive response among the mass but mass discontent was focused in a search for sympathetic spokesmen.

Finally, the structure of opportunities for elites is a function of attitude patterns of a fundamental nature (as opposed to attitudes toward particular issues). These fundamental attitudes have to do with the nature of the political system and support for it. We shall explore these attitudes in terms of the idea of political integration later on.

Whether or not a polity is integrated politically depends in part on the extent of diffuse support for—that is, favorable attitudes or goodwill toward—the political system.[32] Supportive attitudes of this sort are predicated on the assumption that systematic bias against the interests of any one particular group does not prevail in the political system. In such a nonbias situation, members of the mass exhibit high levels of trust in political elites. This trust is a factor that facilitates elite initiatives; *it represents an opportunity in itself.* The absence of trust is a constraint. William Gamson puts the matter this way:

> The effectiveness of political leadership, then, depends on the ability of authorities to claim the loyal co-operation of members of the political system without having to

[32] David Easton, *A Systems Analysis of Political Life* (New York: Wiley, 1965), p. 63.

specify in advance what such co-operation will entail. Within certain limits, effectiveness depends on a blank check. The importance of trust becomes apparent: the loss of trust is the loss of system power, the loss of a generalized capacity for authorities to commit resources to attain collective goals.[33]

To summarize, this section has been devoted to a brief theoretical exploration of the ways in which mass behavior and belief help to structure the opportunities for elite ascendance and to provide opportunities, support, and constraint for elite initiatives. We have seen that elites and masses are mutually dependent. This dependence has important implications for the range of options available to elites in the conduct of interracial politics.

The Elements of Racial Conflict and Cooperation

If we are to speak of the ways in which mass patterns of behavior and belief affect the alternatives open to elites in establishing interracial political relationships—relationships both of conflict and of cooperation—then we must specify the crucial elements of those mass patterns and relate them to operational indicators. In doing so, it must be kept in mind that we are seeking dominant or modal elements of behavior and belief within respective mass-level racial samples. This strategy represents a permissible simplification, to the extent that we are attempting to describe the major avenues of opportunity and sources of constraint that elites confront within the two racial communities. Since these elements of mass behavior and belief may not be distributed monolithically within each of the racial communities—suggesting that, while there may be a dominant set of opportunities and constraints, there may also be other sets of lesser importance—we shall analyze the respective mass samples for variation in belief and behavior among class and political activity strata.

The argument up to this point is that elements in the patterns of mass belief and behavior in the two racial populations constitute pressures that help to determine the nature of the elites who arise and that influence the strategies of those elites in dealing with the elites of the other race. Given a particular configuration of mass patterns, we can say that a particular. variety of conflict or cooperation between the races is more likely to occur than are others.

Which patterns of mass belief and behavior are important to examine? Students of conflict are in general agreement that basic relationships of conflict can be understood as struggles to implement competing values[34] or to control status, power, and other scarce resources available to some but not all of the contestants. This notion of conflict suggests, in Ralf Dahrendorf's terms,

---

[33] William Gamson, *Power and Discontent* (Homewood, Ill.: Dorsey, 1968), p. 43.

[34] Lewis Coser, *The Functions of Social Conflict* (London: Routledge and Kegan Paul, 1956), p. 8.

"incompatible objectives," or *goals*.[35] Where there are differences among groups regarding the goals to be won through politics, we may say that the potential for conflict is present. We are satisfied here with measuring the "potential" for conflict; our purpose in this study is not to measure manifest or active conflict but, rather, to measure mass-generated pressures that bear on elites' decisions to engage in particular types of conflict or cooperation. Conversely, political cooperation among groups implies at least mutual coordination in the pursuit of similar goals. As E. E. Schattschneider notes, "Political conflicts are waged by coalitions of inferior interests held together by a dominant interest."[36]

Thus, the extent to which there appears to be a relative similarity or dissimilarity of certain political goals between the black and white mass samples is a key factor in determining whether the structure of mass pressures is likely to impel racial elites into conflictual or cooperative relationships with one another.

It seems evident that groups with similar goals may, if they decide to cooperate in the pursuit of these goals, establish different sorts of cooperative relationships. Coalitions may be more or less tightly organized; cooperation may be tacit or explicit. Likewise, the quality of competition among groups whose goals differ is likely to vary. Competition may be pursued uncompromisingly, or it may be pursued across a bridgeable gulf. In short, similarity or dissimilarity of goals does not tell us much beyond the shape of the basic pressures that influence the establishment of intergroup political relationships. Other elements help to mold variations of the fundamental pressures for conflict or cooperation.

We can identify at least two elements (there may of course be others) that, in a political relationship, might drive competitors farther apart and cooperators closer together. One element involves the notions of the respective groups concerning appropriate and permissible modes of goal seeking in politics. What strategies do group members prefer? What are the permissible limits of political action? It is not hard to see, for example, that, while two groups may share the same goal, one may wish to seek it through the electoral process, while the other may wish to pursue it through protest tactics. Cooperation between such groups is likely to differ in quality from the relationship between groups whose members share a preference for one type of goal-seeking activity. To measure this element, we shall examine mass-level political behavior and preferences and support for various types of action.

Another element of importance has to do with the mass-level beliefs and attitudes that form a framework for political intercourse. These beliefs and attitudes may be understood for the moment as the normative mechanisms that regulate and contain political interchange; that is, mechanisms that perform

[35] Ralf Dahrendorf, *Class and Class Conflict in Industrial Society* (Stanford, Cal.: Stanford University Press, 1959), p. 135.
[36] E. E. Schattschneider, *The Semisovereign People* (New York: Holt, Rinehart, and Winston, 1960), p. 69.

integrative functions for a political system. One group, for example, may trust the political system, while the other does not. This may not eliminate the possibilities of cooperation, but it probably will change the character of the relationship, as we shall see. These various beliefs and attitudes may, of course, be examined through the use of a survey instrument.

To summarize, I have suggested that mass populations establish a context of pressures on elites and would-be elites that is a function of three elements: *goals, behavior patterns* (which we also may term *styles*), and *integrative attitudes*. The nature of this context is likely to encourage certain types of elites and discourage others. The degree of racial similarity and dissimilarity of mass patterns in each of these three elements establishes a unique mix or set of pressures for the establishment of corresponding types of conflictual or cooperative political relationships, as we shall see in the next section.

General Implications of Convergent–Divergent Patterns

Before turning to a specification of the possible types of interracial conflict and cooperation, it is worth exploring briefly some of the implications of mass similarity or dissimilarity of these elements and their conditions.

One implication of a high degree of convergence of all three elements, in the short run at least, is the lesser likelihood that racial considerations will structure political conflict. Interracial conflict will be muted, and political issues will be contested among biracial groups. General agreement on broad priorities and processes will obtain.

A high degree of general convergence is likely under several conditions. Where blacks are heavily dependent on white political figures or organizations for benefits from the political system, as they were in Chicago during the heyday of the Dawson machine, patterns of black behavior and belief—at least as they are publicly evident and thus as they affect the structure of elite opportunities—are likely to resemble those of whites. In the long run, the state of black dependence that usually characterizes generally convergent political patterns may lead eventually, when blacks begin to assert themselves, to serious disruption and breakdown in interracial cooperation. If dependence has been imposed on black communities, the eventual development of black independence and solidarity is likely to be accompanied by a bitter break with whites. Convergence is not simply a result of structural conditions, however. It may also reflect traditional efforts to arrive at racial accommodation in the search for mutual benefit or social peace.

A major implication of generally divergent racial tendencies in the short run is that racial claims and interests will structure local political conflict. This may be costly for the city. If these interests are well defined and command broad acceptance within their respective racial groups, they will be difficult to relinquish. Stalemate, violence, or some form of racial majority tyranny are potential results in a city in which the races differ on goals and behavior and in their fundamental beliefs about the nature of government and the political process.

On the one hand, divergence may be a function of social structure; if the two racial groups possess widely different resources or if one group has favored status in the political system, then we may expect some degree of divergence. On the other hand, divergent patterns may reflect some degree of intentionality, a conscious attempt to establish a distinctive style. Deliberate divergence in this instance may be a consequence of strategic choice, distinctive cultural predispositions, or hostility toward other actors in the political system. Certain forms of black and student protest, for example, may serve to express all of these elements. Divergence is often an imperative of organizational mobilization: It may be necessary to establish distinctive patterns in order to strengthen group identity and cohesion and isolate antagonists. Naturally, intentional efforts to establish divergent or convergent patterns often are related to structural conditions in such a way that the latter encourage and reinforce conscious efforts.

Analysis of the ways in which and the extent to which mass patterns of behavior and belief converge or diverge can tell us much about the role and impact of race in the political life of the city. For example, the degree and quality of interracial conflict or cooperation is related to the quality of dynamism in urban government, that is, primarily, the ability of elites to mobilize and aggregate the resources of diverse groups in the city and bring them to bear on common problems. Extreme or polar conflicts hamper these efforts by making accommodation and broad-based collective enterprises difficult to achieve. Conversely, high levels of interracial cooperation eliminate one serious source of cleavage and potentially make for a greater ability to aggregate and concentrate the resources of the two racial communities.

This is not to say that racial conflict is always dysfunctional for the political system, nor that interracial political cooperation is an unmitigated good. Some types of conflict between the races may in fact serve a variety of useful functions for both whites and blacks,[37] and some types of cooperation may be thoroughly suffocating to the independent development of the weaker group. Both possibilities are important to keep in mind as we analyze the context of interracial political relationships in Milwaukee and its implications for elite strategies.

Alternative Relationships in the Politics of Race

The different types of possible political relationships between the races are a function of the particular pattern of convergence or divergence in three different

---

[37] See Lewis Coser, "Some Functions of Violence," *The Annals* 364 (March 1966): 8-18; and Joseph S. Himes, "The Functions of Racial Conflict," *Social Forces* 45 (September 1966): 1-10.

areas, each area corresponding to one of the three elements discussed in the previous section. These areas include political goals; styles of political action or behavior; and attitudes and cognitions important for political integration. The degree of convergence or divergence may be ascertained by interracial comparisons of mass survey data. At any given time, the prevailing pattern of convergence or divergence helps to determine the context—relatively conflictual or relatively cooperative—within which elites must work as they pursue their political objectives.[38] Our task in this final section is to delineate the variety of possible relationships.

This mass contribution to the context of elite interaction is not simply a function of how many persons of each race conform to divergent or convergent patterns of behavior and belief but also of *which* persons of each race diverge or converge. For example, if political activists of both races agree on the norms important for political integration while the inactives of the two races disagree, the possibilities for political cooperation are high, even if those activists are minorities of their respective races. Activists, after all, are those who are most likely to be visible to elites and responsive to them. Their behavior and beliefs, then, are relatively more important than those of the inactives in determining the structure of the context of elite interaction.

A Typology of Political Relationships

The various alternative relationships may be placed on a continuum ranging from what I shall call convergent cooperation to divergent conflict. Convergence and divergence must, of course, be understood empirically in relative terms. At the convergent end of the continuum, pressures and opportunities for elites to seek close cooperative relationships are high. Toward the divergent end of the continuum, mass differences are so pervasive that the maintenance of leadership status will most likely require active pursuit of aggressive, conflictual strategies.

Table 1.1 identifies four basic interracial political relationships, each of which has two variants. Where patterns of behavior or belief between the two racial groups converge, relatively, the word "same" is entered in the table, where they diverge, the word "different" is entered. It must be kept in mind that both words are used relatively in the context of survey data analysis.

For empirical purposes, the description of integrative commitment, goals, and behavior must focus selectively on a sample of indicators. The degree to which a city is politically integrated may be determined by comparing *(1)* normative

---

[38] Other factors besides mass behavior and belief patterns contribute to the structure of the context. These include institutional factors, demographic characteristics, and the economic status and basis of the jurisdiction in question. These are, however, outside the scope of this study. Our interest is in the contribution that mass behavior and opinion make to this context.

TABLE 1.1 FOUR TYPES OF INTERRACIAL POLITICAL RELATIONSHIPS,
DEFINED IN TERMS OF AGREEMENT ON INTEGRATIVE NORMS,
POLITICAL GOALS, AND POLITICAL BEHAVIOR

Type of relationship	Degree of understanding of commitment to integrative norms	Nature of political goals	Behavior styles in politics
Convergent cooperation			
Strong coalition	same	same	same
Broad coalition	same	same	different
Accommodation			
Pragmatic coalition	different	same	same
Tacit coalition	different	same	different
Institutionalized competition			
Parallel pluralistic competition	same	different	same
Stylized pluralistic competition	same	different	different
Divergent conflict			
Pragmatic conflict	different	different	same
Polarized conflict	different	different	different

evaluations of government, *(2)* attitudes toward various norms that govern the processes of conflict resolution, and *(3)* beliefs about the role of the individual in politics.

From the multitude of possible political goals, we shall select only one—but one with several facets—of central importance. A number of prominent students of urban politics have contended that the failure of community is the major problem of urban life and that the quest for it—a quest that, as we shall see, can take several forms—is a dominant preoccupation of urban dwellers. Our examination, then, will focus on the extent to which the races agree that the reestablishment of community is a prime goal and on whether or not the way in which this goal is defined differs by race.

To determine divergence and convergence in political behavior, we shall assess participation rates in, and sympathy for, two distinctive modes of political action: conventional activity centered on the electoral process, and protest.

Let us explore briefly the nature of each variant in the spectrum of political relationships.

Convergent Cooperation When members of the mass of each race exhibit similar patterns of commitment to integrative norms and seek similar goals in politics, the major stimulants to a politics based on racial interests are absent. The races agree, in other words, on the basic rules of political interchange and the nature of the governmental context within which such interchange takes place. In addition, there is racial consensus on the identity and nature of the fundamental problems facing people in the city.

Although members of either race may still have a sense of racial identity in politics and a need to express that sense, elites will be under pressure to work for or maintain close cooperative political relationships. The structure of conflict in such a setting will reflect the greater importance of cleavages other than race.

There are two variants of convergent cooperation. One may be called *strong coalition*. Not only do similar goals and identical patterns of commitment to integrative norms exist, but the masses of the two races behave similarly. Elites in this setting are likely to find little encouragement in the form of mass response for strategies—cooperative or conflictual—that emphasize racial distinctiveness. Strategies that deemphasize the racial cleavage are likely to meet with the greatest response, resulting in the consistent formation of racially integrated political groupings and coalitions. The traditional Democratic party coalition on the national scene or the Daley machine coalition on the urban scene are good examples of such coalitions.

The other variant is represented by a situation in which *broad coalitions* are possible. Commitment and goals converge, but modes of political expression, or styles, differ between the races. This difference reflects a situation in which blacks especially have forged a distinctive racial identity in politics, largely for reasons of pride, strategy, tradition, or historical factors. Where the political environment is relatively congenial, they generally choose to manifest this identity largely in symbolic terms involving characteristic forms of expression, such as through the use of "down home" or ghetto rhetoric in politics. In a less self-conscious way, blacks may also differentiate themselves by expressing sympathy for unconventional and occasionally even violent forms of political action. Such sentiments are a product of the black experience and may represent a realistic assessment of certain political necessities as well as an homage to black history. Finally, this differentiation may depart from the purely symbolic and, whether through necessity or preference, take an active form. Blacks may use protest, for example, as a routine way of pursuing the goals of their white allies, either because they are impatient or because they feel they have no other way of attracting attention. Since basic agreement obtains between the races concerning norms and goals, differences of style, however starkly contrasting, are generally not sufficient to constitute barriers to cooperation. The great civil rights coalition of the 1960s, which brought together a large, developing protest constituency and a host of northern liberal white groups that pursued more conventional political strategies, is a good example of a broad coalition.

Accommodation Pressures on elites for accommodation are strongest in a situation in which members of the two races diverge in their commitment to and understanding of integrative norms and definitions but agree nevertheless on the basic goals to be sought through political action.[39] Divergence in commitment to integrative norms occurs when members of one racial group have little faith in the neutral operation of the processes of decision making and hence believe that the political system is stacked against them. In such a case, we find that people are suspicious of the integrative norms that support the mechanisms worked out by society for the resolution of conflicts. The operation of these mechanisms, such as bargaining and compromise, is viewed as biased. Despite these differences, the similarity of substantive interests may be strong enough to generate pressures for accommodation of some sort in order to consolidate resources.

Working out acceptable and stable coalitions is difficult under these conditions, because each racial group represents a potential liability for the other when the two are linked together in a mutual political effort. Consider a situation in which it is blacks who reject integrative norms and whites who adhere to them. For blacks, the white masses are a liability because of their commitment to bargaining norms, central to an integrated system of conflict resolution. Compromise in an interracial coalition may be viewed by blacks as a potential device for "selling out" black interests. For whites, alienated blacks represent a risk insofar as their behavior is unpredictable or unconventional (because it is not bound by a commitment to a set of process norms and to the prevailing system of conflict resolution) and may discredit the coalition. Under these conditions, interracial cooperation is likely to take one of two forms, one of which is explicit but of short duration, the other of which is unacknowledged or tacit.

Pragmatic coalition is possible in a situation in which elites of the alienated racial group (the one less committed to the integrative norms) seize the opportunity to ally themselves with the racial group committed to conventional norms, in order to gain legitimacy in the political system. Taking the case again in which it is blacks who reject the norms, while whites do not, the elites of each race are presented with the opportunity for pragmatic coalition when whites are interested in gaining black resources to augment the strength of their own and blacks are interested in allying with a legitimate and powerful partner. Alliance of this sort is possible not only because the racial groups seek the same political goals but also because, for the moment, their similar behavior styles provide a basis for the pursuit of a coordinated, joint strategy.

This common endeavor is the result of largely pragmatic and short-term considerations. These may be compelling enough to obscure fundamental problems of normative integration; but the coalition will be unstable, because most of the efforts at conflict resolution will be governed by normative conventions that black elements in the coalition reject. Given the inherent necessity of compro-

---

[39] Such a situation probably occurred in Michigan during the fight to decentralize the Detroit public schools. See William R. Grant, "Community Control vs. Integration—The Case of Detroit," *The Public Interest* (Summer 1971): 62-79.

mise in politics as a means of resolving differences peaceably, certain interests are likely to suffer. Groups that admit the necessity of compromise and acknowledge that their interests may be subject to compromise will not necessarily feel betrayed when adjustment is the price of social peace. But if a group believes that compromise always hurts its interests, and thus rejects the compromise norm as self-defeating, then resort to compromise, which is inherent in the pragmatic coalition, will evoke cries of betrayal and will threaten to shatter the coalition.

Another form that accommodation may take is called *tacit coalition*. Here the two racial groups coordinate their efforts implicitly to seek the same goals. Thomas Schelling writes of the situation in which parties have identical interests but face the problem of coordinating their actions for their mutual benefit when communication is impossible; concerted action still may take place, however, if each group knows that the other group wants the same thing.[40] The situation that I have characterized as tacit coalition is not entirely analogous to Schelling's case, but it is based on similar principles: The two racial groups share the same goals. This they make public. Yet the elites are reluctant to attempt an explicit coalition because their respective groups differ not only in their commitment to the prevailing norms of the political process but also in their preferred styles of political behavior. For example, blacks whose behavior is distinctive and whose attitudes are characterized by distrust, alienation, and rejection of bargaining processes do not appear to whites as attractive partners for a public alliance. Hence, the two groups are in a situation in which joint action of an explicit nature is politically ill-advised, a condition analogous in some sense to Schelling's case in which communication is impossible. To communicate would be to make explicit the association. Yet, if both groups continue to seek the same goals by their own means, without formally allying with one another, the effect is one of tacit coalition.[41]

An illustration of this type of situation occurred in Milwaukee during the Reverend James Groppi's protest campaign to secure open-housing legislation in the city. The Catholic church did not wish to ally itself openly with Groppi and his young black followers, primarily because their tactics involved repeated provocative street protests. On the other hand, the archbishop wished to aid the cause. He did so by writing in the editorial column of the *Catholic Herald Citizen*, the weekly archdiocesan newspaper, that, Groppi and his tactics notwithstanding, Christians must favor the cause of "freedom and human dignity."

---

[40] Schelling calls this situation "tacit co-ordination." Thomas C. Schelling, *The Strategy of Conflict* (New York: Oxford University Press, 1960), pp. 54-57.

[41] Lipsky understands protest as a means of gaining the attention of sympathetic groups with political resources to stimulate their entry into the political conflict. This takes place without direct communication. The situation is analogous to tacit coalition in some cases. Lipsky, "Protest as a Political Resource."

In this case, the archbishop disavowed Father Groppi's behavior but pointed out that this was not the issue. At the same time, he implicitly declared himself and the church in favor of racial equality.

Institutionalized Competition   A third pattern is likely to occur when both racial groups have a similar understanding of and commitment to the norms of political integration. Competition in the political arena may proceed according to a set of ground rules by which all parties abide. Political conflict is regularized, or stable, and the parties in conflict may be expected to adhere to a predictable range of behaviors. Victory or defeat is not only likely to be moderated by compromise; it is also unlikely to change fundamental attitudes of commitment to the prevailing norms. Losing parties in any given conflict are not likely to resort to violence, secession, or quiescence. When behavior falls within a predictable range in a recognized framework of rules, we may speak of institutionalization. Coalition between the races is unlikely, however, because goals differ.

When racial groups pursue different goals in conflict with one another but within a framework of rules that govern the process and when, at the same time, they exhibit similar (parallel) behavior patterns, then the situation may be characterized as one of *parallel pluralistic competition*. One example of this occurs when the races clash in electoral competition, with blacks and whites voting in racial blocs. Behavior is similar (voting) and losers and winners accept the rules of elections that govern the outcome. Goals, represented here by competing candidates, differ. Other examples of classic pluralistic competition are those in which conflicting parties seek various access points in the political system and pursue their goals through lobbying, public relations, and constituent communications to relevant elites.

If the two racial groups use different methods of political expression, the races compete in what may be termed a system of *stylized pluralistic competition*. Blacks who use protest methods, for example, still may exhibit commitments to the bargaining process and to other integrative norms.[42]   While protest behavior represents a distinctive style of political self-assertion, competition may proceed nevertheless in an institutionalized context as long as protest remains peaceful and constitutes a form of bargaining.

Divergent Conflict   Divergent conflict, as opposed to what I have called pluralistic competition, implies a situation marked by high instability. Agreement on basic ground rules for conducting political competition and for arriving at resolution is lacking. When the masses differ both in their commitment to integrative norms and on goals, elites are subject to pressures to pursue interracial conflict of a highly antagonistic nature. When mass patterns diverge to this extent, the

---

[42] Peter K. Eisinger, "Protest Behavior and the Integration of Urban Political Systems," *Journal of Politics* 33 (November 1971): 980-1007.

centripetal forces that normally impel elites to seek cooperative relationships are totally absent.

In other situations, agreement either on the basic rules of the political process or on goals tends to mute polar tendencies. Agreement on one of these may offset disagreement on the other, bringing about a basis either for cooperation, where agreement on goals obtains, or for institutionalized competition, where agreement on the rules of the conflict resolution process exists. Where agreement of neither kind exists, racial blocs in politics are well defined and antagonistic.

Where behavior patterns are similar, elites may discover that their most natural course is to pursue what I shall call *pragmatic conflict*. Indeed, this may be their only recourse. While behavior in most instances is likely to take a form related to the group's normative commitments, there may be strong pragmatic reasons for behavior to take other forms. We saw that, in the case of pragmatic coalition, one group may be willing to accommodate to the style of its coalition partners, in order to combine strength, even if its normative commitments dictate other strategies. The same general proposition may hold for the pursuit of conflict.

Let us take the case in which one racial group is deeply suspicious of the conventional bargaining and electoral processes that characterize the conduct of much of local politics. The normative commitment of the group differs, then, from that of groups that trust these processes. However, to follow up actively the logical implications of the rejection of these norms—that is, to deviate in some way from conventionally accepted styles of political expression—may damage beyond repair any hopes of winning concessions in the political system. One may speculate, for example, that Bobby Seale's decision to invest his resources and those of his followers in electoral politics in Oakland was the product of this sort of calculation. Thus, a group may choose to work through the electoral process even though its members suspect that the process is biased, and it may shun an aggressive and uncompromising protest strategy or even a strategy of violence—either of which may be more consistent with its own normative commitments. The danger of pursuing the protest strategy is that the style of expression itself may become the important issue in question, destroying or diverting the effort to press the substantive issues that gave rise to conflict in the first place. Similarity of mass behavior styles in this case represents an implicit, pragmatic mass response to a situation in which local government is extremely hostile to unconventional political behavior. Such a response on the part of members of the disaffected mass reflects partly fear of the consequences of pursuing a protest strategy and partly the realization that "working within the system" in that particular setting is more likely (even if only marginally more likely) to yield results. Such fears and realizations will naturally act as a constraint on elites in formulating their decisions about the strategies by which to pursue conflict.

At other times or in other places, masses alienated from integrative norms may be unafraid to give free rein to their preferences for active political expression. Where the races differ on integrative commitment, goals, and styles, elites must operate in a system where pressures push toward what may be termed *polarized conflict.* Potential outcomes of political conflict in the case of polarization include stalemate, majority tyranny, and violence. A political system marked by either type of divergence is unlikely to move toward mutually agreeable solutions to collective problems; its actors are likely to expend their energies, instead, on matters of survival in conflict.

Uses of the Typology

This typology of political relationships has several uses. First of all, it provides an organizing matrix for the analysis of mass survey data. It suggests not only how these elements of mass belief and behavior may relate to one another but also what role the various elements may play in influencing the quality of interracial political relationships.

The typology is also useful as a means for estimating the relative stability of interracial political relationships, if stability is understood as a function of interracial agreement on integrative norms. Clearly, all cooperative relationships are not equally stable (nor are all conflictual relationships equally unstable). The degree of stability of intergroup relations in politics has important implications for the viability of the political system within which those groups exist.

Finally, the typology makes clear the variety of pressures that may form the empirical context within which elites arise and seek to survive. Each of the eight variations in the patterns of interracial mass relationships provides a setting especially favorable to a certain type of elite interaction. Conditions are less favorable, by varying degrees, to other elite strategies in the pursuit of political objectives through intergroup conflict or cooperation. Choosing the strategy most congruent with the existing configuration of mass patterns is the most likely way to gain mass support. It is also the surest method of solidifying the leader's status, and, in addition, is the path with the fewest constraints. Elites are by no means bound by mass patterns to follow a particular strategy; they may have sound reasons for going against mass desires and habits, and they often do so. Indeed, they may not even discern or interpret those patterns and desires correctly. But we may assume that, given correct understanding of mass behavior and belief, they are less likely to take the difficult path than the easy one, over time. And we may further assume that, if they habitually pursue a strategy against the grain of mass preferences, they probably will not last as leaders.

I state these propositions in general terms, fully aware not only of exceptions but also of complexities gone unexamined. Thus, as an example of the latter, leaders who lose their status because they oppose mass preferences may still retain leadership positions with groups of followers that dissent from the bulk of the mass. But, despite all possible modifications, the general principle of elite dependence on masses still offers a strong theoretical context for examining the conditions of race relations in urban politics.

In part, this is so because black elites are likely to present a united front in important controversies, especially where racial interests are perceived to be at stake, even if they have differences among themselves. If black elites are not united, each leader probably will command only a small following and none will succeed in gaining serious attention.

The proposition also holds true if we take as our theoretical focus of examination *any given conflict* between the races, rather than the whole panorama of racial politics. In the former case, the number of actors is more limited and more clearly defined; the options for conflict or cooperation between the races are relatively concrete, and it is probable that mass interest and opinions will be more clearly focused. It remains for elites to judge how they best can muster support for their initiatives in a particular conflict, given the general predilections and habits of their followers in relation to those of the masses of the other race.

In describing mass patterns of behavior and belief, we must necessarily be selective in choosing empirical indicators. Thus, the patterns of mass relationships are ideals. Empirically, mass convergence or divergence can only be stated as tendencies.

The plan of the book is as follows. Chapter 2 presents a methodological discussion of surveys in the urban setting and provides a glimpse of Milwaukee as a research site. In Chapter 3, the mass attitudes and cognitions important for political integration are examined. Political goals are the subject of Chapter 4. Chapters 5 and 6 concern political behavior styles, with particular focus on conventional action and on protest activity. In each of these substantive chapters, the masses of the two races are compared, in an effort to characterize the pattern of their relationship as generally divergent or convergent. The final chapter, Chapter 7, draws this material together, in order to summarize the nature of the context within which the elites of each race must work in pursuing the political interests of their respective followers.

The Survey
and the City

2

Despite their widespread use in public affairs and academic research, sample surveys still labor under the burden of suspicion in the United States. While a number of social scientists have generally come to take the technique for granted and no longer customarily spend much time in their work justifying it, the questions raised by the suspicious are significant enough to warrant our attention. There are especially strong reasons to discuss a survey conducted at a single point in time in a single city, with a large portion of the sample composed of black ghetto dwellers.

After thirty years' use of surveys by public and private institutions, certain popular doubts about their validity still linger tenaciously. For the present study, such doubts are not very damning, but they bear passing mention. Most people, for example, have never themselves been interviewed for any purpose,[1] nor do they know friends who have been, yet polls of all varieties are continually reported in the media. People are prone to wonder, then, and not unreasonably, just whose opinions these surveys reflect. It can be said in response that evidence based on more than thirty years' experience with surveys has convinced most

---

[1] Elizabeth Hartman, H. Lawrence Isaacson, and Cynthia M. Jurgell estimated on the basis of data drawn from a national survey that about 35 percent of their sample had been interviewed before by some method (mail, telephone, or personal interview). The likelihood of being included in a sample survey of any kind varies by region of residence and social class. "Public Reaction to Public Opinion Surveying," *Public Opinion Quarterly* 32 (Summer 1968): 296.

social scientists that sampling techniques based on the laws of probability have been developed to the point at which they do tend to produce representative subject populations, relatively small in number, whose characteristics, opinions, and behavior reflect, within tolerable limits of error, those of the whole from which they are drawn.[2]

If most members of the academic community no longer share these popular suspicions, some nevertheless have their own misgivings. In the last decade, for example, it was not uncommon to be told that survey techniques simply would not work in black ghettos. Alienated and angry blacks would refuse to talk to interviewers working for a white (or any other) scholar. If they did talk, they probably would distort or hide their true opinions. Furthermore, there would be operational difficulties associated with the ghetto's high rate of residential and social instability, the consequence of which would be to produce low response rates and final samples with disproportionately low numbers of young men, poor people, and drifters. Some critics are doubtful of the utility of surveys taken at a single point in time; others are wary of the meaning and significance of surveys conducted in a single city.

To some degree these are all reasonable concerns, especially given the context of this present survey. The questions raised require to be answered, and that is the purpose of this chapter.

At the outset, we must recognize two preliminary and basic points. The first is that surveys are not perfect instruments; they do have built-in difficulties relating to their administration and interpretation. The question to which we must address ourselves is, Just how imperfect for our purposes are surveys of this type? The second point is a related one: For someone wishing to explore opinions and behavior among members of a mass population, no better device than the sample survey has yet been invented.[3] Thus, at our point of departure, we must recognize both the limitations and the need of such methods.

Basic Methods of the Survey

Selection of the Sample Population

The population sampled for this study included all inhabitants of the city of Milwaukee who were eighteen years of age or older. The study design was constructed to yield two separate probability samples, one of the black population

---

[2] Charles H. Backstrom and Gerald D. Hursch, *Survey Research* (Evanston, Ill.: Northwestern University Press, 1963), pp. 23 ff.

[3] Some mass behavior, such as voting and criminal activity, is recorded by official sources with varying degrees of accuracy. These records yield aggregate data, which involve their own difficulties of interpretation and manipulation. Much behavior we are interested in here is not recorded even in aggregate form by official record keepers.

and one of the white population, the two being as close in size as possible. The final samples numbered 246 blacks and 331 whites.

From the 1969 Milwaukee City Directory, 608 clusters of street blocks were randomly selected without replacement. In order to draw two separate racial samples, these 608 clusters were divided into strata that were based on census tract data according to whether households in those areas were predominantly black or predominantly white. Households in the strata were sampled randomly. Respondents in the sampled households were chosen by the Kish technique.[4]

The survey was conducted over the summer of 1970 by professional interviewers from the University of Wisconsin Survey Research Laboratory. In all cases, the race of the interviewer and the race of the respondent were matched.

The survey itself was preceded by a pretest in the late spring of 1970. Prior to being contacted by the interviewer, the respondents finally chosen received a letter explaining their selection and providing a brief description of the survey. The response rate among the black sample was 80 percent; among the whites, it was 70 percent. An impressionistic explanation for the lower white response rate, based on reasons given for refusal to participate in the survey, is that a significant number of Milwaukee whites were angry at the state university and hence at any enterprise associated with it. The survey went into the field immediately on the heels of violent protests at the University of Wisconsin–Madison campus over the Cambodian invasion by American troops. Given what I later found to be much higher levels of antipathy toward protest in general among whites than among blacks, the response of many potential white respondents, that they wanted nothing to do with a university that harbored rioting students, is not surprising. Such, apparently, are the intrusions of history on scholarship.

The Sample and the Universe

Comparing certain demographic and socioeconomic characteristics of the sample population with those of the universe from which it was drawn provides one means by which to assess the representativeness or reliability of the sample. In Table 2.1 the sex, education, occupation, and income of the sample respondents are compared to the corresponding 1970 Census categories for the Milwaukee population as a whole.

The fit of the sample with its universe is relatively high, except in a few cases. Some of the discrepancies may be attributed to the fact that the census population categories do not always match those used for this study. The sample was drawn from a pool that included all adults age eighteen and over. The census, however, compiles education statistics only for those twenty-five and over, thus

---

[4] See Leslie Kish, "A Procedure for Objective Respondent Selection within the Household," *Journal of the American Statistical Association* 44 (September 1949): 380-387.

TABLE 2.1   CHARACTERISTICS OF THE MILWAUKEE
POPULATION (1970 CENSUS) AND THE SAMPLE POPULATION
(1970 SURVEY), BY RACE

Characteristic	Black population		White population	
	1970 Census (%)	Sample (%)	1970 Census (%)	Sample (%)
Sex				
Male	39.4	38.6	47.7	41.0
Female	60.5	61.3	52.2	58.9
Education				
Less than high school	66.0	55.0	49.0	37.0
High school graduate	24.0	30.0	34.0	36.0
More than high school	10.0	14.0	17.0	26.0
Occupation				
Professional	7.0	5.0	13.0	11.0
Manager, official	2.0	6.0	6.0	8.0
Clerical, sales	15.0	13.0	29.0	28.0
Skilled	10.0	5.0	14.0	13.0
Semiskilled	34.0	42.0	21.0	29.0
Service	33.0	39.0	18.0	12.0
Annual income				
$0-$3000	20.0	16.0	6.0	7.5
$3000-$7000	27.0	23.0	16.0	23.0
$7000-$10,000	22.0	26.0	22.0	25.5
$10,000+	32.0	24.0	55.0	35.0
No answer	0.0	11.0	0.0	8.0

discriminating against the more highly educated younger population. This would help to account for the apparent oversampling of more highly educated people. The census also records the occupation of everyone over sixteen, although the effects of this discrepancy are not obvious. In general, the sample fits best in the middle categories of these socioeconomic variables, while the upper and lower ends show somewhat greater discrepancies, depending on the variable. However, except for the undersampling of high-income whites, no case of undersampling or oversampling is serious enough to question seriously the representativeness of the survey data.

Surveying in the Ghetto

Warnings about the problems of conducting surveys among black ghetto residents abound in the literature on survey techniques. Yet there is reason to believe that careful and sensitive survey administration, coupled with moderate expectations about what may be gained from the data, can serve at least to minimize whatever problems do exist.

One set of problems has to do with the difficulty, imposed by the ghetto setting, of meeting the necessary methodological requirements for a successful and reliable survey. By comparison with that in most white neighborhoods, life in the black ghetto tends to be disorganized in at least two ways that might hinder survey research. For one thing, ghetto dwellers tend to change residence within the city more than do members of the white population.[5] Thus, life is disorganized to some extent because of a high degree of residential mobility. Life in the ghetto is disorganized also because of what Kenneth Clark has called its "institutionalized pathology"—its high rates of poverty, drug use, crime, and mental illness.[6] Both sorts of disorganization are presumed to cut into the population available for interviewing. Respondents may be difficult to find, not only because they change addresses but also because many do not want to be found by inquisitive emissaries from the world outside the ghetto. If they are found, it is thought that many may refuse to be interviewed.

Although we naturally have no data on the characteristics of those Milwaukee ghetto dwellers who refused to be interviewed or on those who could not be found at all, it seems logical to expect that if this had been a serious problem in the Milwaukee survey it would have shown up both in the response rate and in the fit of the sample with the universe in the lower-status socioeconomic categories. In fact, however, the black response rate was relatively high (80 percent), and the lower-status group was in no case badly undersampled.

Once agreements to be interviewed have been obtained from an adequate sample, there is always the possibility that ghetto residents, alienated by their life condition, may, through malice or fear, distort their answers or lie. Evidence to this effect in other ghetto surveys is not convincing, however. Clark found, in a survey of Harlem, that

> the presence of a . . . tape recorder and the inevitable microphone did not inhibit the response of these subjects even when they were discussing drug addiction or police graft. On the contrary, it seemed that the starvation for serious attention and respect which characterizes so many of the forgotten people of the ghetto . . . encouraged free expression.[7]

---

[5] Census surveys suggest that approximately one out of every eight whites changes residence locally (within metropolitan areas) every year. The annual rate for blacks, however, is one out of five. These figures have held constant at least since 1949. Bruce C. Straits, "Residential Movement among Negroes and Whites in Chicago," *Social Science Quarterly* 49 (December 1968): 573.

[6] Kenneth Clark, *Dark Ghetto* (New York: Harper and Row, 1965), pp. 81-97.

[7] Ibid., p. xix.

It has long been thought that one way to ensure such free expression among blacks is to use black interviewers in the ghetto. Yet researchers fear that distortion will then occur in a different way. Suppression of true opinions will no longer be the problem; rather, the pressure to meet the standards of racial orthodoxy may produce falsely militant responses. A pair of scholars interested in this problem conducted an experiment in which they randomly divided a black sample into two groups, one of which was interviewed by whites, the other by blacks. Among their conclusions was the following: "So far as we can tell from indirect evidence, race-of-interviewer effects involve primarily black suppression or repression of existing attitudes when interviews are carried out by whites, rather than the arousal of more militant sentiments when interviewers are black."[8]

By the use of black interviewers in black areas, then, all types of distortion and falsification can be minimized. Since this procedure was followed in the Milwaukee survey, we can be reasonably confident that the black respondents did not systematically distort their answers by telling the investigator what they thought he or she wanted to hear or by attempting to protect themselves by offering innocuous but false opinions.

Another set of problems associated with ghetto surveys has to do with the difficulties of communicating with people of low and peripheral social status. Edith Fein is concerned, for example, about the lack of identification among ghetto residents with the idea of research itself, both as an establishment institution and as a way of explaining phenomena.[9] Whether or not this is a problem peculiar to the ghetto is hard to say; one suspects that it applies equally to lower-class whites. In any event, there are several strategies one can use to foster identification with the survey or at least to combat the sense of estrangement. One strategy is to emphasize the potential material utility of such research for the respondent's life in the city. This is not, perhaps, the strongest strategy, for the respondent is likely to realize that this is at best a marginal, if well-meaning, truth. Another way is to alert interviewers to the social distance problem; status differences between interviewer and respondent can be bridged by tact and training. Still another is to be extremely sensitive to the implications of language used in the survey instrument. To give one example, many of the questions used in the pretest employed the standard survey phrase, "people like yourself," as in "Voting is the only way people like yourself can influence government in the city." The phrase drew repeated negative reactions. People asked frequently what was meant by "people like myself." It seemed in some covert way to function as a code for classifying respondents, especially those who were black. It carried a connotation

---

[8] Howard Schuman and Jean M. Converse, "The Effects of Black and White Interviewers on Black Responses in 1968," *Public Opinion Quarterly* 35 (Spring 1971): 68.

[9] Edith Fein, "Inner-City Interviewing: Some Perspectives," *Public Opinion Quarterly* 34 (Winter 1970-1971): 626.

of inferiority or, at least, of difference. In the final survey that phrase was changed to "the average person." No one was recorded by interviewers as having objected to being average, nor did the word need interpretation.

A second aspect of the problem of interviewing lower-class respondents is their alleged lack of verbal facility. Open-ended questions, especially, place a premium on articulateness. Their use with people who do not express themselves readily or well can be damaging to the respondent's self-esteem and, in turn, to whatever rapport the interviewer has succeeded in establishing.

In response to this allegation it should be said, first, that in fact many lower-status ghetto residents *are* articulate and *do* express themselves readily. Like members of other groups, some of them indeed are verbally ornate, others are garrulous, and many are thoughtfully expressive. It is true, however, that some cannot deal with open-ended questions, beyond supplying overly simplified monosyllabic answers; but this is a problem in surveying any population. In the present study, this difficulty does not appear to be any more serious among the black respondents than among the white. To minimize disparities in verbal capability, the analyst is advised, in any case, to keep his coding categories simple and few in number. There is a temptation, however, for sympathetic scholars to attribute monosyllabic answers simply to problems of articulation, rather than to ignorance or unawareness. Hence, the analyst is likely to see, behind such responses, complexities that actually are not there. Although I have tried to keep this problem in mind, there are undoubtedly instances in the book in which I have sought to wring more meaning from the responses than even the most trusting reader would allow. The book must be read with this caveat in mind.

In sum, survey research in the ghetto perhaps is not so fraught with difficulties as some might argue. People do wish to tell their stories, and they usually tell them well and accurately. With the possible exception of quasi-anthropological methods, such as those used by Elliot Liebow to study ghetto life on Tally's Corner[10] or by Lee Rainwater in the Pruitt-Igoe projects,[11] the survey offers the best means for finding and then listening to the ghetto dweller. If it is not a perfect tool, it is nevertheless a rich one, and its potential for some degree of scientific rigor makes it well worth the price of whatever problems cannot be minimized by careful administration and analysis.

The Cross-Sectional Survey

A survey conducted over one narrow range of time provides a snapshot, or cross-section, of social patterns, beliefs, and relationships. The one major limitation of the cross-sectional survey is that it does not allow one to make judgments about trends or changes. This problem naturally affects the interpretation of the

[10] Elliot Liebow, *Tally's Corner* (Boston: Little, Brown, 1967).
[11] Lee Rainwater, *Behind Ghetto Walls* (Chicago: Aldine, 1970).

survey results; one cannot know, to give one example, whether the 48 percent of the black sample that evinces a willingness to consider the use of political violence is higher or lower than it used to be. For this sort of information a longitudinal survey is necessary, that is, one that takes place at several different points over a span of time. By comparing the patterns of response in surveys conducted over an extended period, one may not only make statements about the degree of stability or the direction of change of patterns but also relate such patterns to external historical conditions or changes in the social and economic environment.

Longitudinal surveys are clearly richer than those that illuminate only a cross-section in a society's life, but this must not be taken to mean that the latter have no valid uses and reasonable justifications. Furthermore, there are various ways by which to establish grounds for speculating about trends and for assessing the possibility that the findings derived from a cross-sectional survey are anomalous and unrepresentative.

Perhaps the major justification for cross-sectional surveys is that they are much cheaper than those conducted longitudinally. While the costs of longitudinal surveys may be reduced by reinterviewing the same panel of respondents rather than drawing new samples each time, the major expense in any survey project is still the cost of interviewing itself. In a period of declining support for large-scale academic enterprises, cost considerations must be taken seriously.

A second justification for cross-sectional surveys is that the research and analysis can be completed in a relatively short time. For surveys that develop data of interest to policymakers, this is an obviously important criterion. To be sure, it would not be especially wise to formulate definitive policies on the basis of cross-sectional data, but policy experimentation, planning, and speculation may all proceed more soundly with even limited information.

The relatively short length of time it takes to complete and analyze cross-sectional survey data may be equally pertinent for scholars in the area. The cross-sectional survey may be likened in some respects to a case study, for its virtues are similar. It may suggest relationships hitherto unsuspected or untested; it may lead to other avenues of inquiry; and it may help in the development of hypotheses. In short, it has heuristic value. The cross-sectional survey is not designed to be definitive; it is tentative and exploratory. Because it does not involve massive expenditure of resources and a long duration of time, the investigator can take certain intellectual risks, follow tentative leads and hunches, and even make a false start here and there without great cost.

But, like the case study, the cross-sectional survey need not be an expedition wholly devoted to breaking trail in virgin territory. It may and should build on other work and establish comparisons with other bodies of data where possible. Ideally, the survey does not stand in isolation, without a context by which to judge its import and its contribution.

The cross-sectional survey poses the greatest problem, perhaps, in the study of opinions, for it reveals the structure of opinion at only one particular time. In contrast, such surveys are useful to a limited extent, to study changes in *behavior* patterns. Behavior in the past may be recalled—recalled, moreover, with some degree of accuracy. Naturally, the further back in time one goes, the less reliable is the recollection of behavior. But for major and relatively recent events (voting in the last two presidential elections, for example) recall is fairly accurate. Aage Clausen estimates that *at the most* 8 percent of the University of Michigan Survey Research Center's national postelection sample lied or reported inaccurately about their voting in the 1964 election, and the figure was probably smaller.[12] Where particular acts cannot be recalled, general trends may be. It is standard procedure to ask in voting surveys whether the respondent always votes for one party or whether he or she leans one way most of the time. Some reports of behavior can even be checked with official records. For example, the percentage of those who report having voted in an election may be compared to aggregate turnout figures.

The point made here is that it is possible at least to reconstruct, and even to check to some degree, the past behavior of respondents, individually or in the aggregate, in a single survey. In contrast, past opinions are not so readily remembered, especially when they have undergone change. Change may have occurred gradually and more or less imperceptibly. Many people are not even aware of opinion change in themselves, nor could they pinpoint the moment of change with any accuracy. Moreover, past opinions may represent a current source of embarrassment. In brief, the cross-sectional survey is a valid enough instrument for illuminating the recent history of respondents' behavior, but it cannot be used with much confidence as a tool for tracing opinion development and change.

Even this drawback does not invalidate the employment of opinion batteries in cross-sectional surveys. Trends and development are not the only aspects of importance in the study of mass beliefs. The aim in the Milwaukee survey was to make intergroup comparisons between blacks and whites. One need not posit a static structure of opinion patterns to compare groups at a single point in time and comment upon the significance of the differences and similarities between them. To recall an earlier example, the discovery that 48 percent of the black sample are willing to consider political violence gains meaning and significance when it is compared with the 10 percent of the white sample that feel this way. *This comparison is important in itself as a snapshot of opinion structure at a given time.* Whether the gap between the races is widening, remaining constant, or decreasing represents a further dimension of the questions as to *what situation exists* and what its consequences for the present might be. All is not lost by our inability to move to that further dimension; the prior questions are significant as they stand. Having made clear this limitation, however, it should be said

[12] Aage Clausen, "Response Validity: Vote Report," *Public Opinion Quarterly* 32 (Winter 1968-1969): 601-602.

that several brief surveys of Milwaukee citizens were conducted by others in the five-year period prior to the present investigation. Some of the questions asked are comparable to some used in this study. Hence, short-term trends at least can be established on some dimensions, providing a rough reliability check of a general nature.

The City as Laboratory: The Problem of Anomaly

Surveys conducted in a single city are always open to the charge that since no American city is "typical," the survey results have little significance beyond their particular setting. It is small consolation to know that single-locale surveys account for a substantial majority of such academic research efforts.

One way to answer this charge, assuming one is interested in the general significance of his research, is to stress the similarities among cities. One big city *is* very much like other big cities in certain important respects. The distinctions among local political cultures, even across regional boundaries, are rapidly giving way to the nationalizing influences of the mass media, high rates of residential mobility, and national economic forces. In addition, the sorts of problems cities must deal with also are similar from city to city, and the major differences among the problems that cities confront are most often differences of degree and not of kind. One of the dominant themes that emerged at the 1972 Conference of U.S. Mayors in New Orleans, for example, was the sense that both big- and small-city mayors share difficulties to an extent they had never imagined.[13] Even the solutions to those problems tend to converge, as cities become increasingly dependent on federal money and federal definitions and perspectives. And, if there are qualitative differences among cities in the problems they face, it is likely that some cities simply move faster on a common path of development, along which other cities may expect eventually to travel.[14]

This argument hardly settles the issue, however, for one may just as easily embrace the perspective that stresses the remaining distinctions among cities. Even granting that these distinctions are diminishing, the fact is that they have not vanished entirely. Some important differentiating factors, such as economic base and demographic makeup, seem relatively stable or at least slow in changing.

There seem to me to be at least two ways by which to mitigate the implications of remaining intercity differences and to establish a more general context in which to assess the typicality of the data gathered in a single-city survey. Neither way offers a definitive answer to the problem, but both supply bench-

[13] Reported in the *New York Times*, June 25, 1972.

[14] Kenneth Gibson, mayor of Newark, is fond of saying that wherever American cities are going, Newark got there first. This is a bitter reference to the fact that Newark leads the nation's cities in a number of indicators of social decay and pathology.

marks in time and place for comparative purposes. The first involves comparison with survey data collected by other investigators in other cities. This is necessarily a piecemeal process, since a given survey almost never is an exact replica of any other survey. But some similar questions are asked time and again. In this study, comparable data are used where possible.

The second method involves establishing the nature of the relevant particulars of the research setting in such a way as to illuminate the areas and degree of typicality and distinctiveness that must bear on the interpretation of the general applicability of the results. Since this is a study of the context of interracial conflict and cooperation, we naturally must be interested, in the remainder of this chapter, in the extent to which Milwaukee resembles other large American cities in matters related to the politics of race. But we also must understand the particular context and shape of Milwaukee politics that form the backdrop for racial conflict and cooperation. Thus, while the present inquiry is not a study of Milwaukee per se, any judgment about the general import of the findings presented here must be informed by a knowledge of the setting itself.

A Milwaukee Profile: The City, Its Politics, and the Role of Race

Those who write about Milwaukee often begin by stressing its essential conservatism, its comfortable complacency, its working-class industriousness and resulting modest affluence, and its curiously intimate small-town ambience and manners.[15] As a consequence of these features, life for most people in this "village metropolis"[16] is normally manageable, pleasant, and unthreatening to the basic assumptions by which people order their existence. Yet, it is not hard to see that the same character traits that, under certain circumstances, may make life uncomplicated easily can give rise to the sorts of social neglect and self-righteousness that stimulate sharp class and racial animosities. The dilemma of how to deal with these ugly by-products of an otherwise comfortable life style confronted Milwaukeeans through the decade of the 1960s and into the 1970s and, among other things, made racial antagonism a persistent feature of the city's politics.

In terms of racial composition, Milwaukee very closely resembles other northern cities of its general size. In 1970, the city ranked twelfth in the nation in total population, with 717,000 people, of whom 105,000, or 14.7 percent, were black. If we compare Milwaukee to those other cities whose populations placed them, in 1970, among the second ten of the twenty largest cities in the country

---

[15]See, for example, Henry J. Schmandt, John C. Goldbach, and Donald B. Vogel, *Milwaukee: A Contemporary Urban Profile* (New York: Praeger, 1971), pp. 6-10; Robert W. Wells, *This Is Milwaukee* (New York: Doubleday, 1970); and Frank A. Aukofer, *City with a Chance* (Milwaukee: Bruce, 1968), pp. 31 ff.

[16]The term is used by Schmandt, Goldbach, and Vogel, *Milwaukee*, p. 3.

TABLE 2.2 DEMOGRAPHIC COMPARISONS AMONG THE SECOND
TEN LARGEST CITIES IN THE UNITED STATES

City	1970 population (in thousands)	1970 black population (in thousands)	Black (%)	Increase in black population 1960-1970 (%)	Residential segregation 1970[a](%)
Indianapolis	745	134	18.0	34.4	89.0
Milwaukee	717	105	14.7	68.3	85.0
San Francisco	716	96	13.4	29.2	66.0
San Diego	697	53	7.6	53.8	78.0
San Antonio	654	50	7.6	20.3	87.0
Boston	641	105	16.3	65.8	81.0
Memphis	624	243	38.9	31.6	89.0
St. Louis	622	254	40.9	18.6	87.0
New Orleans	593	267	45.0	14.4	83.0
Phoenix	582	28	4.8	33.4	83.0
Average	*659*	*133*	*20.7*	*38.0*	*82.8*

Sources: Census figures were obtained from the U.S. Department of Commerce News Release, February 10, 1971. Segregation figures are from Pierre De Vise, "Chicago's Widening Color Gap: 1971 Status Report" (Paper presented before the South Side Planning Board, Illinois Institute of Technology, May 19, 1971).

[a] Indicates the percentage of blacks who would have to move to all-white blocks to produce a racially proportionate residential distribution in the city.

(thus avoiding the potential skewing effects of making comparisons with the very large cities), we find that it closely resembles the other northern cities that fall into this category: The percentage of blacks in Boston is 16.3; in San Francisco, 13.4; and in Indianapolis, 18.0 (see Table 2.2). Averages of the racial composition figures for the entire second-ten group of cities are skewed to the high side by the heavy concentration of blacks in the three southern cities in this group, but even so they do not diverge sharply from the Milwaukee figures.

Milwaukee's black community is relatively new. At the turn of the century, there were fewer than 500 blacks in the city; by 1930, their number had grown to 7500. The decade of the Depression was a stagnant period; at the onset of World War II, only 8800 blacks lived there. Until this period, the presence of Chicago directly to the south had effectively blocked further migration up the lakeshore. The war industries, however, brought increased migration, and by 1950 there were 21,772 blacks, who represented only 3 percent of the city's population.

In the ensuing decade, nearly 25,000 blacks moved into the city,[17] bringing the total to 62,458, or 8.4 percent of the population. By 1970, the number of blacks had increased by 68.3 percent over the 1960 figure, *the largest percentage increase among all of the cities in this second-ten group.* The rapid transition from relative black invisibility to a substantial black presence perhaps was more

[17]Henry J. Schmandt with William H. Standing, *The Milwaukee Metropolitan Study Commission* (Bloomington, Ind.: Indiana University Press, 1965), p. 11.

sharply felt in Milwaukee than in most other cities. The fact that deeply felt racial antagonism has persisted in the politics of a city in which the black community is still relatively small is in part a function of the speed with which the city had to deal with the problem of race and the fact that it was relatively unprepared by its past experience to do so.

Like most of the other cities in the second ten, Milwaukee is heavily residentially segregated. The black population is concentrated in an area adjacent to the downtown and north of the Menominee River valley. The ghetto is known locally as the Inner Core. Using an index of residential segregation developed by Karl and Alma Taeuber,[18] which measures the percentage of blacks who would have to move to presently all-white blocks in order to produce a racially proportionate residential distribution in the city, Pierre De Visé calculates that Milwaukee is the tenth most segregated big city in the country.[19] According to his data, it ranks as the fifth most segregated city among those in the second-ten group—behind Indianapolis and Memphis, which are tied for first, and San Antonio and St. Louis, which are tied for second (see Table 2.2). The average residential segregation index for these second ten cities in 1970 was 82.8; for Milwaukee it was 85.0.

To the south of the Menominee Valley lie Polish and other Eastern European ethnic neighborhoods. Several bridges, or viaducts as they are known in Milwaukee, span the valley and its railroad yards. The Sixteenth Street Viaduct is the bridge over which the Reverend James Groppi led his black demonstrators in 1967, in quest of open-housing legislation. In Milwaukee a joke has it that the viaduct is the longest bridge in the world: "What else," the comic asks, "could connect Africa and Poland?" There is an edge of tension in the joke, for the physical barrier of the valley is symbolic of the distance between these two ethnic groups in the city.

Although most people associate Milwaukee primarily with its great brewing industry, the economy of the city rests much more on heavy industry. Milwaukee firms are major international suppliers of construction equipment, tractors, cranes, diesel engines, and generators. Beer brewing employs only 2 percent of the labor force of the entire county within which Milwaukee is located.[20] More than one-third of the city labor force is engaged in manufacturing, a statistic in which Milwaukee leads all of the other cities in the second ten (see Table 2.3). In this group of cities, only St. Louis has fewer people employed in white-collar occupations.

[18] Karl E. Taeuber and Alma F. Taeuber, *Negroes in Cities* (Chicago: Aldine, 1965), pp. 29-34.

[19] Pierre De Visé, "Chicago's Widening Color Gap: 1971 Status Report" (Paper presented before the South Side Planning Board, Illinois Institute of Technology, May 19, 1971).

[20] Schmandt, Goldbach, and Vogel, *Milwaukee*, p. 18.

TABLE 2.3 SELECTED SOCIOECONOMIC COMPARISONS AMONG POPULATIONS OF THE SECOND TEN LARGEST CITIES, 1970

City	Schooling completed (median years)	High school graduates (%)	Unemployed (%)	Employed in manufacturing (%)	Median annual family income (in dollars)	Below poverty line (%)	Employed in white-collar occupations (%)
Indianapolis	12.1	54.8	4.3	27.9	10,754	7.1	23.1
Milwaukee	11.9	49.2	4.1	34.8	10,262	8.1	17.8
San Francisco	12.4	61.8	6.4	27.9	10,503	9.9	25.5
San Diego	12.5	66.2	6.6	17.7	10,166	9.3	29.5
San Antonio	10.8	42.7	4.3	12.1	7734	16.1	21.1
Boston	12.1	53.5	4.3	17.5	9133	11.7	22.5
Memphis	12.0	50.1	4.7	20.6	8646	15.7	21.9
St. Louis	9.6	33.1	6.4	27.8	8182	14.3	15.5
New Orleans	10.8	42.3	5.8	11.9	7445	21.6	23.6
Phoenix	12.3	58.9	3.9	20.3	9956	8.8	25.3
Average	11.7	51.3	5.1	21.9	9278	12.3	22.6

Source: U.S. Bureau of the Census, Census of Population, 1970, General Social and Economic Characteristics (Washington, D.C.: U.S. Government Printing Office).

At the close of the 1960s, Milwaukee was not only a prosperous city but one that ranked high on a variety of indicators of "quality of life." The city had a lower unemployment rate than all but one of the cities in the second ten, it had the third highest median annual family income, and only Indianapolis had a smaller percentage of people below the poverty line. In addition, a 1973 report by the Urban Institute in Washington showed that the Milwaukee metropolitan area ranked especially high on a combined index of fourteen indicators of "quality of life."[21] Among eighteen metropolitan areas for which comparative data were available, Milwaukee ranked third, behind Minneapolis—St. Paul and Dallas. The index is composed of rankings on such indicators as cost of housing, crime rate (Milwaukee had the lowest in the nation for cities of its size), infant mortality rate, suicides per 100,000 people, transportation costs, air quality, and poverty-level population. In light of all these statistics, the self-satisfaction Milwaukeeans are said to feel about their city[22] comes as no surprise.

In seeking to protect and nurture the good life, Milwaukeeans have pursued a stable and cautious course in local politics. One manifestation of this husbanding effort has been the tendency of local voters to keep incumbent mayors in office for long periods of time. Daniel Hoan, a Socialist known more for his scrupulous honesty than for his socialism, served from 1916 to 1940. Frank Zeidler, another nominal Socialist, occupied city hall from 1948 to 1960. Henry Maier won the mayoralty in 1960, and began his fourth four-year term in 1972. Of all incumbent big-city mayors in 1974, only Richard Daley of Chicago had served longer in office than Henry Maier.

The politician Maier was very much a product of Milwaukee's working-class culture, and he exemplifies its virtues and problems. After a youthful flirtation with the Socialists, Maier became a Democrat in the postwar years and developed close ties with several big industrial unions.[23] Organized labor remained the central element of his successful coalition.

Maier often fought Milwaukee's civic and social elite. His first opponent for the mayoralty was Congressman Henry Reuss, a member of the North Side establishment. Maier ran a frugal and folksy campaign. Reuss was endorsed by nearly all of the city's leading figures, but Maier won by more than 35,000 votes.

Maier always enjoyed the role of workingman's champion. In the 1972 campaign for a fourth term, for example, he promised to build a lakefront recreation center "where the working people and their families can relax." In Maier's view, the established cultural groups had been insensitive to the recreational needs of

---

[21] Reported in the *New York Times*, October 21, 1973.

[22] A 1965 survey commissioned by the *Milwaukee Journal* revealed that 83 percent of the black sample and 90 percent of the white sample said they liked living in Milwaukee. Bisbing Business Research, *Attitude Study among Negro and White Residents in the Milwaukee Negro Residential Areas* (Milwaukee, 1965), p. 27.

[23] Much of the following account relies upon Ralph Whitehead, Jr., "Milwaukee's Mercurial Mayor Henry Maier," *City* 6 (March-April, 1972): 11-20.

the working class: "All they care about is classical music for suburbanites," he was quoted as saying.[24] While Maier was successful in his identification with Milwaukee's white ethnic working people, his relationship with black Milwaukee was never smooth. Maier's hatred of Father Groppi, his opposition to a local open-housing ordinance, his refusal in 1970 to take the lead in settling a protracted dispute over scattered-site public housing,[25] his support for the tough and aggressive police chief, Harold Brier, and his carefully planned and vigorous response to the 1967 riot[26] (but not to its underlying causes) are among the factors that strained Maier's relations with the black community. Through 1972, at least, Maier had never established lines of communication with recognized black leaders in the city.[27] Although he expected a riot in the city in the summer of 1967[28] and developed elaborate contingency plans for handling it, he scarcely set foot in the Inner Core during the year prior to the disturbance.[29] He was never the sort of mayor to take Lindsay-like walks in the ghettos.[30] Even while the brief riot was actually in progress, he refused to meet with spokesmen from the Inner Core whom he considered militant.[31]

One of the tactics Maier often used was to avoid assuming active political leadership functions in tense interracial disputes by claiming that he had no formal jurisdiction in the area. This was the case when blacks asked him, in the school boycott of 1964, to intervene with a recalcitrant school board. It was also the case during the later open-housing conflict; Maier claimed that a metropolitan area open-housing law, not a city-only law, was the only proper legislative solution to the problem. The metropolitan area was, of course, beyond his jurisdiction. He employed the tactic again when he was asked to support federal guidelines concerning the diffusion of public housing throughout the city, the so-called scattered-site housing program. Only the Common Council, he claimed, had jurisdiction in this area. The consequence of this formalistic strategy was to place himself, at least by implication, on the opposite side from blacks in a variety of issues.

[24] Ibid., pp. 19-20.

[25] Reported in the *Milwaukee Journal*, April 12, 1970.

[26] For a good account of Maier's handling of the riot itself, see H. R. Wilde, "Milwaukee's National Media Riot," in *Urban Government*, ed. Edward C. Banfield (New York: Free Press, 1969), pp. 682-688.

[27] Ibid., p. 686; and Whitehead, "Milwaukee's Mercurial Mayor," p. 17.

[28] A week before the riot occurred, Maier canceled plans to go east to a convention in the expectation that violence was imminent. The *Milwaukee Journal* quotes him after the riot as saying, "I am not astonished we had a riot. I am astonished it did not come sooner. I had it down to about one week." *Milwaukee Journal*, August 6, 1967.

[29] Wilde, "Milwaukee's Riot," p. 686.

[30] See John Lindsay's account of one of his famous 1968 ghetto walks in his book *The City* (New York: Norton, 1970), pp. 97-100.

[31] *Newsweek*, August 14, 1967, p. 20.

One of the reasons why Maier made few overtures or commitments to blacks was that he did not need them politically. He put together, without the aid of blacks, a more than minimum winning coalition. Black support was superfluous. He saw clearly that to take strong positions in favor of such black causes as open housing would alienate those very groups on whom he always relied for his major support.[32] Any black support he might gain would not be great enough to replace the white support he would inevitably lose by such a strategy.

Maier's position in Milwaukee politics was a commanding one. His position, however, owed little to the formal dimensions of the office. Milwaukee has a weak-mayor system. The chief executive has little independent appointive power; most appointments must be ratified by the Common Council. The major officers of his administration—city attorney, treasurer, and comptroller—are independently elected by the voters. The mayor's office has no executive budget.

The political structure of the city is also unfavorable to the accretion of significant individual power. Milwaukee is formally nonpartisan (although Maier did draw on the resources of the county Democratic party), which means that a political leader has no stable institutional apparatus to dominate, to use in pulling together resources, or to draw upon. In addition, the informal structure of power in the city is what has been described as "polynucleated," or pluralistic.[33] A mayor's aide has complained that Milwaukee is "a veto-oriented town."[34]

Despite these handicaps, Maier pyramided power by courting the Common Council; he frequently appointed former councilmen to administrative and regulatory boards, having, through a series of governmental reorganization schemes, placed new agencies and some old ones under the authority of the mayor. And he built a state- and nation-wide consituency for his role as expert on, and champion of, the cities. Mayor Richard Daley was impressed enough to suggest Maier as a vice-presidential possibility in 1972. By 1974, Maier was the most active single participant in Milwaukee decision making[35] and master of the city's most powerful coalition.

In 1970, only four of the second-ten cities had better ratios of black officeholders to black population than did Milwaukee. In absolute terms, however, Milwaukee at that time had only three black officeholders—two aldermen and one school board member. Interpreted in the starkest of racial terms, this meant one black alderman for every 52,500 blacks, but one white alderman for every 35,900 whites. Milwaukee has a total of nineteen aldermen, each based in a ward.

[32] Schmandt, Goldbach, and Vogel, *Milwaukee*, p. 101.
[33] Ibid., Chapter 4; and Schmandt with Standing, *Milwaukee Metropolitan Study Commission*, pp. 24-25.
[34] Whitehead, "Milwaukee's Mercurial Mayor," p. 18.
[35] Schmandt, Goldbach, and Vogel, *Milwaukee*, p. 96.

Nearly all of the significant figures in Milwaukee's pluralistic structure of power are white. Black political capabilities have been limited by a variety of factors, not the least of which is the relatively small size of the black community; black political influence is a rare ingredient in the calculus of decision making in the city. Nevertheless, the emergence of a black political community has been proceeding at a steady pace over the past ten years. Milwaukee blacks have in no sense been isolated from the main current of the developments that have shaped black politics nationally. If anything, black political efforts in a few areas have been marginally more successful in Milwaukee than in cities of similar size, and Milwaukee blacks certainly have been more actively militant within the context of the civil rights movement than have blacks in many other cities.

Black political success must often be measured in the most modest terms. If we compare the ratios of black officeholders to black population among the second ten largest cities, we find that in 1970 Milwaukee's representation ratio was slightly better than the average (Table 2.4).

Six of these ten cities experienced civil disorders during the summer of 1967,[36] and a seventh, Memphis, saw major violence in 1968. These outbreaks varied in intensity. Of the 1967 riots, the eruption in Milwaukee was considered by the Kerner Commission to be among the most severe in the nation (a "major disorder," according to the commission's classification scheme), those in St. Louis and San Diego were "minor disorders," and the remainder fell in between.[37]

Milwaukee also has a history of black protest. Systematic comparison with other cities is difficult, since records of protest incidents have not been compiled. In one study of protest in forty-three large American cities, however, five of the second-ten cities fell within the sample: Milwaukee, San Francisco, Boston, Phoenix, and New Orleans. Over a six-month period in 1968, the first three of these cities recorded more protests, and more black protests, than any of the other forty cities in the sample. Milwaukee in fact had the most of all.[38]

Milwaukee's most notable protest campaign involved six months of daily street marches in 1967 and 1968, led by the Reverend James Groppi, a white priest, to secure an open-housing ordinance. These protests attracted national attention, and, in the end, were successful in their basic objective. Other major black protests included school boycotts in 1964 and 1965 by a civil rights coalition called Milwaukee United School Integration Committee (MUSIC), protesting racial imbalance in the inner-city schools. And, during 1969 and 1970, various welfare groups, including the National Welfare Rights Organization, be-

---

[36] The four that did not have riots were Indianapolis, San Antonio, Memphis, and New Orleans.

[37] *Report of the National Advisory Commission on Civil Disorders* (New York: Bantam, 1968), pp. 158-159.

[38] Peter K. Eisinger, "The Conditions of Protest Behavior in American Cities," *American Political Science Review* 67 (March 1973): 28.

TABLE 2.4 RATIO OF BLACK OFFICEHOLDERS TO BLACK
POPULATION IN THE SECOND TEN LARGEST CITIES, 1970

City	Number of black officeholders[a]	Ratio
Indianapolis	9	1:15,000
Milwaukee	3	1:35,000
San Francisco	2	1:48,000
San Diego	3	1:18,000
San Antonio	1	1:50,000
Boston	1	1:105,000
Memphis	4	1:61,000
St. Louis	16	1:16,000
New Orleans	2	1:133,000
Phoenix	2	1:14,000
Average ratio		*1:49,000*

Source: *National Roster of Black Elected Officials* (Washington, D.C.: Joint Center for
Political Studies, March 1971).

[a]Officeholders include city councilmen, municipal judges,and school board members.

came active in Milwaukee and helped to sponsor a series of militant demonstrations, including a march of local welfare recipients to the state capitol in Madison. Other institutions, including the Eagles Club, a major supermarket chain,
and the largest manufacturing employer in the city—Allis-Chalmers—have also
been the targets of much-publicized protests by black organizations in recent
years.

In a broad sense, going beyond the details of these confrontations, such
events do not distinguish Milwaukee. The city has no special reputation as a
harbinger of racial developments. But neither is it a sleepy backwater. The city's
residents did once cherish the view that they lived in a "village metropolis,"
friendly, unsophisticated, and conservative in its general character. But, as Henry
Schmandt and his colleagues observe, reflecting on the experience of racial confrontation in the city: "Milwaukeeans, looking in the mirror of events, saw
themselves to be little different from their counterparts in other urban areas.
The image of *Gemütlichkeit*, of a city of friendly people, was shattered."[39]

Milwaukee as a Sample City

How does this brief profile of Milwaukee bear on the problem of the reliability of this survey as a means of interpreting developments beyond this Wisconsin city? Clearly, one must be very cautious. Milwaukee is not an entirely
"typical" city. Its personalities, its recent political history, and its sense of itself

[39]Schmandt, Goldbach, and Vogel, *Milwaukee*, p. 156.

are elements characteristic of that city alone, emerging from its particular culture and heritage. But of course that is true of any city. However, in casting about for particular characteristics to serve as a context in which the survey results may be interpreted, we would not, I think, select the city's exemplary working-class solidity or its lack of sophistication, but rather, the fact that blacks are a small minority there.

Aside from this feature, the particular character of Milwaukee is not, I would argue, very important for our purposes. In certain important ways, the city is a laboratory, much like other laboratories. What is important is not the existence of certain distinguishing characteristics and traditions but the fact that, in a variety of respects, Milwaukee cannot be distinguished *systematically* from other American cities. If it does not "stand for" other cities or all cities, neither does it stand alone. What we find here, then, is surely suggestive, substantively as well as theoretically, for the politics of other big cities in other parts of the country.

Political Integration in the City

3

On the evening of August 28, 1967, a column of several hundred young black people, conspicuously led by a white priest, marched into Milwaukee's Polish South Side neighborhood to dramatize their demands for a local open-housing ordinance. Their intrusion was met by residents of this working-class district, who came armed with racially insulting placards and assorted missiles. For a while, the police contained the confrontation, but it soon became clear that they would not maintain control for long. After a brief, symbolic picnic in Kosciuszko Park, the black marchers quickly left the South Side, pursued by taunting youths and a barrage of rocks.

The young black people, members of the National Association for the Advancement of Colored People (NAACP) Youth Council, and their white adviser, the Reverend James Groppi, returned the next night and the next and for approximately 230 nights thereafter. A white counterprotest organization—also led by a white priest—was formed in September and named Citizens for Closed Housing. This group marched too, but only for a short period, before altering its tactics and changing its name to Milwaukee Citizens Civic Voice, to present a more moderate image.

This was a tense period in Milwaukee, and few public figures were interested in conciliation or compromise. Mayor Maier, who refused to support a city open-housing ordinance, referred to the marches as "Groppi's unworthy cause"[1]

---

[1] Frank Aukofer, *City with a Chance* (Milwaukee: Bruce, 1968), p. 113.

and called Groppi himself a hatemonger.[2] Groppi in turn responded with the promise, "There'll be no peace in this city until a bill is signed."[3] "We are going to keep marching," he announced, "until we get fair housing so we can move in here with these white bigots or wherever we want."[4]

During this period, pressure in the white community in favor of open housing was modest at best. A survey conducted during the heat of the controversy showed that while 90 percent of the blacks polled favored an open-housing law, only 43 percent of the whites polled did so.[5]

When Alderwoman Vel Phillips, the first black on the Common Council, first proposed open-housing legislation in 1962, hers was the only vote to be cast in its favor.[6] This set a pattern of white intransigence that marked the conflict over open housing until April 1968, when the Common Council, with seven new members and in the wake of federal open-housing legislation, finally passed a tough local law. Until this abrupt and unexpected ending, however, the issue was debated in an atmosphere marked by considerable violence on both sides and by a general unwillingness, especially on the part of city officials, to compromise on or even to debate the matter. This is not to say that no one tried conciliation. A number of predominantly white groups—church and civic groups, some labor and business organizations, the media, and a committee of prominent and very moderate white and black citizens—all came out in favor of some type of open-housing law. Several of these groups proposed compromises, and many suggested meetings between the major antagonists. None of these pressures succeeded in moving the mayor or the Common Council.

In general, such intransigence and unpredictability signal a weakness in a political system. When parties to a conflict are persistently unwilling or unable to resolve issues through established institutions or to meet to discuss their differences in a setting governed by ground rules that delineate permissible modes of conflict resolution and norms of accommodation, we may speak of political malintegration. The open-housing controversy was undoubtedly the most intensely felt and divisive issue of the decade in Milwaukee politics, but it is, I think, illustrative in some measure of the consequences of a particular attitudinal context within which elites engaged in interracial politics operate.

Our task in this chapter is to explore the nature of that attitudinal context as it bears on political integration. The time at which this survey took place was

---

[2]*Newsweek*, September 18, 1967, p. 32.

[3]Ibid.

[4]*U.S. News and World Report*, September 25, 1967, p. 24.

[5]Jonathan Slesinger, "Study of Community Opinions concerning the Summer 1967 Civil Disturbance in Milwaukee" (Unpublished report, Office of Applied Social Research, School of Social Welfare and Institute of Human Relations, University of Wisconsin–Milwaukee, April 1, 1968), p. 18.

[6]In at least three subsequent attempts to get an open-housing ordinance passed, Phillips was defeated 18–1 each time.

a more peaceful one for the city than was 1967, but some of the pressures and constraints under which its elites had dealt with the issue of open housing were still much in evidence.

The Meaning of Political Integration

Political integration refers to a situation in which diverse groups in a political system have been successful in developing common institutions and norms by which to settle conflicts peacefully or to pursue collective goals cooperatively, depending on the particular circumstances of the situation. Integration is built on the fact of diversity, the need for mutual accommodation, and the desire of parties in the system to maintain the integrity of competing groups.

Scholars have shown particular interest in the extent to which nation-states manage to achieve integration in the international system and in the ability of diverse subnational groupings in the "emerging states" to achieve national unification peacefully. The problem of political integration in the United States as a whole and in its cities in particular has virtually been ignored. This is attributable, no doubt, to the persistent myth of assimilation, which assumed either that various ethnic groups and races lost their political identity in the melting pot or that, maintaining their sense of cultural distinctiveness, they nevertheless came to accept the prevailing norms and institutions of American politics. If the lessons of the racial confrontations of the last decade and the recent reexamination of the history of domestic political violence[7] have taught us anything, it is that neither of these assumptions is entirely valid. The concept of political integration, it would appear, has vital relevance for understanding interracial politics in America.

In terms of the argument presented in Chapter 1, the types of interracial political relationships that elites may establish most easily are in part a function of the extent to which the masses of the two races accept and adhere to the common institutions and norms designed to regulate and manage the process of conflict resolution. For our purposes, then, the pattern of mass commitment to these norms has important strategic implications for elites.

Interracial consensus on the validity of the norms implies a certain stability in the political relationships established between the racial groups. Elites and followers can expect certain responses from competing elites and followers and are, in turn, expected to deal with those responses in generally prescribed ways. To give one example, a commitment to the necessity of compromise represents a norm designed to facilitate conflict resolution; parties in competition or groups

---

[7]See, for example, Ted Robert Gurr and Hugh D. Graham, eds., *Violence in America: Historical and Comparative Perspectives* (Washington, D.C.: National Commission on the Causes and Prevention of Violence, 1969).

considering coalition expect each other to work toward an ultimate accommodation lying somewhere between their respective initially preferred positions. Refusal to negotiate or willingness to use violence in an attempt to impose a
preferred position indicates a lack of general commitment to the norm of compromise. Normative divergence, then, injects a degree of instability into the
conflict process, in the sense that it deprives competitors or potential coalition
partners of mechanisms for the mutually satisfactory solution of differences. The
absence of shared expectations forces parties to engage in political interchange in
a context that is without orderly structure. Elites, of course, are seriously constrained by an unstable situation. Even if they themselves are committed to a
politics of compromise and negotiation, they cannot guarantee the behavior of
followers who disavow the norms that underlie such principles of interchange.

An example of this sort of situation occurred during the open-housing controversy. A prominent white public relations counsel, working out of the public
eye, had sought to establish a special committee composed of citizens and members of government, to work out a compromise.[8] His efforts found favor both
with the Common Council Judiciary Committee and with several citizens' organizations, including the NAACP Youth Council. A committee was formed, and
its members worked out a series of alternative proposals to present to the Common Council as a whole. Negotiation and compromise were proceeding in good
faith. A day before the Common Council was to consider the various proposals,
however, the Milwaukee Citizens Civic Voice, the South Side organization opposed to open housing, presented a petition bearing 27,000 signatures that directed the Common Council to submit to public referendum a resolution prohib-
iting the passage of open-housing legislation for at least two years. This was
meant to be—and would have been, had the referendum been held—the death
blow to open housing. Without examining the legality of such a referendum (it
was later declared unconstitutional in the courts), the Common Council dropped
its plans to consider the special committee's proposals and ordered the referendum held. Elite efforts to arrive at a compromise had been rendered ineffective,
at least temporarily, by the pressures generated by mass intransigence.

How can we begin to measure attitudes important for political integration?
The theme of political community emerges persistently, although students differ
on the precise definition of that term.[9] The notion of political community
implies a set of shared norms on the one hand and a set of common institutions
and processes on the other, all for the management of political conflict. For
example, Claude Ake writes:

[8] Aukofer, *City with a Chance*, pp. 132-133.
[9] Fred Hayward surveys various definitions in "Continuities and Discontinuities between Studies of National and International Political Integration," *International Organization* 24 (1970): 917-920.

A political system is integrated to the extent that the minimal units (individual political actors) develop in the course of political interaction a pool of commonly accepted norms regarding political behavior and a commitment to the behavior patterns legitimized by these norms.[10]

And Karl Deutsch suggests that political integration implies "the attainment, within a territory, ... of institutions and practices strong enough and widespread enough to assure, for a 'long' time, dependable expectations of 'peaceful change' among its population."[11]

These norms and institutions are products of certain implicit value premises that form the ideal basis of an open political society. One such value is expressed in the form of a commitment to the survival of competing political interests, both during and after the pursuit of a particular political goal. Another value concerns the desirability of settling conflicts in ways at least minimally tolerable to contending parties. While these values may reflect unattainable ideals, even in relatively well-integrated societies, they are nevertheless grounded on the twin realizations that conflicts are inevitable in society and that absolutely satisfactory solutions to such conflicts are virtually impossible to find.

In general, then, one may say that a polity is politically integrated if diverse groups support and work through the common institutions designed to deal with conflict (namely government) and agree upon and act upon the norms implied by the basic value premises. Thus, there are two dimensions of integration: shared attitudes and norms on the one hand and action congruent with those attitudes and norms on the other. Our immediate interest is in attitudes and norms, for we are concerned with the strategic *possibilities* available to elites as they seek to mobilize and lead mass followings in interracial politics. The specific purpose of this chapter is to explore the differences and similarities in professed commitment to governmental institutions and integrative norms between the two racial groups in Milwaukee.

There are, I believe, several aspects of this commitment, if the term "commitment" is broadly construed. One involves basic evaluations of government that relate ultimately to trust or support. A second concerns adherence to various logically related norms governing the pursuit and resolution of conflict. A third relates to beliefs about the centrality of the individual citizen's role in politics. The nature of these aspects and the way in which they are interrelated require detailed examination before we turn our attention to the data.

If we are to assess the extent to which people accept common governmental institutions (one of whose functions is to mediate and decide conflicts among groups), then we must devise ways of testing their support and trust of those institutions. It is not difficult to see that groups that in some fundamental sense

[10] Claude Ake, *A Theory of Political Integration* (Homewood, Ill.: Dorsey, 1967), p. 3.
[11] Karl Deutsch, "Political Community and the North Atlantic Area," in *International Political Communities: An Anthology* (Garden City, N.Y.: Doubleday, 1966), p. 2.

do not trust government will scarcely feel confident about taking their differences with other groups into the governmental arena for resolution. In such a case we cannot speak of an integrated conflict process, because at least some of the parties in conflict have no faith in the institutions designed as the focus of that process.

One way to arrive at an assessment of a generalized sense of trust is to determine basic evaluations of "government." These are not evaluations of specific policies or acts of government, nor of specific actors or regimes, but rather of that vague set of institutions and symbols as seen in the mind's eye of the citizen. In this survey I have used several means to measure this sense of support or trust; one of the most fruitful involves providing an opportunity for the respondent to give a free-association response to the term "government." Answers can be coded, as we shall see, as positive, neutral, negative, or prescriptive. "Prescriptive" involves evaluations of what government could or should be doing, or suggestions for action.

A second characteristic of politically integrated societies is consensus on certain essential rules and modes of functioning in the process of conflict resolution. This consensus includes a variety of commitments and judgments, stated in normative terms, that comprise an objective understanding of how things ought to be in the political process and a subjective sense of how they are. It includes, more specifically, commitment to norms defining the boundaries and mechanisms that govern the means by which politics may be pursued, support for the political system, and assessments of the manner in which the system, as it relates to conflict management, operates. In a polity in which such normative consensus is high and cuts across diverse groups, basic ideological disputes and disagreements over policy may both be resolved in ways that preserve social peace and protect the survival of the respective parties.

The most important norm, to which all others are connected in one way or another, is the commitment to peaceful politics, or conversely, the unwillingness to use violence to achieve political ends. Assuming a society in which groups are relatively free to participate in peaceful politics, it can be seen that this norm limiting strategic options is of profound importance. Crossing the boundary represents a real threat to the integrity and survival of competing groups.[12]

Given a commitment to avoid violence, it follows that groups must work out formal and informal mechanisms to maintain peace. Peace is more likely to be

---

[12] To state this does not necessarily bring an ethical judgment to bear on the use of political violence. As Ted Robert Gurr writes, "specific acts of political violence can be good, bad, or neutral according to the viewpoint of the observer. . . . But it does not require an ethical judgment to observe that intense violence is destructive: even if some political violence is valued by both citizens and rulers, the greater its magnitude the less efficiently a political system fulfills its other functions. Violence generally consumes men and goods, it seldom enhances them." *Why Men Rebel* (Princeton, N.J.: Princeton University Press, 1970), p. 4.

maintained if decisions made by government are perceived as fair or at least fairly reached. To some degree, fairness is a function of compromise. As Deutsch points out, the norm of compromise is a crucial aspect of political integration.[13] Compromises are outcomes that represent adjustments of competing interests; they mark some middle ground. Unsatisfactory as compromise may be to those who seek decisions based on "pure" (meaning uncompromised) criteria, the logical implications of peaceful conflict resolution require a readiness to consider compromise as a general principle.

Compromises themselves may be deemed "fair" or "unfair," however. These characterizations of outcomes represent normative judgments levied by the parties to conflict. Their judgments are not always a function of the extent to which the outcome favors their interests. Frequently, in fact, parties to conflict will believe that the outcome is fair simply because the authoritative decision-makers have heard all points of view and followed regularized, neutral procedures—even if the substance of the outcome is in some measure unfavorable to their interests.

In a broad sense, then, the general view that government is usually fair is an important aspect of political integration; and it is a sign of system support, in the sense that the attribution of fairness is also an attribution of legitimacy.

More specifically, both the government itself and the compromises it proposes probably will be perceived as fair if all interested parties have, and believe they have, free access to decisionmakers. A belief that the society is open is therefore another essential aspect of political integration. The belief that one can gain a hearing from authority figures not only reflects some degree of openness but also helps to maintain it. The fact that one believes he can gain access, even if he does not seek or use it, in itself helps to maintain certain expectations on the part of citizens and officials alike. Citizens expect to be able to make demands on or talk to public officials; officials are aware of this. To deny that right is to risk destroying citizen expectations that the system indeed is open. And to destroy such expectations is to jeopardize support for the system. Hence, the belief that one can gain the opportunity to make demands on officials if one wishes constitutes latent pressure to maintain an open political system and contributes directly to political integration.

Political integration also requires that citizens agree on formal mechanisms for ending conflicts. A mechanism for peacefully ending one type of conflict—competition for public office—is the vote. The belief that voting is legitimate and decisive is important for integration. In other words, citizens in an integrated society agree not only that voting is a valid method of making collective choices about officeholders but also that it makes a decisive difference, in the sense that

---

[13] Karl Deutsch, *The Analysis of International Relations* (Englewood Cliffs, N.J.: Prentice-Hall, 1968), p. 199.

the course of action pursued by government probably would be different if the vote had gone another way.

It should be said that these normative commitments, even when widely held, do not invariably govern the political process. In other words, consensus on the norms themselves is not to be taken as a reliable reflection of the nature of political interchange. Citizens pledged to the maintenance of an open political society may nevertheless spend their energies preventing the consideration of all relevant viewpoints in a dispute. And many of the decisions reached in such conditions are not genuine compromises. People are quick to take advantage of the built-in biases in the system that favor their interests. Finally, even those who most strongly profess a commitment to peaceful politics may resort to the most blatant violence.

But the object of studying the patterns of a society's normative commitments and judgments is not to describe the way in which that social order actually operates. Rather, in a general sense, one examines the norms in order to comprehend the standards of the society and the degree to which behavior is congruent with these standards. More specifically for our concerns, such an examination provides an indication of the extent of mass support that elites can count on when selecting alternative strategies in the pursuit of intergroup politics. Presumably, the normative commitments of the masses provide potential support for some behaviors (such as bargaining) and not for others (such as violence). The options that are most likely to command mass support, then, tell us much about the potential quality of interracial political relationships. It is obvious that when substantial portions of both racial populations agree on integrative norms, there are good possibilities for close cooperation and for the regulated and stable resolution of conflict.

A third aspect of the integrative matrix of commitments and judgments concerns beliefs about the centrality and effectiveness of the individual citizen in politics. These beliefs are subsumed under the notion of "political efficacy"—the sense that an individual can master intellectually, in a general way, the complexities of politics, that a range of possible strategies is available to him, that the strategy chosen will effectively influence government. A widespread sense of efficacy is important for political integration because it lies at the foundation of individual political participation. Efficacy constitutes an expression of confidence that makes the act of political self-assertion possible. Participation, in turn, is central to politically integrated democratic systems because it supports, informs, and constrains elites in the processes of political interchange. A politically integrated system is an open one, in which competing views may be heard. The participation of individual citizens helps to make views visible and lends those views force and legitimacy. While participation itself is the subject of later chapters, the attitudes that underlie it are appropriately discussed here.

To recapitulate, there exists a matrix of evaluations, attitudes, and beliefs, and the degree of consensus on them helps determine the extent to which a society is politically integrated. The degree of mass-level convergence is one determinant of the type of political relationship that blacks and whites are likely to establish with one another. In a society in which the citizens of both races agree generally on the worth and integrity of government, the limits and mechanisms of the conflict resolution process, and the value of individual political participation, conditions are such that blacks and whites can form cooperative or competitive relationships that do not weaken the essential framework within which politics operates. Such a situation serves to confine behavior on the part of potential allies and antagonists to a predictable and consensual range. A state of political integration does not eliminate conflict; rather, it makes it possible for parties to proceed with conflict under a set of similar basic assumptions. In the following sections we turn to an examination of the survey data to explore interracial similarities and differences with regard to these key integrative elements.

The Measurement of Integrative Elements

Free-Association Evaluations of Government

To ask survey respondents outright whether they support or trust government would seem to introduce numerous possibilities for misunderstanding. What is meant by "trust" and "support"? As for "support," does it refer to feelings toward a particular regime or administration? Does it involve support for particular actions? And what does it entail? One strategy to determine basic levels of trust or support that avoids some of these ambiguities involves allowing people to summon up whatever images of government they wish and then coding the emotional or evaluative terms in which they express those images. This course proceeds on the assumption that a free-association test produces, in the first response, certain dominant emotional reactions to a given substantive term or idea. While this strategy has the drawback of allowing the respondent to specify the object of his own emotions (that is, he supplies what he means by "government"), it has the advantage of not suggesting to him that the investigator is interested in something called "support" or "trust."

Respondents were asked: "When you think about the government, what comes to mind?" Later in the interview they were asked specifically: "When you think about government in Milwaukee, what comes to mind?" Such questions have been employed before to determine cognitive associations with the term "government,"[14] but they have not been employed to tap evaluative orientations.

---

[14] See Jack Dennis, *Political Learning in Childhood and Adolescence: A Study of Fifth, Eighth, and Eleventh Graders in Milwaukee, Wisconsin*, University of Wisconsin, Wisconsin Research and Development Center for Cognitive Learning, Technical Report No. 98 (Madison, Wis., October 1969).

TABLE 3.1 SURVEY RESPONSES INDICATING DIFFERENT
EVALUATIVE ORIENTATIONS TOWARD GOVERNMENT, BY
RACE

| | White respondents | | | | Black respondents | | | |
| | "The government" | | "The government in Milwaukee" | | "The government" | | "The government in Milwaukee" | |
Response	%	N	%	N	%	N	%	N
Positive	7	22	18	54	2	4	12	22
Neutral	70	212	55	162	49	92	24	44
Negative	19	56	20	59	44	84	53	98
Prescriptive	4	12	6	17	5	9	11	20
Total	*100*	*302*	*99*	*292*	*100*	*189*	*100*	*184*

Note: Differences between racial orientations toward "the government" are significant at .001 level ($\chi^2 = 42.08$). Differences between racial orientations toward Milwaukee government are significant at .001 level ($\chi^2 = 70.10$).

For approximately half the black sample, both "the government" and "the government in Milwaukee," especially the latter, evoked negative emotions. For a substantial majority of the white respondents, the same terms elicited either outright praise or neutral statements. What has striking implications for the city is that negative black reaction increased when "the government in Milwaukee" was substituted for the more abstract "the government," while for whites the introduction of the specific governmental reference brought a sizable increase in distinctly positive statements (see Table 3.1).

Responses were classified as affectively positive when they were overtly approving, laudatory, admiring, or trustful. Neither racial group was generous with spontaneous admiration in response to either question, but close to one-fifth of the white sample praised Milwaukee government, answering that what came to mind was that it was "a good system," or that "they are doing a pretty good job."

Neutral responses usually contained no value statements; in some cases they presented a balanced view, as in the following: "Government is usually honest, but sometimes it isn't." The majority of white responses fell in this neutral category, and most of them may be characterized as value-free descriptions of government institutions or functions.

Expressions of anger, bitterness, hostility, scorn, and dissatisfaction, or outright condemnations citing government failures and incapacity, were classified as affectively negative. The tone of white responses was only slightly more critical toward "the government in Milwaukee" than toward "the government," while for blacks the increase in negativism toward the city government was substantially sharper.

More than one-half of white, but fewer than one-quarter of black, answers were neutral regarding Milwaukee government. A small portion of both racial samples commented on what government could or should be doing. These were classified as prescriptive responses. While critical in tone, they included suggestions of what courses of action government might take. Some respondents, for example, were reminded by the term "government" that it should be doing more for black people or that it did not hire enough blacks.

Data from surveys conducted in Detroit in 1967 and 1971 reveal the same general patterns, using different questions, of a low level of black trust in government.[15] The racial differences in evaluative orientations in both Milwaukee and Detroit contrast sharply with older research findings on the subject. In 1958, the Survey Research Center at the University of Michigan developed a scale of positive–negative feeling toward government based on a series of questions concerning ethical qualities of public officials, government efficiency and honesty, and the "correctness" of policy decisions. Donald Stokes analyzed these national data for variations in evaluative orientations by social group, and he discovered that there were no differences. Not only were strong negative feelings absent generally, but those that did exist were not concentrated in particular racial, religious, or ethnic elements in the population.[16]

While the Survey Research Center data are not strongly comparable to the Milwaukee data, both sets tap basic affect toward government, and a comparison of the two reveals an apparent change in black attitudes. Of the variety of factors that might account for this change in black feelings since the 1950s, the development of independent black political strength and aspirations and the frustration felt by black ghetto dwellers at the slow and often reluctant pace of government action on their behalf[17] certainly are important ones. These were essentially the factors Stokes cited, in less specific form, as a theoretical explanation of variations in affective attitudes within a population.

> The more central and enduring the group basis of conflict and the more the state is an instrument of the dominant social forces, the more extreme will be the differences in the attitudes different groups have toward government. Certainly examples are plentiful enough of societies in which deep hostility toward the regime has developed in racial or class or ethnic groupings that feel themselves lastingly cut off from political power.[18]

[15] Joel Aberbach and Jack Walker, *Race in the City* (Boston: Little, Brown, 1973), pp. 182-184.

[16] Donald E. Stokes, "Popular Evaluations of Government: An Empirical Assessment," in *Ethics and Bigness*, ed. Harland Cleveland and Harold Lasswell (New York: Harper, 1962), p. 65.

[17] As California State Senator Mervyn Dymally, a black, has written, "the Black man in America has been condemned to seek radical ends within a political framework which was designed to prevent sudden radical social and economic changes." "The Black Outsider and the American Political System," in *The Black Politician: His Struggle for Power*, ed. Mervyn Dymally (Belmont, Cal.: Duxbury, 1971), p. 118.

[18] Stokes, "Evaluations of Government," p. 62.

Although blacks in contemporary America may not feel "lastingly cut off from political power," they chafe at least at the slow-coming effects and the resistance that meet their attempts to acquire it. To the extent that whites appear to wield the power of the state to protect their own interests, the state—that is, as it is represented by the government—becomes an object of revulsion and distrust for blacks.[19]

If political integration depends on the resolution of intergroup conflicts through the acceptance of common institutions—which in turn involves trust in or support for those institutions—then it may be said that these data signal a major racial difference that is likely to make stable modes of interaction difficult. One logical implication of black negativism is that existing arrangements are not satisfactory. Whatever images the term "government" evokes, they are images colored by negative emotional associations. Blacks are not only less likely to trust government as a common set of institutions for conflict management; they are also unlikely to be able to coalesce easily with groups that feel differently.

Normative Consensus on the Nature of the Conflict Process

Given the ubiquity of political conflict, men in democratic societies devise formal and informal rules for the mutual protection of parties in competition. Elites who initiate and pursue conflict depend in some measure upon general adherence to these rules, both by other elites and by their respective mass constituencies, as a condition of survival. These rules, or norms, serve to moderate the processes by which conflicts are resolved and to set limits on the nature of the demands competing elites may pose to one another. Furthermore, the norms are designed to ensure a certain degree of equity in the decision-making procedures.[20] Such norms apply not only to elites in formal government positions (elected officials and bureaucrats) and their constituencies (electors and clients) but also to leaders of nonofficial interest aggregations and their followers.

My aim in this section is to bring data to bear on an assessment of the degree of interracial agreement on several logically related normative commitments and judgments relating to the pursuit and resolution of political conflict. The findings here complement, enlarge upon, and make specific the previous findings on the patterns of sentiment revealed by the free-association tests.

It should be emphasized at the outset that, when substantial segments of the

---

[19] In the 1967 Slesinger survey, respondents were asked how much they thought the city government was doing to encourage racial integration. While 66 percent of the whites thought it was doing the right amount, only 13 percent of the blacks were equally satisfied. However, 73 percent of the black sample thought the city government was doing too little, compared to 15 percent of the white sample that thought so. Slesinger, "Study of Opinions," p. 28.

[20] The notion of equity applies here only to the nature of the procedures used to reach decisions, not to the nature of the outcomes.

population disagree on norms that limit the ways in which conflict ought and ought not to be carried out, then the very survival of competing interests, especially those of minority groups, is called into question. This is the case when competitors on both sides of a cleavage line reject the norms, as may have been the situation in some measure during the early stages of the open-housing controversy in Milwaukee. But it is also the case if only one side, the dominant or majority population group, is committed to the norms in principle, as our survey data suggest. This paradox is not difficult to understand. If the majority segment, for example, is committed in principle to peaceful modes of political interchange, while the minority segment is not, then the majority segment is likely to feel constrained to respond in practice, as a matter of survival, with counter or preemptive violence. In the same way, if the majority group is committed to a politics of compromise and accommodation, while the minority segment is rigid in its political postures, then compromise on mutually agreed-upon grounds is virtually impossible. Hence, in order to describe a polity as politically integrated, we must find that agreement on the normative commitments and judgments is general among competing groups. Commitment to the norms by one group only is insufficient to ensure a peaceful, equitable politics, and it presages obvious difficulties in the formation of certain types of coalitions.

However, general agreement, in principle, on the norms guarantees neither that conflicts will be resolved fairly nor that coalitions will be stable or mutually satisfactory. Majorities may impose their version of accommodation on minorities so consistently that, even if the minorities are also committed to compromise, that commitment may gain them so little as to be meaningless in practice. How politics operates in practice is yet another question and one that serves to obscure the present problem, which is the degree of consensus on those normative principles that provide standards for political conduct and exert pressure on elites.

The predominant pattern that emerges in the following data does not bode well either for integrated modes of interracial conflict resolution or for stable interracial coalitions. At the mass level, blacks and whites diverge sharply in their normative commitments and assessments. To the extent that racial divergence does in fact exist, elites in the two racial groups are unlikely to establish interracial political relationships, of conflict or of cooperation, in which their mass constituencies hold similar assumptions about the conduct of politics. What is especially striking is that the patterns of white adherence to the norms and black rejection of them appear to cut across class lines, leaving the racial factor as the more significant discriminating variable.

Take, for example, the problem of the role of violence in American society. To pursue violence as a political strategy is to attempt, through the use of force, to destroy, or render impotent, opponent groups. Even the ostensibly restrained use of violence, such as that employed by police in "riot" or "mob" control, clearly abnegates the immediate if not the long-range possibility of reasoned accommodation.

Blacks and whites in Milwaukee tended to differ sharply in their views of violence. The results shown in Table 3.2, involving responses to a statement in which violence was placed in a concrete context associated with black deprivation, perhaps are not surprising.[21] But in the statement covered in Table 3.3, the question of violence was posed in more abstract terms, testing a generalized commitment to peaceful politics. Racial differences were still strong. A significant portion of the black population either condoned violence or was willing to consider it, at least in the abstract, as a political tactic. In no sense did the two races share a notion of the permissible limits of the political conflict resolution process.

It legitimately may be asked whether the responses to these two questions reflect an assessment of Milwaukee's own experience with collective violence or a more generalized sympathy for violent modes of political action. A survey conducted in Milwaukee by Jonathan Slesinger several months after the riot occurred in that city provides some perspective on the data offered in Tables 3.2 and 3.3. Slesinger's data suggest that most blacks did not think the Milwaukee riot was very effective: Only 35 percent of his black sample thought the Milwaukee riot in particular helped the "Negroes' cause."[22] Yet, three years later, 76 percent of the blacks in my sample thought that "some good" had come of riots "like those that happened in Detroit and Newark."[23]

Slesinger's black respondents were much more sympathetic to the idea of violence in general than their assessment of the Milwaukee riot itself might suggest. Of the blacks in the 1967 survey, 57 percent agreed that "Riots are unpopular but an effective method for bringing about desired changes," and 40 percent agreed that "Negroes have more to gain than lose by resorting to violence in the civil rights movement."[24] Those figures are consistent with the 48 percent of the blacks in my sample who responded favorably to the idea of political violence.

Attitudes toward the use of violence may be a function, to some extent, of

[21] Gary Marx asked essentially the same question in 1964, substituting Harlem for Detroit and Newark, and found that over one-half of his urban black sample (52 percent) answered that no good could ever come of such riots. The contrast over time is striking. Gary Marx, *Protest and Prejudice* (New York: Harper and Row, 1967), p. 32.

[22] Slesinger, "Study of Opinions," p. 33.

[23] Lest one suppose that during this time great changes took place that changed blacks' assessments of the impact of the Milwaukee riot, he should read David Olson's account of the meager response to the problems assumed to lie at the root of the disorders. David Olson, "Racial Violence and City Politics: The Political Response to Civil Disorders in Three American Cities" (Ph.D. dissertation, University of Wisconsin, Madison, 1971).

[24] Slesinger, "Study of Opinions," p. 32. Corresponding percentages of agreement among the white respondents were 17 percent and 3 percent on the respective questions.

TABLE 3.2 RESPONSES, BY RACE, TO QUESTIONNAIRE ITEM 37

Response	Black respondents		White respondents	
	%	N	%	N
"Some people say that no good can ever come from riots like those that happened in Detroit and Newark a few years ago. Other people say that such riots do some good. Which comes closest to the way you feel?"				
Some good	76	186	24	78
No good	13	31	66	220
Don't know; no answer	12	29	10	33
Total	*101*	*246*	*100*	*331*

Note: Differences are significant at .001 level (χ^2 = 178.10).

assessments of the degree of justice with which government carries out its role as mediator and ultimate decisionmaker in intergroup conflict. This assessment involves, among other things, perceptions of the openness of the political system, one indicator of which is the sense of the public's ease of access to political officials. To be sure, to gain access is simply to gain the opportunity to make a case. The availability of public officials tells little about their responsiveness— that is, their willingness to meet or treat demands. Nevertheless, if the routes of access are free, then petitioners may feel assured at least that their demands will be heard, and that they will be heard without resort to the drama of violence. On the other hand, if the system is perceived as closed to those seeking peaceful access, then the attractiveness of violence as a device to gain attention for demands increases.

Blacks and whites in Milwaukee differed in their perceptions of the availability

TABLE 3.3 RESPONSES, BY RACE, TO QUESTIONNAIRE ITEM 39

Response	Black respondents		White respondents	
	%	N	%	N
"A lot of people get so angry about certain things that they think that violence is the only way to get the government to do something. Have you ever felt this way?"				
Yes	48	118	10	34
No	50	122	89	295
Don't know; no answer	2	6	1	2
Total	*100*	*246*	*100*	*331*

Note: Differences are significant at .001 level (χ^2 = 104.91).

TABLE 3.4   RESPONSES, BY RACE, TO QUESTIONNAIRE ITEM 41

Response	Black respondents		White respondents	
	%	N	%	N
"If a group of people have a problem · *here in Milwaukee, it's pretty easy to get* *somebody in the city government to* *listen to them."*				
Agree	20	49	37	123
Agree and disagree	24	60	19	63
Disagree	45	111	39	130
Don't know; no answer	11	26	5	15
Total	*100*	*246*	*100*	*331*

Note: Differences are significant at .001 level (χ^2 = 24.37).

of local government officials, as we see in Table 3.4. They also varied in their estimates of their respective capacities to take part in the system. The admission that one does not feel free to talk to public officials (Table 3.5) may represent not only a failure of the system to provide evidence that it is open but also the absence of attitudes that would help to sustain or even stimulate such openness.

Although segments of the white population shared with many blacks doubts about the openness of the political system in the city, the answers of a majority reflected confidence that government officials were easily approachable. To most blacks, the routes of access appeared closed.

Those who believe that the system is a relatively closed one are also likely to believe that the system does not work in their favor. If people believe that opportunities to make their position heard are restricted, then it follows that they will not believe that equity governs political decision making, because equity requires hearing all sides of an issue. In such a case, generalized support for the

TABLE 3.5 RESPONSES, BY RACE, TO QUESTIONNAIRE ITEM 61

Response	Black Respondents		White Respondents	
	%	N	%	N
"Suppose a group around here wanted to *get the government of Milwaukee to do* *something for this neighborhood. Would* *you feel free to go talk to someone in* *the government about it?"*				
Yes	46	112	72	239
No	54	134	27	89
Don't know; no answer	0	0	1	3
Total	*100*	*246*	*100*	*331*

Note: Differences are significant at .001 level (χ^2 = 43.08).

TABLE 3.6 RESPONSES, BY RACE, TO QUESTIONNAIRE ITEM 64

Response	Black respondents		White respondents	
	%	N	%	N
"The government of Milwaukee is usually pretty fair to the average person."				
Agree	25	62	67	222
Agree and disagree	29	72	20	67
Disagree	40	99	9	29
Don't know; no answer	5	13	4	13
Total	*99*	*246*	*100*	*331*

Note: Differences are significant at .001 level ($\chi^2 = 118.66$).

system probably will be low. The data (Table 3.6) provide a basis for such reasoning.

In a complementary way, generalized attitudes toward compromise as a principle facilitating conflict resolution and coalition come into play here. The data show (Table 3.7) that the races differed strongly in this regard. These data may be interpreted in several ways. On the one hand, if these general attitudes relate to the role of government as mediator and decisionmaker in group conflict (in which it imposes settlements, or compromises), then we may conclude that such attitudes reinforce our finding that the races differ in their support for established governmental institutions. It is likely that blacks do not support government in part *because* it imposes compromises, and compromise, especially for a weak minority group, is not a valued principle.[25] On the other hand, we may also interpret the data as telling us something about the possibilities for welding interracial coalitions. The very notion of coalition normally implies accommodation, or movement from preferred positions to one to which all parties can adhere. For elites who would pursue standard bargaining strategies leading to compromised outcomes, mass support in the black community clearly appears low. To the extent that members of a group reject the principle of compromise as a prescriptive norm, the possibility of their inclusion in a diverse coalition declines.

The preceding tables have shown strong racial differences in adherence to norms of the conflict resolution process and in judgments of the extent to which norms calling for open access to government are operative. The data support the

---

[25] Blacks in the sample were particularly vehement in their belief that blacks should not have to make compromises in politics. Sixty-five percent of the black sample agreed with the statement "Black people shouldn't have to make compromises when they make demands because they've waited so long to be treated fairly." Only 11 percent of the white sample agreed.

TABLE 3.7 RESPONSES, BY RACE, TO QUESTIONNAIRE ITEM 46

	Black respondents		White respondents	
Response	%	N	%	N
"Compromise is a good thing; everybody gets a little of what he wants."				
Agree	24	59	55	182
Agree and disagree	22	54	26	87
Disagree	47	115	13	42
Don't know; no answer	7	18	6	20
Total	*100*	*246*	*100*	*331*

Note: Differences are significant at .001 level (χ^2 = 94.07).

conclusion that the races do not share a common view of the limits of permissible political action or of the desirability of compromise as a device to facilitate conflict resolution. Nor do they share the perception that the political system is an open one and that it is fair. In one area, however, the views of the races converge: They agree that voting, a formal mechanism to resolve contests for public office and provide government with roughly wrought cues, is decisive (Table 3.8). In other words, they agree that voting does have some effectiveness as a means of controlling government.

In general, differences in normative commitment and judgment appear to be predominantly a function of race, rather than of social or demographic characteristics. When age, education, and home ownership[26] were individually controlled for each race, the correlations indicated that these factors, with a few exceptions, had relatively little value in predicting a respondent's position on any given question. In addition, an additive index, designed to provide an overall score to measure the degree to which an individual's preferences on these items are integrative, showed striking racial differences. In Table 3.9, correlations between agreement on the questions and the three status variables are shown for each race.

Older whites were likely to be more hostile to the idea of violent political action than younger whites, and they tended to be more confident that government is accessible and fair. Education, however, did not have much predictive power, nor did the status variable of home ownership.

Age and education both had some small predictive value for blacks in regard

[26] Robert Alford and Harry Scoble employ home ownership as an independent variable measuring community attachment, but it is also clearly a status variable in that it tends to be associated with income and other middle-class attributes. It is used here because Alford and Scoble find that it is one of the most powerful predictors of local political involvement, more powerful in fact than income or occupation. The home-ownership variable used in this present study is based on the question "Do you own or are you buying this home or what?" "Sources of Local Political Involvement," *American Political Science Review* 62 (December 1968): 1192-1206.

TABLE 3.8 RESPONSES, BY RACE, TO QUESTIONNAIRE ITEM 50

Response	Black respondents		White respondents	
	%	N	N	%
"Voting is no use in this city, because the government will do what it wants no matter how you vote."				
Agree	10	25	11	34
Agree and disagree	20	48	14	46
Disagree	66	163	71	234
Don't know; no answer	4	10	5	16
Total	*100*	*246*	*101*	*330*

Note: Differences are not significant (χ^2 = 3.32).

to attitudes toward violence. Age was negatively associated with the feeling that violence occasionally may succeed in getting government to act, while education was positively correlated with such a sentiment. Young, better-educated blacks, then, represent a militant segment of the black community, a finding not inconsistent with studies of riot participants.[27] In general, however, these status variables did not provide strong predictors of position in this matrix of integrative norms and cognitions. Black negativism cut across class and age lines, for the most part; conversely, white positive attitudes were relatively evenly distributed

TABLE 3.9 CORRELATIONS (GAMMA) BETWEEN RESPONDENTS' STATUS AND AGREEMENT ON INTEGRATIVE NORMS, BY RACE

Area of agreement by respondents	Black respondents			White respondents		
	Age	Education	Home ownership	Age	Education	Home ownership
Have thought violence would force government to act	-.46	.39	-.02	-.33	.14	-.18
Easy to get someone to listen	.17	-.15	.01	.31	-.16	.08
Feel free to talk to someone in government	-.04	.26	.30	.12	.33	.21
Government is fair to average person	.20	.06	-.01	.41	-.19	.24
Compromise is a good thing	-.10	-.08	.20	.01	-.16	-.04
Voting is no use in this city	-.06	-.06	-.03	-.08	-.29	-.21

[27]The Kerner Commission found, for example, that while the typical rioter had "not, usually, graduated from high school, he was somewhat better educated than the average inner-city Negro, having at least attended high school for a time." *Report of the National Advisory Commission on Civil Disorders* (New York: Bantam, 1968), p. 128.

TABLE 3.10 POLITICAL INTEGRATION INDEX: DISTRIBUTION
OF RESPONSE SCORES INDICATING COMMITMENT TO
INTEGRATIVE NORMS, BY RACE

Score Range[a]	Black respondents		White respondents	
	%	N	%	N
High	7	16	37	121
Medium	43	106	52	173
Low	50	124	11	37
Total	*100*	*246*	*100*	*331*

Note: Differences are significant at .001 level (χ^2 = 133.96).

[a]Score numbers began at 0 and ended at 45. High range was 34-45; medium, 25-33; low, 0-24. Points were assigned each respondent according to his or her answers on nine agree-disagree questions. See Footnote 28 to Chapter 3 for a fuller explanation of the derivation of the scores.

throughout the sample. Thus, the attitudinal differences we have observed in the preceding tables must be attributed to the different collective experiences of the two races and not to social status or life cycle factors.

The view that the nature of normative understanding is a function of race rather than of class was reinforced by a cross-tabulation of race and scores on a summary index of attitudes toward political integration.[28] Scores ranged from a possible low of 0 to a high of 45. Respondents were grouped into three categories, denoting high (34-45), medium (25-33), and low (0-24) integrative normative commitment. Table 3.10 shows the distribution of scores by race.

The two races showed substantial overlap in the medium category but sharp polarity at the extreme ends of the scale. High scores were not strongly related to two status variables, age and education; home ownership showed some relationship, but not a strong one (see Table 3.11).

---

[28] The index was constructed by assigning a score of 5 for each answer that indicated high commitment to the norm or a high sense that the norm was operative in the political system. A score of 1 was given for answers that indicated low commitment or a low sense that the norm was in effect. Intermediate responses on the agree strongly/disagree strongly continuum were scored accordingly. "Don't know" responses were scored 0. A total of nine questions was used to construct the index, including all six of those in Table 3.9. The following were also used:

"A good many local elections aren't important enough to bother with."
"Most of the people running the government in Milwaukee are honest."
"A group has to compromise too often to get what it wants from government."

Two questions were not scaled in the interview schedule along the five-point agree strongly/disagree strongly continuum. These were the question inquiring about personal feelings toward the use of violence and the question asking people whether they felt free to contact government officials. Both were answered either yes or no. A "yes" response to the violence question was scored 1, and a "yes" answer to the contact question was scored 5. "No" answers were scored 5 and 1, respectively.

TABLE 3.11 CORRELATIONS (GAMMA) BETWEEN HIGH INTEGRATION SCORES AND STATUS VARIABLES, BY RACE

Respondents scoring in high range on political integration index	Status variables		
	Age	Education	Home ownership
Blacks	.18	.08	.34
Whites	.12	.17	.27

The Individual Role: The Question of Political Efficacy

Democratic societies place a high value on citizen participation, on the assumption that widespread involvement in decision-making processes enhances a population's sense that the system and its outputs are legitimate.[29] Broad participation offers a kind of proof of the theory that everyone has had a chance to make his influence felt, although opportunities for participation may in fact be strictly regulated by elites. Nevertheless, widespread citizen participation is one hallmark of an open political society (though not a sufficient indicator of such)[30] and is a virtual requirement for a system in which collective decisions are to be the product of bargaining among diverse citizen interests.

Political integration cannot genuinely be said to exist when participation in politics is limited to certain social segments of the population while other social segments remain essentially inactive. The interests of the inactive cannot be represented forcefully by elites because the inactive provide no mass support; even if elites can make a good case for such interests, they are unlikely to prevail.

An important psychological variable underlying individual participation in politics is the sense of political efficacy. A sense of efficacy is the feeling that one can comprehend the political system in a basic way and accomplish things, as a citizen, through political action. In this book I have chosen to distinguish between two types of political efficacy: conventional efficacy and protest efficacy. The first implies a belief in the effectiveness of voting and other conventional modes of participation, while the second implies a belief that protest is an effective means—perhaps the most effective means—of wielding political influence. Although the two types are not necessarily mutually exclusive, blacks and poor people generally have tended to score low in conventional efficacy, leading scholars to conclude that efficacy itself is a white, middle-class property.[31] However, when we introduce the idea of protest efficacy, we discover that there

[29] Gabriel Almond and Sidney Verba, *The Civic Culture* (Boston: Little, Brown, 1965), p. 191.
[30] Robert Dahl, *Polyarchy* (New Haven, Conn.: Yale University Press, 1971), pp. 3-7.
[31] Lester Milbrath, *Political Participation* (Chicago: Rand McNally, 1965), pp. 57-58.

is a more widespread sense that things can be accomplished through political action.

Political efficacy is important for biracial political integration; unless feelings concerning efficacy are generally shared, interracial cooperation is difficult to achieve and maintain. If the members of one group feel politically efficacious, in whatever way, while those of the other group do not, or if the two groups differ in the *type* of political efficacy their members feel, or if neither population feels efficacious, then a major assumption underlying political cooperation—that people can get what they want through the political process by joining together to pursue collective goals—is absent. Cooperation, if it is achieved at all, is likely to be highly unstable.

In the Milwaukee sample, neither blacks nor whites exhibited very high levels of belief in efficacy when measured by conventional questions. Three standard questions were used to test degree of efficacy.[32] Table 3.12 shows the racial distribution on each question.

The races diverged in their estimates of the centrality of the individual and his concerns in city politics, but they were in substantial agreement on the murky nature of the political process. The races also agreed that voting is the only means for wielding political influence. Agreement on this point has been treated in the literature as an inefficacious response because it indicates a limited grasp of the variety of possibilities for political self-assertion. Black agreement in this case appears to be inconsistent with black attitudes toward the utility of protest, as is discussed in greater detail in Chapter 6.

White conventional efficacy was moderately related to education. Negative correlation coefficients (gamma) indicate that better-educated white respondents were likely to disagree with statements that voting is the only means for making citizen influence felt (-.41), that politics is too complex for the average man to comprehend (-.28), and that government officials do not care about the average man (-.22). No such relationships held for blacks.

While neither race exhibited high feelings of efficacy when tested on traditional questions, blacks showed a strong faith in the efficacy of protest methods, as Table 3.13 shows.

For both races, then, the psychological supports for conventional political participation were comparatively weak; but the black respondents believed that individuals have an effective means of political self-assertion through protest.

Conclusions

In general, the races diverged in their basic attitudinal support for common institutions for the management of conflict and in their normative commitment

---

[32] Their source is Milbrath, *Political Participation*, pp. 156-157.

TABLE 3.12 RESPONSES, BY RACE, TO STATEMENTS
CONCERNING ATTITUDES TOWARD CONVENTIONAL POLITICAL
EFFICACY

Response	Black respondents		White respondents	
	%	N	%	N
A. People in the government in this city don't care much what the average person thinks."				
Agree	53	130	31	104
Agree and disagree	27	66	21	71
Disagree	15	37	44	146
Don't know; no answer	5	13	3	10
Total	*100*	*246*	*99*	*331*
B. "Politics is so complicated that the average person can hardly understand it."				
Agree	61	151	59	195
Agree and disagree	20	48	18	61
Disagree	15	37	21	68
Don't know; no answer	4	10	2	7
Total	*100*	*246*	*100*	*331*
C. "Voting is the only way the average person can influence government in this city."				
Agree	62	152	58	191
Agree and disagree	22	53	15	49
Disagree	15	36	25	83
Don't know; no answer	2	5	2	8
Total	*101*	*246*	*100*	*331*

Note: Part A—Differences are significant at .001 level $(\chi^2 = 57.10)$.
   Part B—Differences are not significant $(\chi^2 = 4.40)$.
   Part C—Differences are significant at .01 level $(\chi^2 = 11.58)$.

to rules for solving political differences. The differences that emerged in the data on evaluative orientations toward government, on commitment to integrative norms, on expectations of access, and on protest efficacy are primarily racial differences and cannot be adequately explained by controlling for status variables. The data presented here indicate that in all probability the masses of the two races in Milwaukee are unlikely to succeed in establishing politically integrated or stable relationships.

This divergence creates a context that poses certain obvious problems for the elites of both races. At the mass level among blacks, many of the standards that help to regulate the conflict process are absent, as is basic support for government as an institution for conflict management. Even for black elites committed to a politically integrated polity, it seems unlikely that they will find much broad-based and sustained support for attempts to establish stable competitive

TABLE 3.13 RESPONSES, BY RACE, TO QUESTIONNAIRE ITEM 49

Response	Black respondents		White respondents	
	%	N	%	N
"Demonstrations and mass marches are one good way to get the city government to listen to you."				
Agree	69	169	23	75
Agree and disagree	19	47	20	66
Disagree	9	23	54	179
Don't know; no answer	3	7	3	11
Total	*100*	*246*	*100*	*331*

Note: Differences are significant at .001 level (χ^2 = 151.54).

(bargaining) or cooperative relationships with white groups. The possibilities, for example, for a coalition of blacks and poor whites, appear dim, leading one to conclude that a politics based on racial division is more likely to persist in the city than is a politics based on class.

Since mass attitudes provide opportunities for certain types of elites and militate against others, the structure of the Milwaukee situation, characterized as it is by mass divergence in the integrative matrix, would seem to work against elites who are committed among themselves to similar assumptions about the context and conduct of politics.

Yet, the situation in Milwaukee appears to be exacerbated if not indeed caused by the fact that a significant and vocal portion of the white community has rejected the norms of accommodation and peaceful politics on those occasions when racial questions have been at issue—as is vividly illustrated by the case of the open-housing controversy with which we opened this chapter. Setting this particular case within the whole history of race relations in this country, it seems entirely reasonable to conclude that the black disaffection observable in the data presented here is a *product* of the failure of whites to act on the basis of their stated normative pretensions. From this perspective, the onus for the failure of whites and blacks to pursue political relationships within a framework of regulative norms and commitments falls ultimately on those vocal and inconsistent segments of the white community and on the elites who cater to them.

Political Goals: The Quest for Community

4

In describing the typology of different modes of political conflict and cooperation in Chapter 1, I suggested that the *stability* of interracial political coalition or competition depends in large measure upon the degree to which the members of the two racial groups share commitments to a variety of integrative norms. In this chapter we shall examine the nature of some of the underlying pressures that help to determine whether those relationships will tend, in the main, to be cooperative or competitive.

An obviously central factor in determining whether groups are potential contestants or partners in politics in any given instance is whether they find themselves competing for resources to realize incompatible goals or whether their goals are complementary or identical.

In some measure, conflict and cooperation are tied to specific issues. We can point to a number of instances in Milwaukee in which the two racial communities have come into conflict over the past ten years, most of them having to do with schools and housing. The fight in 1964-1965 over de facto segregation and the policy of "intact bussing," which kept black children in segregated classrooms in the white schools to which they had been bussed, the dispute in 1970 over changes in school district boundaries that would have altered the racial composition of a number of public schools, the battle in 1970 over the attempt to locate public housing outside of the northside ghetto, and, of course, the

This chapter originally appeared in slightly different form as "The Urban Crisis as a Failure of Community," by Peter K. Eisinger, and is reprinted from *Urban Affairs Quarterly*, Vol. 9, No. 4 (June 1974), pp. 437-461, by permission of the publisher, Sage Publications, Inc.

confrontation over open housing are all examples of situations in which the two racial communities sought incompatible goals.

Identifying particular controversies to provide a picture of the political goals of the two racial communities has several drawbacks. First, there is the problem of selecting which issues to analyze. By what criteria does one choose? What are the important issues? What constitutes a representative sample? These are difficulties that bedeviled the pluralist community power investigators ten years ago, and they have never been satisfactorily resolved.[1] Second, by concentrating on actual instances of conflict (or cooperation), one has to focus on the issues that have mobilized groups to pursue their goals. We are interested, however, in the goals that may or may not impel elites to attempt mobilization.

For these reasons, I have sought to investigate political goals by focusing on indicators of *underlying preferences*. Such preferences may cut across specific issues and controversies, and they may or may not, depending on the circumstances, give rise to mobilization efforts. These preferences, or generalized political goals, have to do with the nature of community and the means to realize it. While the quest for community has been seen by a number of observers of the city as the central goal of contemporary urban dwellers, it also subsumes a wide range of specific issues. If the races define community differently or seek community in radically different ways, then we might conclude that pressures for racial conflict are deep and generalized, coloring perceptions of interests across a wide range of specific controversies that might arise or actually do arise.

The Nature of Community

As any current textbook on domestic politics assures us, America's cities are in a state of crisis. This has become a conventional bit of wisdom, and it commands nearly universal acknowledgment. Like many ideas that become widely used in the language of politics, however, it has become a rhetorical formula, a cliché, and its precise meaning varies according to the identity of the particular commentator. Thus, the specific nature of the "urban crisis" as well as solutions to it are matters of much disagreement.

In public discourse, the phrase "urban crisis" is generally followed by a list of discrete problems, some of which seem constant from list to list and others of which owe their mention to the particular list maker's concerns. Poor housing, crime, and the lack of public transportation may be considered part of the same crisis as drug abuse, riotous youth, and official corruption. The urban crisis is thus defined inductively, in the press and in political circles, as the conglomerate threat and challenge posed by the deterioration of the city's physical plant, the

---

[1] For a discussion of these particular problems, see Peter Bachrach and Morton S. Baratz, "Two Faces of Power," *American Political Science Review* 56 (December 1962): 948.

failure of its public services, and the decay of moral standards among its populace.

Some observers, dissatisfied with a definition so diffuse, have sought common threads that bind together the potentially endless range of problems that people living in the city encounter. Many of these problems, they believe, may be traced in one way or another to lack of money. Not only are monetary resources scarce but the revenue-raising capacity of cities is greatly limited by the states. Hence it is not unusual to find the urban crisis defined as being, at base, a fiscal crisis.[2]

For a number of scholars, however, the nature of the crisis lies beyond the more immediate difficulties of revenue raising. For these scholars, the major symptom of the urban crisis is a crisis of mood, a pervasive unease, a sense of isolation, estrangement, and helplessness.[3] This mood stems most significantly not from poor services, urban congestion, and deterioration or from the burdens involved in the cities' taxing and spending problems *but from the failure of community-sustaining norms and institutions.*

In essence, their viewpoint is that the urban crisis in its basic form is nothing especially new; twentieth-century man has long been said to be in quest of community. What is novel in the current situation is, first, that this quest is taking place mainly in the cities and, by definition, involves more people than ever before. Second, the failure of community in the city has a compounding effect that seems to have brought on a massive sense of powerlessness and also, in a much more immediate sense, seems actually life-threatening in the daily course of events. Thus it is that fear of crime has become an obsessive preoccupation for many city dwellers.

The notion that the urban crisis in fact is attributable to the failure of community or that it may be understood in these terms has been emergent in American scholarship for over a decade. Edward Banfield and James Q. Wilson saw the political ascendance of "private-regarding" ethnics as a signal of the loss of power of the "public-regarding" cosmopolitan middle class.[4] Parochial and group self-seeking considerations had come, in their view, to animate big-city politics at the expense of community-wide concerns.

Daniel P. Moynihan has offered a more extensive analysis, which takes the failure of urban community as its point of departure. It is his thesis that the whole set of federal initiatives in urban policy in the last decade as well as the movement for community control are responses to the failure of community. Drawing heavily on Robert Nisbet's general discussion of the quest for com-

---

[2]This is an underlying theme in John Lindsay's book *The City* (New York: Norton, 1969). See also Douglas M. Fox, "Federal Aid to the Cities," in *The New Urban Politics*, ed. Douglas M. Fox (Pacific Palisades, Cal.: Goodyear, 1972) for an academic version of this argument.

[3]James Q. Wilson, "The Urban Unease: Community vs. the City," *Public Interest* (Summer 1968): 25-39.

[4]Edward Banfield and James Q. Wilson, *City Politics* (Cambridge, Mass.: Harvard University Press, 1963).

munity as a central enterprise of modern man, Moynihan reviews the familiar argument concerning the erosion of the institutions by which people in the mass relate to one another. "The authority of small groups such as the family, the local community, and other traditional associations," he writes, "had eroded because their functions had eroded."[5] This deterioration of primary associations has left individuals isolated, and it is this isolation, exacerbated and accentuated in the city, that constitutes, in his view, the crisis of urban life.

In the late 1950s, Moynihan continues, academics and others came to view juvenile delinquency as symptomatic of this breakdown,[6] and their analyses helped to lead, first, to federal legislation to combat youth crime and later, in a more or less natural progression, to antipoverty legislation and other urban social programs. Central-city dwellers were not entirely passive recipients of government aid in the face of this general social deterioration; during the 1960s, activists in the cities developed a loosely structured ideology based on the notion of community self-determination or community control, which Moynihan has called the "quest for specific community."[7]

If a number of scholars have come to agree that the urban crisis may be defined in terms of the absence of community, their notions of what constitutes community vary to some degree. For Wilson, community consists of the mutual observance and maintenance of "standards of right and seemly conduct in the public places in which one lives and moves."[8] Community refers here not to place or affinity, but rather, to shared expectations and obligations about behavior in public. The failure of community, then, is seen as a breakdown of community-sustaining norms of behavior.

For others—notably the proponents of community control—the idea of community involves shared identity, common values, and political self-rule in face-to-face (neighborhood) settings. Community in this distinctly political sense has also come to imply a special sort of politics—humane, democratic, responsive, flexible—whose characteristics distinguish it from what are perceived to be the rigid, impersonal, and elitist political relationships of larger jurisdictions. The ethnic neighborhood and the ghetto are thought to provide ideal bases for the establishment of such community.[9] From this perspective, the failure of community lies in the impersonality of increasing scale and in the loss of political control. That is to say, the failure is a failure of community-sustaining political institutions.

[5] Daniel P. Moynihan, *Maximum Feasible Misunderstanding* (New York: Free Press, 1969), p. 10.

[6] Ibid., p. 14.

[7] Daniel P. Moynihan, "Toward a National Urban Policy," in *Toward a National Urban Policy*, ed. Daniel P. Moynihan (New York: Basic Books, 1970), p. 5.

[8] Wilson, "The Urban Unease," p. 27.

[9] Wilson explicitly dissents from this point of view. See especially his *Varieties of Police Behavior* (Cambridge, Mass.: Harvard University Press, 1968), Chapter 9.

To summarize, several prominent students of city life have proposed the failure of community as the defining feature of the contemporary urban crisis. Of the many definitions of community, two have been offered here. On the one hand, community is said to exist to the extent that people living together share norms governing social interaction. On the other hand, community is said to involve shared political identity and some measure of autonomous control and responsibility.

It is important to realize that, in seeking to confront the urban crisis, Americans have agreed for the most part that the city's problems are amenable to political solution. That is to say, the difficulties cities face generally are not thought to be a function of the failure of character, culture, or the free market, or of deterministic processes of decay—all of which are more or less immune to the effects of political action. Thus, if the response to the urban crisis has been a quest for community—either a search for order or a search for political autonomy—then the object of that quest and the way it is defined may be viewed as a primarily, indeed an overridingly, *political* goal. The task we face in the remainder of this chapter is to determine whether blacks and whites in Milwaukee are in fact in quest of community in some sense and whether they share common definitions of what they have lost and are searching for.

Community as Shared Norms

According to James Q. Wilson, the common man's view of the central urban problem has very little to do with issues like housing, tax inequities, poverty, unemployment, or pollution. These are the issues that interest scholars and political elites, but they are national problems and scarcely unique to the cities. The issues that concern the common man are "crime, violence, rebellious youth, racial tension, public immorality, delinquency. However stated, the common theme seem[s] to be a concern for improper behavior in public places."[10]

The spread of "improper behavior" signals a failure of community, if community is understood as the collection of shared norms that govern social interaction in public. Significant numbers of urban dwellers are rejecting those norms in a variety of ways. Some have embraced what has come to be called a "counter-culture"; others have taken the route of political dissent; and still others have turned increasingly to such forms of antisocial expression as crime and drug usage.

Wilson argues that the failure of community is a problem that not only dominates the common man's conception of the urban crisis but is felt equally by blacks and whites. In addition, he argues that the common man's understanding of the urban crisis is opposed to the elite view. By the use of terms such as "common man" and "elite," he implies two differing, class-based definitions of the urban crisis. The propositions in his argument are open to test.

[10] Wilson, "The Urban Unease," p. 26.

Wilson distinguishes between "conventional" urban problems (those that concern elites) and those that have to do with the failure of community, which I have called "behavior" problems. The latter category achieves coherence to the extent that it includes problems having to do with the breakdown of shared norms of behavior. The former category is largely residual in character, since it includes all other problems.

Respondents in the Milwaukee survey were asked what they thought were some of the most important problems faced by the city—the same question asked by Wilson in a survey he conducted in Boston in 1966–1967. The results of the two surveys are quite different. In the Milwaukee survey, responses to those questions that dealt with police protection, crime, rioting and demonstrations, and drug use—all except the last of which were listed by Wilson—were classed together and interpreted as expressions of concern over a breakdown of behavior norms, a signal of the perception of the failure of community. All other problems were considered "conventional," that is, unrelated to the particular concerns over community norms. Table 4.1 shows the distribution of responses.

It is apparent that, in Milwaukee, citizens are primarily concerned with "conventional" sorts of problems. By Wilson's criteria, concern over a community of shared norms was not a significant preoccupation for more than one-fifth of the sample population. Other data from the Milwaukee survey support this finding. When people were asked, at another point, which of the problems facing the city they thought was the most important, 64 percent of the blacks and 58 percent of the whites mentioned "conventional" problems.

TABLE 4.1   RESPONDENTS' IDENTIFICATION OF PROBLEMS FACING THE CITY OF MILWAUKEE, BY RACE

Classification of problems	Black respondents				White respondents			
	First response[a]		Second response[b]		First response[a]		Second response[b]	
	%	N	%	N	%	N	%	N
Conventional problems[c]	62	155	42	103	74	245	50	167
Behavior problems[d]	17	41	11	27	21	70	21	69
Other	1	3	2	4	*	1	1	4
Don't know; no answer	19	47	45	112	5	15	27	91
Total	*99*	*246*	*100*	*246*	*100*	*331*	*99*	*331*

[a]The first response was the first problem mentioned by the respondent.
[b]Second responses were occasionally mentioned spontaneously but were more often answers to interviewer probes.
[c]*Conventional problems* included housing, taxes, cost of living, education, unemployment, highways, traffic problems, poverty, pollution, mass transit, sanitation, street maintenance, lack of revenue, and waste of money.
[d]*Behavior problems* included racial tension, crime, inadequate police protection, rioting, demonstrations, drugs, the behavior of young people and students, and corrupt city officials.
*Indicates less than 1 percent.

Only 13 percent of the blacks and 25 percent of the whites mentioned problems that indicated, in Wilson's sense, a concern over the failure of community-sustaining norms.

Among blacks, housing and unemployment were cited most frequently as the single *most important* problem (25 percent and 20 percent, respectively), while whites thought that housing and taxes were the most crucial (17 percent and 14 percent). Not a single black respondent thought that crime was the *most important* problem facing the city, and only 5 percent of the whites thought so. The most pressing "behavior" problem was racial tension, which ranked as the third most frequently cited item for both races.

In Wilson's Boston survey, only 27 percent of the entire sample mentioned "conventional" problems, while the rest, presumably (Wilson does not give the actual breakdown of the data in his article), gave answers relating to community norms and behavior. What makes the differing Milwaukee data even more intriguing is the fact that Wilson believes that the patterns he found in Boston are not peculiar to that city but have more general application.

It is clear that neither the Boston nor the Milwaukee survey can settle the matter. There is tangential support for the Milwaukee findings in the University of Michigan Survey Research Center's fifteen-city survey, in which the investigators found that *satisfaction* with police protection was much higher in both the black and the white communities (a desire for more police protection is classified as a "behavior" concern by Wilson) than was satisfaction with such services as schools, parks and playgrounds, and recreation centers—all of which have to do with "conventional" problems.[11] In other words, the need for more police protection did not rank high as a problem. Gallup poll data of 1969 also show that blacks still ranked jobs, schools, and housing as the first three most important problems "facing Negro people."[12]

If Wilson is not convincing about the general applicability of his data, it is still a fact that the Boston patterns revealed in his survey differ from those in Milwaukee. One is compelled to wonder why the two surveys, conducted in cities of similar size and makeup, should produce such different results. The fact that Boston's crime rate is nearly double that of Milwaukee may offer one explanation for the Bostonians' apparently greater concern with crime. But there are other factors that may neutralize the net impact of the differing crime rates of the two cities. Milwaukee, we may recall, had a severe riot in 1967; similar disturbances in Boston were mild and received less national attention. And the middle western city appears to have experienced somewhat more black protest activity than the eastern city.[13] Without knowing how citizen concerns over these

[11] Angus Campbell and Howard Schuman, *Racial Attitudes in Fifteen American Cities* (Ann Arbor: University of Michigan, Institute for Social Research, July 1969), p. 40.

[12] Peter Goldman, *Report from Black America* (New York: Simon and Schuster, 1969), pp. 46-47.

[13] Peter K. Eisinger, "The Conditions of Protest in American Cities," *American Political Science Review* 67 (March 1973): 28.

TABLE   4.2 CORRELATIONS (GAMMA) BETWEEN STATUS
VARIABLES AND IDENTIFICATION OF URBAN PROBLEMS IN
CONVENTIONAL TERMS, BY RACE

Social class indicator	Black respondents	White respondents
Occupation	.06	.28
Income	.23	.23
Education	.18	.41
Number of group memberships	.23	.33
Home ownership	.30	.17

events are balanced, one against another, one can reach no convincing conclusions. However, Boston does not appear to be significantly more normless, anomic, or socially fragmented than Milwaukee—or at least not to an extent that would account for the disparity in the survey results.

The Milwaukee data do provide modest support for Wilson's assertion that there exist class differences in the perception of urban problems. When asked what were the most important problems facing Milwaukee, a majority of respondents at all status levels cited "conventional" problems; but the size of that majority steadily increases as one moves up the status ladder. This is especially the case in the white community, as the gamma correlations in Table 4.2 show.

That greater numbers of lower-status people should be concerned with behavior norms, such as crime, has reasonable explanations. They are, for example, the chief victims of crime, in part because they live in the local communities from which criminals derive. They are also more likely to live in neighborhoods tense with the pressures of racial transition and thus to feel the burden of racial fear and antagonism in their daily lives.

In general, the relationship between status and the perception of the urban crisis in "conventional" terms is weaker among blacks than among whites. One reason is that blacks of all social classes live in close proximity in the ghetto, while whites are more likely to live in class-differentiated neighborhoods. Thus, members of the black middle class probably are more likely to fall victim to crime or be subject to the pressures of racially changing neighborhoods than are those of the white middle class, which successfully isolates itself in more favored, class-homogeneous areas of the town. Hence, the degree of concern over the failure of community exemplified, say, by fear of crime or by dismay at racial tension, decreases more sharply as status increases among whites than it does among blacks, in part because whites are less exposed to the sources of these problems.

One conclusion in regard at least to Milwaukee is clear: Blacks and whites in that city share a concern for the "conventional" problems of urban life. Concern over community as defined by normative consensus does not appear to enter into the political relationships that blacks and whites establish with one another. What we do find, however, is that the priorities of the two races differ in regard to the "conventional" problems they care about. This suggests, as will be dis-

TABLE 4.3 FREQUENCY OF MENTION OF CONVENTIONAL
TYPES OF URBAN PROBLEMS, BY RACE

Black respondents			White respondents		
Rank of problem	Problem	Frequency of mention (%)	Rank of problem	Problem	Frequency of mention (%)
1	Housing	25	1	Taxes	23
2	Unemployment	15	2	Housing	17
3	Racial tension	10	3	Pollution	11
4	Pollution	7	4	Racial tension	7
5	Schools	6	5	Rioting, demonstrations	5
6	Taxes	4	6	Schools	4
6	Cost of living	4			

cussed at greater length later, that conflict and cooperation across racial lines are tied to immediate issues and do not spring from major disagreement about the quality of community; essentially, both groups put a premium on order and predictability.

As the figures in Table 4.3 show, after housing, black concern was greatest about unemployment, while whites worried more about their tax burden than about anything else. In each case, these are intensely personal concerns, connected with the races' differing problems of economic survival.

It is evident that solutions to the problems of economic survival—jobs for blacks, lower taxes for whites—may call for very different government strategies. Furthermore, the fact that more than anything else whites want lower taxes makes it doubtful that solutions to the concerns that blacks express, which involve public expenditures, can be the common focus of interracial political efforts.

Community as Local Control-Sharing

If the survey data reviewed so far give little evidence that Milwaukeeans are concerned about the failure of community as defined by sharing the norms that govern social interaction, to what degree are they preoccupied with the notion of community defined, alternatively, in political terms? Are Milwaukee residents interested in the idea of community control, and would they support efforts to achieve it for their neighborhoods?

Although some of the impetus for community control or, better, control-sharing arrangements[14] has diminished in the mid-1970s, such reforms were the

[14] I have used the term "control-sharing" to suggest a more accurate and inclusive description of these political-administrative reforms than the more common phrases currently in use, such as "decentralization" or "community control." Decentralization is simply one variant of control-sharing. Community control is, properly speaking, a misnomer, since it obscures the fact that, whenever public funds are involved, such communities

subject of much excitement at the beginning of the decade. The movement for the inclusion of lay citizens in the formal policy-making apparatus responsible for urban service delivery and administration—especially for school and police systems—engaged the imagination of reformers, activists, and policy planners and promised for a brief time to restructure the American city.[15]

To test the version of the failure-of-community thesis that suggests that one major consequence of this failure is the quest for political community through the control-sharing movement, we shall seek to determine the degree to which blacks and whites at the mass level understand the notion of control-sharing, the extent to which there exist mass demand and support for such arrangements across race and class lines, and the nature and focus of that support.

One series of questions was designed to discover the extent to which respondents were familiar with control-sharing ideas and institutions. This part of the inquiry provides an opportunity to assess the extent to which control-sharing is a potential focus of the search for community. In some of these questions people were asked if they had heard of any of several prominent programs and experiments involving a control-sharing component. Other questions dealt with comprehension of control-sharing on a more abstract level; interviewers simply asked people what the terms "community control" and "citizen participation" meant to them. In general, the degree of familiarity with both the concrete and the abstract manifestations of control-sharing was modest.

The concrete manifestations chosen included three well-publicized and controversial experiments and programs. Each constituted, in effect, a model of control-sharing—a point of reference by which an individual might understand the concept in concrete terms. One such model was the Milwaukee Organization of Organizations, or Triple O, a federation of various private social welfare and ghetto groups from which representatives of the poor to the antipoverty community action board were chosen.

Triple O, led at the time by an outspoken young black man named Larry

---

invariably share control over a designated function with superior governmental jurisdictions. Control-sharing may be defined as a political and administrative arrangement in which authority over policy decisions—such as the establishment of program priorities, service levels, and personnel choices—is shared among professional bureaucrats, elected and appointed officials, and citizen representatives of geographical neighborhoods or particular client groups. For an extended discussion of the origins of the movement for control-sharing and the characteristics and consequences of such reforms, see Peter K. Eisinger, "Control-Sharing of Administrative Functions in the City" (Paper delivered at the American Political Science Association meeting, Los Angeles, Cal., September 1970); and Peter K. Eisinger, "Control-Sharing in the City: Some Thoughts on Decentralization and Client Representation," *American Behavioral Scientist* 15 (September–October 1971): 26-51.

[15] See Peter K. Eisinger, "Support for Control-Sharing at the Mass Level," *American Journal of Political Science* 17 (November 1973): 669-671, for a discussion of the scope of these proposals.

Harwell, was an aggressive, militant organization committed, among other things, to community organizing and to community control over federal programs like Model Cities and Community Action. Since it often had to fight the mayor on the issue of control, its name and exploits were often in the press. Its potential for visibility was high.

A second point of reference was the Model Cities program itself. Few other cities in the country seemed to have such difficulty in agreeing upon a division of representation on the governing board among residents and public officials. Whereas Milwaukeeans fought heatedly for well over a year during 1968-1969 about how control should be shared, the average time it took to settle this question in other cities was 5.1 months.[16] Only 12 percent of the cities responding to an Urban Data Service questionnaire took longer than 9.0 months. Most cities (90 percent) reported that they resolved the problem of how to share control over the program without major controversy.[17]

Milwaukee missed out on the first round of Model Cities grants because the Common Council refused to endorse the application. Aldermen thought the mayor was seeking excessive power over the program.[18] When the Council finally approved the planning grant application a year later, organizations like Triple O immediately charged that the mayor was after "complete dictatorial power" over Model Cities.[19] The Housing and Urban Development (HUD) regional office, too, apparently thought that Maier's plan, whereby one-third of the governing board seats would go to representatives of the residents, was inadequate, and pressured him to compromise. Maier finally yielded. Elections took place at last, resulting in a governing board split relatively equally between pro- and anti-Maier factions. As a result of this long struggle, and indeed of the problems caused by the factional split that occurred in the first year (1970) over program planning, Model Cities received extensive news coverage and publicity in Milwaukee.

A third point of reference used in the survey was the New York City school-decentralization program. Decentralization in New York was accompanied by great controversy, including two bitter teachers' strikes, in 1967 and 1968. These were covered thoroughly in the Milwaukee and national news media. The New York City plan was visible not only because of the tensions it exposed but because it was the first such experiment in the country. It prompted similar programs and proposals in other cities, including Milwaukee, although none, with the exception of the one in Detroit, was on such a large scale.

[16] The figure is based on a study conducted by the Urban Data Service. Only 65 of the 148 planning grant recipients responded to the questionnaire, not including Milwaukee. Urban Data Service, *Citizen Participation in Model Cities* (Chicago: International City Management Association, July 1970), p. 15.

[17] Ibid.

[18] Henry J. Schmandt, John C. Goldbach, and Donald B. Vogel, *Milwaukee: A Contemporary Urban Profile* (New York: Praeger, 1971), p. 161.

[19] Ibid., p. 162.

In Milwaukee there were several moves to establish "community-controlled" or decentralized schools, or pilot programs in that direction. One effort involved federal funding of advisory councils, with elected representatives of parents, teachers, students (in secondary schools), and administrators for five Inner Core schools. The purpose of the councils was to make policy recommendations to the central school board, which retained control in all matters.[20] The affected schools served 15,000 students, comprising over half of the "economically deprived" student population.

Another project, funded largely by private donations but with some federal Title I money, was the Federation of Independent Community Schools. The federation, consisting of seven schools with a total of 2300 children at all levels, was designed and aided by the University of Wisconsin–Milwaukee, Marquette University, and the Council on Urban Life—the activist civil rights arm of the Milwaukee Catholic archdiocese. Each school was an autonomous corporation controlled by people elected from the neighborhood and from the school staff, many of whom were volunteers. The federation has survived and flourished since 1969.

The Milwaukee experiments were modest by comparison with the New York City decentralization reform. Because I wished to test familiarity with *models* of control-sharing, I chose in the survey to ask about the New York reforms, rather than about the derivative and less visible local experiments.

In each case, white respondents were more familiar with the control-sharing models than were black respondents, despite the fact that blacks constituted the major portion of the clientele of the Milwaukee Model Cities and antipoverty programs (Table 4.4). However, knowledge of these programs was strongly related to education and was moderately related to occupation. Since a larger proportion of whites than blacks had a higher level of both occupation and education, the differences that emerge in Table 4.5 are probably a function less

TABLE 4.4 PERCENTAGE AND NUMBER OF RESPONDENTS, BY RACE, WHO HAD HEARD OF SELECTED CONTROL-SHARING PROGRAMS

Program	Black respondents		White respondents	
	%	N	%	N
Milwaukee Model Cities	46	112	77	256
Triple O	23	56	29	96
New York City school decentralization	7	18	25	82

[20] Educational Research Service, *Decentralization and Community Involvement: A Status Report*, Circular No. 7 (Washington, D.C.: American Association of School Administrators, 1969), p. 21.

TABLE 4.5 CORRELATIONS (GAMMA) BETWEEN STATUS
VARIABLES AND HAVING INFORMATION ABOUT CONTROL-
SHARING PROGRAMS, BY RACE

Program respondents had heard of	Black respondents		White respondents	
	Occupation	Education	Occupation	Education
Milwaukee Model Cities	.32	.24	.38	.47
Triple O	.39	.67	.38	.48
New York City school decentralization	.43	.74	.38	.48

of race than of class. It is notable that this is virtually the only instance in the
data concerning control-sharing in which any degree of variation by social class
indicators appears.

The figures in Table 4.5 indicate that the potential for thinking about control-sharing by analogy with actual programs is relatively low among the mass
population, and especially low among blacks. These programs do not serve most
people as *models for what could be.* Knowledge of institutions or reforms else-
where may stimulate the quest for the same for oneself, but most people in
Milwaukee would be unable to seek control over schools *in emulation of the
people of New York City.* The major part of the black population would not be
able to transfer either the lessons or the arrangements of the Model Cities or
Community Action programs to other areas of public service because they have
never heard of those programs to begin with.

None of this means necessarily that people do not grasp the *concept* of
control-sharing, nor does it imply that they do not seek community through
such arrangements. It signifies that they are unaware of some of the major
examples of control-sharing. To understand the abstract concept is itself important; it indicates a readiness to engage in discourse and the possibility that elite
initiatives will strike a familiar chord in the mass population. Issue recognition
may be the most basic step on the path to mobilization. If people have heard of
a concept and demonstrate a rudimentary understanding of it, then at least the
problem of recognition is not a significant one for interest-group elites bent on
mobilization.

Understanding may range from an awareness of the principles and dimensions
of an idea to relatively superficial or intuitive comprehension. Respondents were
asked to define two key phrases widely associated with control-sharing, "community control" and "citizen participation." The questions read as follows:

Q. We hear a lot these days about "community control," like for example, community control of schools. What do the words "community control" mean to you?

Q. Some federal government programs, like the poverty program, call for local "citizen participation." What do the words "citizen participation" mean to you?

Specific programs were mentioned in the questions, to provide context.

TABLE 4.6   LEVELS OF CONCEPTUALIZATION INDICATED BY RESPONSES
DEFINING "COMMUNITY CONTROL," BY RACE

Level of conceptualization indicated by response	Black respondents				White respondents			
	Subtotals		Totals		Subtotals		Totals	
	%	N	%	N	%	N	%	N
Level 1								
Community participation in policy making, planning for public services, programs	3	8	4	10	7	22	13	42
Elaboration of neighborhood government, self-rule theme	1	2			6	20		
Level 2								
Community participation in policy making for schools			10	25			18	59
Level 3								
Expressing opinions	1	2			3	9		
Helping out, working together, taking part	9	21	39	94	6	21	27	91
Tautological answers: community control means the community controls the schools	29	71			18	61		
Level 4								
Other (including references to the PTA, disciplining children, the school board, and hostile answers)			13	33			15	49
Level 5								
Don't know			34	84			27	90
Total			*100*	*246*			*100*	*331*

Tables 4.6 and 4.7 supply a breakdown of the answers to these open-ended
questions. The answers are grouped according to levels of conceptualization—
from the most sophisticated level, at the top, to no understanding, at the bottom. We can be relatively sure that those on levels 1 and 2 recognized the terms;
those on levels 4 and 5 surely did not. Respondents whose answers fall on level 3
were probably guessing, in most cases, at the meaning of these terms; but this
classification may be penalizing those who were less articulate. In any case, the
overall degree of recognition and understanding was extremely low.

Sophisticated answers are those that *elaborated* on the notions of control or
participation and *generalized* their application. For example, when respondents
defined either phrase in terms of policy making or policy planning (both are
elements of control or participation) and extended the ideas to other areas of
public service administration, to government programs, or to neighborhood government in general, their answers are included in the top category.

On the second level are those answers that elaborated the notions of control

TABLE 4.7   LEVELS OF CONCEPTUALIZATION INDICATED BY
RESPONSES DEFINING "CITIZEN PARTICIPATION," BY RACE

Level of conceptualization indicated by response	Black respondents Subtotals %	N	Totals %	N	White respondents Subtotals %	N	Totals %	N
Level 1 Citizen participation in planning or policy making for public programs			4	11			6	20
Level 2 Citizen participation in policy making, planning for poverty program or other single analogous program			2	5			1	3
Level 3 Poor people, individuals "taking part" in poverty program	26	64			7	22		
Going to meetings, expressing opinions	1	2			4	14		
People working together	7	16	54	132	5	15	60	198
Tautological answers: citizen participation means taking part	20	50			44	147		
Level 4 Other (includes references to voting, being an obedient citizen, and making laws for the nation, and hostile answers)			12	29			13	44
Level 5 Don't know			28	69			20	66
Total			*100*	*246*			*100*	*331*

or participation but applied them only to the programs mentioned in the questions. Hence, many respondents mentioned that community control implied parental participation in setting school curriculum, hiring personnel, or formulating school policy.

The third level includes answers that were essentially intuitive. Many people simply repeated the terms in the questions: "Community control means the community controls the schools" or "Citizen participation means taking part, getting involved in the cause." The fourth level is a residual category of incorrect or negative or outlandish responses. The fifth and lowest level comprises answers in the "don't know" category.

Most people failed to demonstrate any special comprehension of these ideas. Members of both races responded as they undoubtedly respond to other terms current in the political marketplace. That people apparently are not able to set these ideas into some programmatic context nor to derive from them certain implications for the specific ways in which they or others might act seems to indicate that elites may be relatively free to forge and manipulate their own definitions of the appropriate settings for citizen control-sharing, without pressure from the mass public.

Set in the context of what is generally known about the ability of members of the mass public to recognize and discuss current issues and political ideas, the low levels of conceptualization revealed here are not inconsistent with previous findings. The data are nevertheless important, for several reasons. First, they indicate that elites interested in control-sharing are not successfully communicating either the vocabulary or the principles of the control-sharing movement to large numbers of their potential constituents. The data also show that, of those in the mass who do recognize the terms, the majority can offer only intuitive definitions, that is, definitions derived strictly from common sense or from cues supplied by the questions themselves. This suggests a minimal capacity to engage in discourse or debate over community control and throws doubt on the possibility that elite initiatives toward control-sharing will strike a readily responsive chord in the mass public. Finally, the data show that blacks are less likely than whites to recognize these terms at all and just as likely to offer intuitive definitions. If in fact both phrases represent ideas central to the rhetoric and expectations of control-sharing efforts, then it cannot be said that there is any evidence of active mass pressure on elites to pursue the issue. Active pressure presumes the ability, at the very least, to recognize the terms and to elaborate on them beyond a mere repetition of the phrases used in the questions themselves. In short, the absence of recognition and understanding among the larger parts of both racial groups suggests that control-sharing arrangements are, at best, a poorly articulated focus of the search for community.

The failure to recognize or define control-sharing programs and phrases does not, however, offer conclusive evidence that support for control-sharing is low. Indeed, if we look at the additional data, it appears that the above argument may be on the wrong track. These additional data reveal marked racial differences in what I shall call the "communitarian perspective," that is, the expression of confidence in local people or the neighborhood, rather than in the central-city government or officials, in the conduct of political affairs. Blacks appear much more prone to embrace this perspective than do-whites (Table 4.8).

The expression of such confidence does not constitute the conscious articulation of a desire for control-sharing, but it does suggest that blacks are more concerned with the particular sort of community values associated with control-sharing. It may, then, signify a greater potential receptivity to control-sharing proposals among blacks.

The figures shown in Table 4.8 appear to reflect genuine racial differences. Additional analysis indicated that rejection of the communitarian perspective is not, in either of the two survey questions, a function of income, education, or

TABLE 4.8 RESPONSES, BY RACE, TO STATEMENTS
INDICATING ATTITUDES TOWARD LOCAL COMMUNITY VERSUS
CITY GOVERNMENT

A. *"Which of these statements would you agree with most?"*				
	Black respondents agreeing		White respondents agreeing	
Statement	%	N	%	N
1. "The people in the local community know better than the people in the city government what is best for them."	80	198	42	139
2. "The people we elect to the city government know best what is good for the local communities."	16	39	50	166
3. Don't know	4	9	8	26
Total	*100*	*246*	*100*	*331*

B. *"Would you agree or disagree: It's much better for the city government to decide what's best for everyone rather than letting individual neighborhoods do their own deciding?"*

	Black respondents		White respondents	
Response	%	N	%	N
Agree	20	48	48	159
Depends	11	28	15	50
Disagree	63	155	31	104
Don't know	6	15	5	18
Total	*100*	*246*	*100*	*331*

Note: Part A—Differences are significant at .001 level (χ^2 = 86.62).
Part B—Differences are significant at .001 level (χ^2 = 64.93).

home ownership. Occupation is mildly related (.38) to the notion that local people know better what is best for them, but this is the only figure that approaches that magnitude.

Within the black sample, occupation and income bear no relationship to position on the communitarian-perspective questions, while education (.38) and home ownership (.28) are positively associated, to a moderate degree, with a neighborhood identification (Part B).[21]

[21] The questions in the two parts of Table 4.8, as well as others used in this report, were run against type and degree of political activity. Respondents were divided into four types: those high in conventional political activity (determined by a cut-off point on an additive index of participation in voting, campaign work, talking about politics, and giving money) who had taken part in at least one political protest; those who scored low on the conventional measure but who had taken part in protest; those who scored high in conventional participation but had never protested; and those low in both types of participation. Political activists were equally likely to adhere to the communitarian perspective. Among the activists there were no differences among protesters, conventional participants, and those active in both types of participation. These uniformities held for both races. In general, type and

In short, the differences that appear may be attributed more accurately to racial than to socioeconomic factors, since attitudes are distributed relatively equally among class strata within each racial sample. Controlling for socio-economic status does not eliminate racial differences.

Additional data indicate, however, that to interpret adherence to the communitarian perspective in terms of actual receptivity to control-sharing may be to state the case inaccurately. While most blacks embraced the perspective, most also showed little inclination to support notions of community autonomy. In addition, position on the communitarian perspective did not serve to distinguish those who favored "community control" in general from those who did not. And there are further indications that blacks in Milwaukee may support actual proposals for control-sharing in particular areas of public service much more selectively than might be anticipated from the proportions adhering to the communitarian perspective.

While blacks fell heavily on the side of the neighborhood in the conflict between neighborhood and city, they had no apparent preferences for community autonomy. Seventy-eight percent of the black respondents believed that local neighborhoods need "a lot" of help from the city government in running poverty programs and Model Cities. Curiously, whites were more confident about local abilities; only 58 percent agreed with the need for a great deal of city government help in running these programs.[22] There is, then, little evidence to support a picture of local black communities yearning for "liberty" and willing to gain it from the city, even at high cost.[23]

Even taking into account the low level of understanding of the term "community control," one might expect, given the currency of the phrase, that people would have responded to it as a "code word"—an undefined symbol connoting a desirable or undesirable state of affairs. Yet a majority in both racial groups claimed that they did not favor *any* type of community control, as we see in Part A of Table 4.9. Adherence to the communitarian perspective does not serve to distinguish those who favored community control from those who rejected it. As we see in Part B, *both black and white adherents to the communitarian perspective were just as likely to reject community control as they were to favor it.*

If any significance at all is to be attributed to the striking racial differences on

---

degree of political activity were not associated with attitudes toward control-sharing. In the rare instance in which there was association, I have noted it specifically.

[22] Data collected by Sidney Verba and Norman Nie reveal a complementary pattern. Their nationwide survey shows that blacks clearly are more likely than whites to believe they need the aid of government in dealing with problems they consider pressing. *Participation in America* (New York: Harper and Row, 1972), p. 167.

[23] Such a picture is painted in Milton Kotler, *Neighborhood Government* (Indianapolis, Ind.: Bobbs-Merrill, 1969), pp. 10, 75-79.

TABLE 4.9 RESPONDENTS' ATTITUDES TOWARD
"COMMUNITY CONTROL" AND THE COMMUNITARIAN
PERSPECTIVE, BY RACE

A. *Responses to question: "Are you in favor of any type of community control?"*

Response	Black respondents		White respondents	
	%	N	%	N
Yes[a]	38	93	38	128
No	61	151	48	158
Don't know	1	2	14	45
Total	*100*	*246*	*100*	*331*

B. *Position of respondents on communitarian perspective, controlling for attitudes toward community control.*

Position	Black respondents				White respondents			
	Favoring community control		Opposing community control		Favoring community control		Opposing community control	
	%	N	%	N	%	N	%	N
"The people in the local community know better than the people in the city government what is best for them."	80	74	79	119	43	55	43	67
"The people we elect to the city government know best what is good for the local communities."	12	11	19	28	46	58	55	87
Don't know	8	8	3	4	11	14	2	4
Total	*100*	*93*	*100*	*151*	*100*	*128*	*100*	*158*

[a]Of the 93 blacks who favored some types of community control, 48 mentioned that local people should control the schools; of the 128 whites who favored some types of community control, 68 mentioned the schools. No more than 6 persons in either sample agreed on any other specific service that should be controlled by the community. To test the possibility that the issue of control-sharing in the schools might be understood better in terms of school *decentralization*, rather than community control, the respondents were asked at another point in the interview if they favored decentralized schools for Milwaukee. Only 7 percent of the blacks (N = 16) and 14 percent of the whites (N = 45) said yes.

the communitarian perspective, it is that they serve notice that the seeds of conflict exist; but they are apparently dormant. These value differences have not yet provided a basis for the mobilization of the black population in Milwaukee on behalf of control-sharing reforms.

In order to explore the possibility that "community control" holds more attraction when linked to specific programs than it does as an abstract idea, the questionnaire sought to tap attitudes toward lay involvement in the school system and with the police. These are the two most sensitive areas in which control-sharing experiments have been considered nationally. In Milwaukee, both races seemed generally satisfied with the school system, and there existed little sentiment within either racial group for decentralized schools.[24] On the other hand, blacks were more attracted than whites to a proposal for introducing greater lay influence over the police.

The school-decentralization movement derives its major impetus from the belief that urban schools have failed in their task of educating children, especially those from minority groups.[25] Without the dynamic of discontent, there seems little chance of mobilizing substantial support for school decentralization. In Milwaukee, 73 percent of the black sample and 83 percent of the white sample believed that the public schools were doing a very good job or a fair job of teaching children.[26]

The failure of the urban school is clearly not the only reason for seeking decentralization. Another motivation has been the desire to devise institutional settings for greater adult participation in making policies that affect the collectivity. Such participation has been deemed of value as a means of enhancing individual political capabilities and confidence.[27] A related motivation has been the desire to challenge what are viewed as the pretensions of professionalism—the belief on the part of professionals that expertise constitutes a superior, even exclusive, claim to power. Marilyn Gittell and Alan Hevesi have written:

> Those who support [school] decentralization criticize centralized control of decision-making because they believe it excludes from participation those elements that are essential to a workable system: the parents and the community. They deny the validity of the concept of professionalism as the absolute and exclusive value on which a power system should be based.[28]

If there exists a strong demand at the mass level for decentralized schools, then we would expect to find major segments of the population advocating a

[24] Joel Aberbach and Jack Walker found similar patterns in their study of Detroit. In their 1971 survey, 37 percent of the whites and 29 percent of the blacks favored decentralized schools. "Citizen Desires, Policy Outcomes and Community Control," *Urban Affairs Quarterly* 8 (September 1972): 55-75.

[25] See Leonard Fein, *The Ecology of the Public Schools: An Inquiry into Community Control* (New York: Pegasus, 1971), for one of the most recent and cogent expositions of the implications of this.

[26] The belief that the schools are doing a good job is negatively related to education (gamma coefficients are -.30 for blacks and -.24 for whites). Those who scored high in both conventional and protest participation were slightly more likely than respondents who were less active in either or both forms of political activity to believe the schools were doing poorly.

[27] For one of the better statements of this classic democratic argument, see Carole Pateman, *Participation and Democratic Theory* (Cambridge: Cambridge University Press, 1970).

[28] Marilyn Gittell and Alan G. Hevesi, "Editors' Introduction," in *The Politics of Urban Education*, ed. Marilyn Gittell and Alan G. Hevesi (New York: Praeger, 1969), p. 9.

TABLE 4.10 RESPONSES, BY RACE, TO QUESTIONNAIRE ITEM 48

Response	Black respondents		White respondents	
	%	N	%	N
"The only way to get quality education for our children is to let professional educators run the whole school system."				
Agree	29	71	39	130
Agree and disagree	21	52	17	57
Disagree	24	59	38	124
Don't know; no answer	26	64	6	20
Total	*100*	*246*	*100*	*331*

greater, if not a dominant, role for parents, in relation to the professional educators, in running the school system. Yet among Milwaukeeans of both races there was only modest sentiment for counterbalancing professional power with parental influence.

Within each racial sample, nearly equal numbers agreed and disagreed that the job of running the schools should be left to professionals (Table 4.10). In fact, more whites than blacks entirely disagreed with the idea of leaving everything to professionals, a finding that undermines the stereotype of the black community in revolt against the educators and bureaucrats of the school system.

Blacks were slightly more prone than whites to believe that "parents who don't know anything about education and teaching should be allowed to have a voice in running the [public] schools," but the low percentage that agreed with this statement (40 percent of the blacks, 35 percent of the whites) indicates that sentiment is not especially strong in favor of lay influence under any and all conditions.

Modal opinion among blacks favored the devolution of major authority over local schools to the lowest functionaries *within the school system,* namely, the teachers and principals (Table 4.11). Within the white sample, more respondents believed that the main control over local schools should be lodged with the central school board. But the data reveal only moderate preference among blacks

TABLE 4.11 RESPONSES, BY RACE, INDICATING
PREFERENCES FOR THE MAIN LOCUS OF CONTROL OVER
LOCAL PUBLIC SCHOOLS

Preferred locus of control	Black respondents		White respondents	
	%	N	%	N
Parents	14	35	9	31
Central school board	25	62	46	151
Teachers and principals	39	95	32	107
All of the above	32	79	21	68

Note: Percentages do not total 100 because respondents could check more than one answer.

for such *administrative decentralization*—a form of downward transfer of authority within the existing formal structure of the bureaucracy, rather than a restructuring of the mechanisms for policy making to include parents in a control-sharing arrangement[29] —and almost an equal percentage of whites as of blacks favored this alternative. Placing the main control in the hands of local parents was favored by extremely small segments of the two racial groups.

In brief, there was only modest sentiment in favor of increased or dominant parent influence in the schools.[30] Whites were slightly more indifferent to the idea of a greater role for parents, although whites in fact were more opposed than blacks to the idea of giving professionals exclusive control of the schools.

The situation was only slightly different in regard to the police. Since the period of intense urban rioting in the 1960s, it has been taken as an article of faith that blacks are overwhelmingly dissatisfied with the quality of police services.[31] If such is the case, then this discontent would provide some evidence of potential for elites to mobilize support for the sort of major reform that police decentralization represents. A substantial body of survey data fails to demonstrate, however, that general discontent about the police is universally felt in the black community. *These data show that there are racial differences in the aggregate level of general satisfaction, but among both races this level is surprisingly high.*

Investigators from the University of Michigan Survey Research Center reported, for example, that only one-quarter of their fifteen-city black sample was "very dissatisfied" with police services in their neighborhoods (compared to approximately 10 percent of the whites). Two-thirds of the whites and approximately one-half of the blacks were "generally" satisfied.[32] Joel Aberbach and Jack Walker collected data in Detroit that show that 51 percent of the black respondents were satisfied with police services, while 43 percent were dissatisfied. More blacks in that city were dissatisfied with parks and teenage recreation centers than with the police.[33] In Milwaukee, 72 percent of the black sample

---

[29] For a succinct discussion of the differences between administrative and political decentralization in the urban context, see Howard W. Hallman, *Administrative Decentralization and Citizen Control*, Center for Governmental Studies Pamphlet No. 7 (Washington, D.C.: Center for Governmental Studies, March 1971).

[30] Milwaukee is apparently not atypical in this regard. The Urban Observatory survey found that, when people were asked what could be done to improve schools in the neighborhood, no more than 1 percent in any of the ten cities suggested an increase in community control; a few respondents (no more than 3 percent in any city) suggested increased parent participation in the educational process. An Urban Observatory Report, "City Taxes and Services: Citizens Speak Out," *Nation's Cities* (August 1971): 28-29.

[31] *Report of the National Advisory Commission on Civil Disorders* (New York: Bantam, 1968), p. 302.

[32] Campbell and Schuman, *Racial Attitudes*, p. 40.

[33] Joel D. Aberbach and Jack L. Walker, "The Attitudes of Blacks and Whites toward City Services: Implications for Public Policy," in *Financing the Metropolis*, ed. John P. Crecine (Beverly Hills, Cal.: Sage, 1970), p. 522.

and 91 percent of the white sample believed that the police in their neighborhood behaved fairly.[34]

In the absence of indications of profound dissatisfaction, it is hardly surprising to find that proposals for changes in police practice and police government did not elicit very wide support. Although there had been resentment expressed over the virtually all-white tactical patrol squads developed by Police Chief Harold Brier to patrol high-crime (ghetto) areas,[35] only 16 percent of the black respondents approved the idea of having only black policemen patrol black neighborhoods and only white policemen patrol white neighborhoods. Only 22 percent of the white sample thought this was a good idea. Most people in both racial groups (57 percent of the whites, 59 percent of the blacks) rejected the idea because of a professed commitment to integration or a belief that segregated patrols would be racist. It should be said, to place these commitments in perspective, that black policemen accounted for only slightly more than 2 percent (51 out of 2200) of the Milwaukee police force in 1972.[36]

Sentiment in favor of the establishment of elected boards of local citizens to watch over the police in each precinct and to handle citizen complaints was modest, in light of the fact that the Milwaukee police had never been noted for their responsiveness to citizen desires and grievances. Chief Brier commanded and controlled his department with a firm and unyielding hand. A 1971 report by the Council on Urban Life stated that "Brier . . . has decided to keep his own counsel on police matters."[37] According to the report, Brier refused to cooperate with the Kerner Commission investigators, resisted statewide efforts to establish a Law Enforcement Standards Board for Wisconsin, refused to give the Police and Fire Commission (which appoints the police chief) a copy of the rule book he used to run the department, and (at least through 1974) successfully fought attempts, including those by the Police and Fire Commission, to develop a police community relations program.[38] None of this is to suggest that the Police and Fire Commission itself had been responsive; although it is empowered

---

[34] Satisfaction cuts across class lines and political activity categories. However, this does appear to contrast with earlier attitudes. The Bisbing survey (1965) showed only 22 percent of the blacks agreeing that the police do an "equal job in all neighborhoods." Bisbing Business Research, *Attitude Study among Negro and White Residents in the Milwaukee Negro Residential Areas* (Milwaukee: 1965), p. 98. The Slesinger postriot survey found that 58 percent of the black sample (compared to only 5 percent of the white sample) found the police "too brutal." Jonathan Slesinger, "Study of Community Opinions concerning the Summer 1967 Civil Disturbance in Milwaukee" (Unpublished report, Office of Applied Social Research, School of Social Welfare and Institute of Human Relations, University of Wisconsin–Milwaukee, April 1, 1968), p. 25.

[35] Reported in the *Milwaukee Journal*, March 8, 1968.

[36] Ralph Whitehead, Jr., "Milwaukee's Mercurial Mayor Henry Maier," *City* 6 (March–April 1972): 17.

[37] Quoted by Whitehead, ibid. See also Schmandt, Goldbach, and Vogel, *Milwaukee*, p. 103.

[38] Whitehead, "Milwaukee's Mercurial Mayor," p. 17.

to hear citizen complaints about police conduct, no patrolman had ever, up to the time of this survey in 1970, been indicted as a result of a citizen accusation.

Slightly more than one-half (56 percent) of the black sample approved the idea of a citizen board, as compared with 26 percent of the white sample. The idea of such a board represents a reform of modest dimensions, yet support for this is not strikingly high.

Conclusion

There is little evidence in the Milwaukee data to support the notion that the failure of community constitutes a central preoccupation of urban dwellers in the modern age. I suggested at the outset that if we found data to indicate that the two racial groups defined community differently or sought to realize some idea of community in different ways, then we could argue that the basic, underlying political goals of the two races were sufficiently divergent to make most encounters in the political arena competitive rather than cooperative. The idea is that underlying goals color perceptions of other, more immediate issues that arise. When these basic goals diverge, racial conflict is built in persistently to each encounter, regardless of the specific nature of the issue. Every question of policy comes to be evaluated, under these circumstances, in light of its effects on the attainment of community, as each racial group defines it.

What we find, instead, is that neither race is substantially concerned with community in either of the ways we have suggested such concern might be manifested. We do find evidence that black and white *issue priorities* diverge. Thus, it would seem reasonable to conclude that, in Milwaukee, racial conflict is likely to be tied to the structure of policy preferences associated with specific issues that arise. Conflict in any given instance results from independent evaluations that, in the situation at hand, racial interests diverge. Conflict as a consequence of racial divergence on generalized political goals having to do with the nature of community is not built into race relations in Milwaukee politics.

The data we have examined here help us to understand some of the pressures that do and do not bear on elites and what sorts of implications the preferences of each racial group in Milwaukee might have for race relations in that city.

It seems apparent that the demand for control-sharing in Milwaukee is an elite demand, not a mass demand. That the demand exists, there can be no doubt. Various groups of black leaders have fought bitter battles with the city administration over the measure of control by the poor in the poverty and Model Cities programs. Other black leaders have been involved in experimentation with school decentralization, and still others have become interested in proposals for lay participation in administrative decisions in the police department.[39] But all

---

[39] Joan McManus, "Police, People and Power" (Report prepared for the Council on Urban Life, Milwaukee, Wis., July 1970).

of these demands appear to have come primarily from elites; pressure from the masses themselves for greater participation does not seem to exist in much strength.

This raises obvious problems for black elites especially. As we have seen, those who are interested in control-sharing reforms confront not only a modest but a highly selective pattern of support from the black community. It is possible that a massive educational campaign or a divisive conflict of the dimensions of the New York City school-decentralization episode could generate and mobilize mass support. But similar cases in other parts of the country have proven otherwise (in Detroit, for example), and for elites to bank their resources on such a strategy has great risks.

Black elites who choose to pursue the control-sharing issue without mass support derive both advantages and disadvantages from the situation. One major advantage is that elites who make the demand for control-sharing institutions are not constrained by mass expectations. There exists no substantial mass following that either expects or desires such reforms or that has an ideal picture in mind of their appropriate form. This frees elites to bargain with those authorities in a position to deal with such demands. In such a case, mass ignorance and apathy may facilitate cooperation between elites, in the sense that bargains may be struck in a negotiation process unhindered by the need to report concurrently to the masses or even to take their desires into account.

This situation has obvious disadvantages, too. The absence of mass support and the level of mass unawareness weaken those elites who demand control-sharing, both vis-à-vis the authorities upon whom they make their demand and in their own community of potential followers. There are few imperatives to induce a response from the elites in city or state government. The demand for control-sharing may be written off without great cost by the mayor and his administration as the demand of an unrepresentative few. There is little basis in our survey data for anticipating sustained negative reactions among the population of either race to such an official response—or, rather, nonresponse—to this demand.

Then, too, elites who pursue goals that generate neither interest nor enthusiasm among the masses run the risk of losing the support they need for survival. Indeed, they are likely to bore the masses; and, of all the reactions that may be evoked in the masses, few are as lethal to the power of a leader as boredom. In sum, the structure of opinion is such that while neither racial community actively supports or opposes control-sharing, the opportunities for elites who seek such reforms are not especially promising. Black elites may find more fruitful ways to attract and hold mass followings. White reform leaders, too, will discover, as John Lindsay did in New York City, that there is no substantial constituency for control-sharing, and, to survive, they will find it necessary to drop the issue. Thus the probability that elites will successfully exploit the attraction of the black masses to communitarian values by seeking control-

LEWIS AND CLARK COLLEGE LIBRARY
PORTLAND, OREGON 97219

sharing reforms, which in turn presumably would generate serious racial conflicts, is not high. Instead, racial conflict is more likely to continue to center
around the achievement of very ordinary welfare goals of the type that Wilson
labeled "conventional," and these are the sorts of issues on which elites of either
racial community may hope to ride to power.

Patterns of Conventional Political Participation

5

When the campaign for mayor began in early 1968, racial tensions in Milwaukee were running high. The city was still experiencing repercussions from the riot of the previous August; whites were reported to be purchasing handguns in record numbers,[1] the Triple O was urging establishment of a "Black Cross" to aid future civilian victims of racial disorders,[2] and litigation challenging the constitutionality of Mayor Maier's citywide curfew during the riot had just come to a close in the Circuit Court with a decision in Maier's favor.[3] "Groppi's Commandos" were still marching for open housing, stopping finally only two weeks before the April 2 election day. In addition, the public schools were in turmoil over black student demands for black history courses and for "soul food" in the cafeterias. Under the circumstances, it was not surprising that, for the first time in the city's history, racial issues took a central role in the mayoral election.

Henry Maier, standing for his third term, was initially opposed by five candidates, including David Walther, a young white attorney who came in second to Maier in the March preliminary vote. Walther was clearly engaged in a losing fight in the runoff campaign in the ensuing month; Maier had won 76 percent of the vote in the primary election. Nevertheless, Walther decided to

---

[1]*Milwaukee Journal*, March 8, 1968.
[2]Ibid., March 28, 1968.
[3]Ibid., March 29, 1968.

pursue an uncompromising course by speaking out for black interests. He argued that Milwaukeeans had to support the idea of black power and autonomy, and he won the endorsement of the black *Milwaukee Courier.* He favored open housing, he attacked the bias of the Eagles Club, and he proclaimed racial discrimination to be the chief moral crisis in America. In a city where blacks constituted only about 10 percent of the electorate, this unpopular strategy could do no less than seal his fate.

Meanwhile, Maier opposed a "city-only" open-housing law, and he was endorsed in late March by the Milwaukee Citizens Civic Voice, the Milwaukee County Property Owners Association, the South Side Neighborhood Association, and the Citizens Association of Wisconsin.[4] Maier touched only tangentially on the issue of equal rights, pursuing, instead, a campaign that he described as a "crusade for jobs and resources." His cause was helped when the city received a $2.35 million federal manpower-training grant just days before the election. The day after the grant was awarded, Maier named to his campaign staff John Givens, a former CORE leader who had once organized a sit-in in the mayor's office. He was the first black to gain such an appointment. On April 2, Maier won, amassing 86 percent of the vote. Walther lost in every ward, including the Inner Core's Sixth, First, and Seventh wards.

Several facts stand out in this tale of the 1968 municipal election in Milwaukee. One is that Henry Maier did not need the black vote, and he did not seek it. A second fact is that he received the black vote, despite the effort his opponent made to get it. A third fact is that Walther, identified as a candidate partial to blacks, was virtually isolated all through the campaign. He received no more than one-quarter of the black vote (according to my survey data, it was even less; only 16 percent of the blacks old enough to vote said they had voted for Walther) and very scattered, token white support. He had failed, in other words, to establish an interracial coalition with a black core of support as the basis.

These features of the 1968 election are not atypical of the ways in which blacks and whites confront one another in the lists of conventional electoral politics in Milwaukee, and they serve to raise some important questions around which our analysis of conventional participation patterns may revolve. First, when a group represents a small minority in a city, what factors enhance or detract from its desirability as a coalition partner? What helps to determine the chances of a black–white coalition in conventional politics? What possibilities do the avenues of conventional politics offer minority groups for winning political conflicts with majority groups? Are blacks doomed always to lose in such situations? An examination of the data on conventional participation patterns throws some light on these problems.

[4] Ibid., March 27, 1968. All these groups, of course, opposed open-housing legislation.

An Analysis of Conventional Participation Data

Some of the most firmly established generalizations in the social sciences have to do with differential rates of political participation among various groups in society. Let us consider here how the rate of such activity among a group's members affects the chances of coalition with other groups. Coalitions are constructed on the grounds of mutual need. The idea at the heart of coalition is the pooling of resources. A group that has little to bring to such a union is obviously an undesirable partner, for in effect that group cannot pay for its share—however big or small—of whatever spoils the coalition may win. Among the important resources are large numbers of followers who demonstrate their support by mobilizing, by supplying money, and by acting in response to elite cues in such a way as to strengthen and illuminate a leader's claims to power. That is to say, when a leader commands a following of politically active or easily mobilizable constituents, his group is, other things being equal, a more desirable coalition partner than groups whose members show a low rate of activity or propensity to mobilize. Thus, determining the rates of black and white mass participation can provide some basis for judging the likelihood of interracial coalition.

The scene is complicated by the fact that, broadly speaking, there are at least two different styles of nonviolent participatory strategies for seeking political goals: a conventional style and a protest style. Before proceeding to distinguish and define these, I would point out that one may distinguish coalitions in part by the styles adopted by the partner groups. There are coalitions in which all parties are committed to conventional strategies, such as electoral coalitions; there are those in which all parties are committed to protest; and, finally, there are hybrid coalitions, in which some groups employ conventional means and others use protest. These hybrids may give rise to forms of cooperation that I have called broad coalition and tacit coalition. If we pursue the analysis of comparative rates of participation across *styles* of participation, then we may develop estimates of probabilities of the kinds of coalitions in which the masses of the two races are most likely to be valuable to one another.

These estimates based on rates of participation have implications for elites of the two races. The particular patterns of mass activity make certain types of coalition easier to imagine and others more difficult to imagine. If, for example, blacks show a high rate of protest and a low rate of conventional participation, while the white masses show exactly the opposite patterns of participation, then it is clear that blacks would represent a liability in an electoral (conventional) coalition. This is scarcely inviting to black elites, even those who are ideologically or pragmatically predisposed to work in biracial electoral politics. The opportunities, on the other hand, for black elites to lead through the formation of hybrid coalitions—that is, by allying their protest constituency with sympathetic but conventionally oriented white groups—are somewhat better, or at least the possibilities for such coalitions are easier to contemplate. It is apparent that the particular rate and style of participation at the mass level create a situation that may encourage some types of elites and discourage others by providing particular sorts of opportunities for interracial cooperation.

Comparative rates of participation can also tell us much about the nature of interracial conflict, *if and when conflict occurs*. It is not clear that specific differences or similarities in rates of activity effectively help to establish specific probabilities for conflict, in the way that they do for cooperation. The most important contribution of an analysis of participation rates is to provide estimates of relative group stength—a factor that obviously can determine the character of conflict in various ways. Of the many factors of which group strength is a function, those upon which the patterns of participation throw light include relative group *visibility, cohesiveness,* and *receptivity to political mobilization.*

To be visible politically is to be conspicuous to decisionmakers when they make decisions. Visibility is, of course, relative. All things being equal, a more visible group is more likely to have its needs and desires enter into the calculus of decision making than is a less visible group. The visibility of a group is a function of a variety of different factors. It may depend, for example, on the social prominence or achievements of its members or leaders. Or it may stem simply from the nature of the problems the group faces, in which case visibility may be related in part to the nature of the burdens a needy group imposes on the society at large. Visibility may also be a function of the things a group does; a group may enhance its visibility by taking certain actions. These may take the form, for example, of bloc voting or the communication to public officials of demands, opinions, or grievances. Voting and contact are both forms of political participation. What we can examine in this chapter, then, is the degree to which blacks and whites contribute by their conventional political activity to the respective political visibility of the two races, that is, to the structuring of the political scene as it is viewed by public officials.

Participation data, especially voting statistics, can also indicate the degree to which the respective mass populations are cohesive. Cohesion here can be defined operationally as a high level of intragroup similarity of behavior in the pursuit of similar goals. Where voting by members of a given group goes heavily in one direction, we may conclude that, at least for that period and in those circumstances, group cohesion was high. Cohesion is a source of group strength and an element in solidifying group identity. It also contributes to a group's visibility. A group whose members cohere in the effort to win some group goal is bound to be engaged in a more intractable form of conflict than one whose members are divided in their loyalties or desires.

A further source of group strength is the readiness of its members to mobilize for political action. We may judge this receptivity not only by inference from the rates of participation but also by assessing the character of the inactive population to determine the nature of the untapped resource they offer elites bent on mobilizing the masses.

To summarize, group strength depends to some extent on relative visibility, cohesion, and the receptivity of the mass to mobilization initiatives. When conflict between mass groups of the two races occurs, the depth, length, and outcome of the conflict will rest, in part, on these factors.

Distinguishing Participatory Styles

If the investigation of differing group rates of participation is important, a problem of equal interest—but one much less often explored—is whether different groups pursue qualitatively distinctive styles of participation. We wish to make a distinction here between conventional and protest styles. The styles may not be differentiated by the ideologies associated with their use, since groups with widely varying ideologies may and do employ both styles. Neither may the styles be distinguished entirely by their characteristic forms of behavior, since certain types of behavior, such as mass rallies, may be included under either style, although different sets of behaviors do provide an important starting point. Rather, the distinction rests ultimately, I believe, on social definitions of what constitute acceptable and unacceptable forms of political self-expression.

It is not clear by what criteria a society makes these particular definitional judgments. To some degree they are probably a function of the degree to which particular behavior is perceived as threatening (which is therefore unacceptable) or not (which is acceptable).[5] Whatever the reasons for social judgments, we can clearly distinguish one category of acts that commands high social approval and another that commands wide social disapproval, and on this difference, empirically established, our distinction between styles will rest.

Stylistic differences alone do not provide a sufficient basis for predicting a competitive political relationship; the strange bedfellows for which politics is famous are often groups whose styles of action are radically different. Neither do stylistic similarities afford enough evidence to consider cooperation a foregone conclusion; perhaps the most common form of political competition among mass groups in the United States involves electoral conflict, in which all parties are strongly committed to conventional strategies. But an examination of stylistic differences and similarities can, like the other elements in our typology, tell us much about the form interracial political relationships are likely to take. This in turn tells us much about the context in which elites must operate, for we

[5] I have offered a discussion along these lines concerning protest in my article "The Conditions of Protest in American Cities," *American Political Science Review* 67 (March 1973): 13-14.

may judge the nature of the alternative choices open to them and the nature of the supports and constraints at work in their environment.

Style is an elusive concept. One thing style implies is that various ways of doing a particular thing exhibit common and distinctive characteristics. Thus, to speak of a style of political participation is to suggest that, in making political demands, the methods employed—which may differ *tactically* from one another—may be distinguished from other methods that constitute a different style. What seems to distinguish the sets of participatory methods that make up a style are the particular levels of societal support and beliefs that sustain and judge such actions. The conventional style includes those forms of political activity that are widely approved. The protest style includes demand-making activities that are widely disapproved but not absolutely forbidden. It is the disapproval such behavior engenders that makes it unconventional.

The tactics that constitute the conventional style include all those that center around the vote, including efforts to affect the vote during electoral campaigns. I have also included, following Lester Milbrath, individual attempts to contact public officials for the purpose of communicating claims, grievances, requests, and opinions. Milbrath has provided what is now a standard list of conventional political acts, of which Figure 5.1 is an adaptation.[6]

```
1. Helping out in a political campaign.
2. Working in a voter registration drive.
3. Giving money to a candidate or party.
4. Contacting a public official.
5. Attempting to persuade someone to
   vote in a certain way.
6. Talking about politics.
7. Voting.
```

Figure 5.1. List of conventional political acts.

Although these particular acts may not invariably exhibit clear tactical similarities to one another (contacting an official is tactically distinct from talking about politics), they are linked by the general cultural or social approval they command. This is in fact what makes them conventional. Voting, for example, commands nearly universal support. This is most strongly expressed as a "personal commitment to the norm of voting obligation."[7] Indeed, the institution of elections—involving a process that encompasses most of the acts on Milbrath's list—enjoys widespread support in America.[8] Gabriel Almond and Sidney Verba have reported that most Americans believe they could and would contact public

---

[6] Lester Milbrath, *Political Participation* (Chicago: Rand McNally, 1965), p. 18. For a similar and more recent list, see Sidney Verba and Norman Nie, *Participation in America* (New York: Harper and Row, 1972), p. 31.

[7] Jack Dennis, "Support for the Institution of Elections by the Mass Public," *American Political Science Review* 64 (September 1970): 834.

[8] Ibid.

officials if they had a grievance,[9] a supposition so widespread as to cloak the act itself in conventional tones.

The unconventional style involves political protest, a form of disruptive behavior that relies on a delicate balance of threat and moral appeal to provide its users with access to decisionmakers and with bargaining leverage in political contests. The particular acts that may be labeled protest need not be analytically distinguished for our purposes; they include protest marches, demonstrations, picketing, and sit-ins—to name some common types of protest.

Protest tactics are clearly considered beyond the established and acceptable norms that govern political participation. A Harris poll conducted in 1965 found that 68 percent of the respondents believed that antiwar picketing and demonstrations were more harmful than helpful; 68 percent believed that civil rights demonstrations likewise were more harmful than helpful; and 65 percent felt the same way about student demonstrations.[10] A 1966 Harris poll asked whites whether, if they were in the same position as Negroes, they would feel justified "to march and protest in demonstrations." Exactly one-half of the sample said they would not feel justified; 35 percent said they would.[11] A later Harris poll, taken in 1968, found that 82 percent of those sampled "disapproved" of Negro "demonstration tactics."[12] Similar data showing high general disapproval of protest were reported in separate studies by Marvin Olsen[13] and Angus Campbell.[14]

The Milwaukee data reveal that, when we control for race in examining attitudes toward protest, striking racial differences appear. These findings will be reported in detail in the next chapter; it is sufficient to note for now that black approval and support for protest were so widespread that we may speak of distinctive subcultural attitudes toward such forms of participation. We also found that blacks, more than whites, believed protest to be effective, and many believed they had a kind of civic duty to take part in such manifestations. If protest is unconventional in the eyes of society at large (white society), it is a relatively normal aspect of black political life.

To distinguish styles of political activity through an examination of attitudes toward forms of behavior has certain advantages that a less complex method

[9] Gabriel Almond and Sidney Verba, *The Civic Culture* (Boston: Little, Brown, 1965), p. 188.

[10] Amitai Etzioni, *Demonstration Democracy* (New York: Gordon and Breach, 1970), p. 10.

[11] William Brink and Louis Harris, *Black and White: A Study of Racial Attitudes Today* (New York: Simon and Schuster, 1967), p. 222.

[12] Etzioni, *Demonstration Democracy*, p. 10.

[13] Marvin Olsen, "Perceived Legitimacy of Social Protest Actions," *Social Problems* 15 (Winter 1968): 299.

[14] Angus Campbell, *White Attitudes toward Black People* (Ann Arbor, Mich.: University of Michigan, Institute for Social Research, 1971), pp. 138-139.

does not offer. One is that the conventional–unconventional distinction, which hinges on social approval or disapproval, provides a connection among discrete acts that goes beyond the intuitive level. Another advantage is that the attitudes toward these forms of action help to explain the inevitable unattractiveness of protest constituencies as partners in conventional coalitions, given the cost in terms of popular support of the social disapproval they engender. Conversely, conventionally oriented groups may be highly attractive to protest groups for the legitimacy-by-association they might be able to offer.

Indices of Conventional Political Participation

The remainder of this chapter is devoted to exploring racial patterns in rates of conventional participation. To facilitate the task of making racial comparisons on a large number of individual items, several composite indices were constructed. These are simply additive measures, developed in the following way.[15] All the individual items of participation (there are nine) were intercorrelated. Clusters were then identified. These clusters are groups that show especially high associations among the individual items. Three distinct clusters emerged: a voting participation cluster, a verbal participation cluster, and one composed primarily of campaign participation items. For purposes of scoring, the items within each cluster were treated as dichotomous variables. One point was awarded for participation on the item, zero for nonparticipation. The three indices that resulted are simple additive scores of conventional participation in three relatively distinct areas. A fourth index, a summary measure, is composed of the scores on all nine items. The items that constitute each index and the range of possible scores are as follows:

Voting Index, score range 0-2: voted for president in 1968; voted for mayor in 1968.

Verbal Index, score range 0-3: talked about presidential election in 1968; talked about mayoral election in 1968; attempted to persuade someone to vote in a certain way.

Campaign–Contact Index, score range 0-4: gave money to a party or candidate; helped out in a campaign in any way; took part in a voter registration drive; contacted any public official.

The distribution of scores on each index is shown in Table 5.1. The finding that black levels of nonparticipation were consistently higher than those of whites is a predictable one.[16] It leads us nevertheless to wonder whether *in fact*

---

[15] A detailed discussion of the derivation of the indices and the raw correlations may be found in Appendix A.

[16] For recent similar findings, using similar indices of black and white conventional participation, see Verba and Nie, *Participation in America*, pp. 151-152.

TABLE 5.1 POLITICAL PARTICIPATION INDEX SCORES, BY RACE

Index of political participation	Score	Black respondents %	N	White respondents %	N
Voting[a]	0	31	67	23	69
	1	22	46	18	54
	2	47	100	59	174
Total		*100*	*213*	*100*	*297*
Verbal participation[b]	0	43	105	26	87
	1	11	28	19	63
	2	20	50	37	122
	3	26	63	18	59
Total		*100*	*246*	*100*	*331*
Campaign–contact[c]	0	70	172	60	200
	1	19	47	27	89
	2	7	18	10	33
	3	2	5	2	7
	4	2	4	1	2
Total		*100*	*246*	*100*	*331*
Composite score[d]	0	22	54	12	39
	1-4	55	134	58	192
	5-9	24	58	30	100
Total		*100*	*246*	*100*	*331*

[a] Differences are significant at .03 level (χ^2=7.01).
[b] Differences are significant at .001 level (χ^2=33.6).
[c] Differences are significant at .10 level (χ^2=7.99).
[d] Differences are significant at .004 level (χ^2=11.63).

black elites have in the inactive black population a significantly larger un-tapped—or unmobilized—potential resource for conventional politics than white elites have among inactive whites. We shall explore this question momentarily.

The finding that a greater proportion of blacks than of whites scored high on the verbal index is also not completely unexpected. Donald R. Matthews and James W. Prothro report, for example, that equal proportions of the two races in the North claim to have discussed with others the presidential election of 1960.[17] Nor is it entirely surprising that blacks and whites were almost equally represented at the most active levels on the campaign–contact index, although, in the case of blacks, this was entirely a product of high campaign, rather than high contact, activity. All these patterns of activity accord nicely with the national findings in the study done by Sidney Verba and Norman Nie, who summarize black participation in the following way:

> One of the interesting facets of the pattern of participation among blacks is that although they are severely *overrepresented* among the inactives, they are not severely

[17] Donald R. Matthews and James W. Prothro, *Negroes and the New Southern Politics* (New York: Harcourt, Brace and World, 1966), p. 44.

TABLE 5.2 VOTING TURNOUT IN MILWAUKEE, BY RACE, 1968

Election	Black adults who reported having voted (%)	White adults who reported having voted (%)
Presidential	66	73
Local	50	63

underrepresented among the complete activists. There is an asymmetry in their level of activity.[18]

We can be confident, I think, that the Milwaukee data are not atypical.

In Milwaukee, white voting in 1968 at both the local and national levels occurred at a higher rate than black voting (see Table 5.2)—a pattern that corroborates other findings on racial differences in electoral behavior in other places and at other times.[19] The level of black participation in local elections, as compared with national elections, dropped more sharply than that of whites, as we can see by the fact that the percentage difference in local and national turnout rates was greater for blacks than for whites. Blacks constituted a less important segment of the local electorate than of the national electorate.

The pattern of lower black voting rates, if unremarkable, leads us to consider the extent to which blacks as a group represent attractive partners to those building nonpartisan electoral coalitions in Milwaukee. The standard analysis of black voting patterns would imply that blacks would be highly desirable coalition partners. On the national level, they comprise an essential part of the Democratic constituency. Even in local arenas in which they are a minority, as in Milwaukee, they would seem to represent a potential swing vote. Despite their potential, I would suggest that, under prevailing circumstances, Milwaukee blacks are not very attractive to white groups as coalition partners. The problem rests substantially on the calculus of political coalitions.

We begin with the observation that the turnout rate of blacks is not as high as that of whites. This indicates that, as a bloc, blacks are not maximizing their impact on the electoral outcome. In a partisan system, the failure to turn out the black vote (that is, the failure relative to the white effort) may be offset to some degree by the fact that blacks vote almost exclusively for the Democratic ticket. But in a nonpartisan system, such as Milwaukee's, there is no continuing

[18] Verba and Nie, *Participation in America*, p. 151.

[19] Survey Research Center data from the University of Michigan show consistently higher rates of black nonvoting in presidential elections through 1968, even in the North. William Flanigan, *Political Behavior of the American Electorate* (Boston: Allyn and Bacon, 1972), p. 23. See also Robert Axelrod, "Where the Votes Come From: An Analysis of Electoral Coalitions, 1952-1968," *American Political Science Review* 66 (March 1972): 14; and Howard Hamilton, "The Municipal Voter: Voting and Nonvoting in City Elections," *American Political Science Review* 65 (December 1971): 1138.

focus for stable loyalties. Blacks cannot be counted upon to turn out in great numbers, and they cannot be expected to vote in a predictable way. Because they are a minority (10 percent of the electorate), they need maximum effort and high cohesion to have any chance of affecting electoral outcomes.

But blacks are unattractive to white coalition makers not simply because they are weak potential partners; their numbers might be adequate to swing a close vote. Rather, they are unattractive because what they must and do demand from a coalition exceeds the measure of their contribution to it.[20] Let us assume that the spoils of electoral victory are parceled out roughly according to a formula based on effort and contribution to the coalition, with some (subjective) need factor taken into account. The only reasonable conclusion is that black needs and demands far outstrip their electoral effort and contribution because *(1)* they do not pull their maximum potential weight in a coalition, *(2)* their weight in a city like Milwaukee is minimal at any rate, and *(3)* their demands are heavy in the eyes of whites—as Walther's failure in 1968 made clear. There is little pragmatic justification to seek blacks as coalition partners, given these conditions.

Black effort and contribution in the 1968 municipal election can be measured relative to those of whites to provide a graphic illustration of the basis of the argument presented above. The electoral effort of a group for a given candidate (or coalition) may be calculated by the following simple formula:

$$\text{effort} = X_i \cdot Y_i,$$

where

X_i = the percentage of a group's turnout,

Y_i = the percentage of a group's vote for the candidate of that coalition.

Perfect turnout and unanimous voting for that candidate yield a score of 1.0. Black turnout among the sample population in the mayoral election of 1968 was 50 percent; 83 percent of the black sample claimed to have voted for Maier—a figure that represents a generous estimate of overall black support. White turnout was 63 percent; 94 percent of the white sample claimed to have voted for Maier. Thus:

$$\text{black effort} = 0.50 \cdot 0.83 = 0.415$$
$$\text{white effort} = 0.63 \cdot 0.94 = 0.592.$$

Conceivably, a victorious coalition might reward a very small group for an extremely high level of effort, but its actual contribution to the coalition is more likely to be the basis for the division of spoils. The relative contribution of a group is a function of the effort score multiplied by the percentage of adults of

[20] William Gamson, writing of an analogous situation, puts the matter this way: "Unrepresented groups tend to be poor in resources and rich in demands, making them poor coalition partners. They will expect to share in the rewards of a coalition disproportionately to the resources they contribute to it." "Stable Unrepresentation in American Society," *American Behavioral Scientist* 12 (November–December 1968): 20.

voting age in the population who belong to that group. The formula is as follows:

$$\text{contribution} = X_i \cdot Y_i \cdot Z_i,$$

where

Z_i = the percentage of adults of voting age who belong to that group.

Contribution is a combination, then, of capability and effort. Again, the highest score possible is 1.0, reflecting perfect turnout and unanimous voting in a perfectly homogeneous electorate. For the mayoral election of 1968 in Milwaukee, we make the following calculation:

$$\text{black contribution} = 0.50 \cdot 0.83 \cdot 0.094 = 0.039,$$

where 0.094 is the percentage of the adults of voting age who are black; and

$$\text{white contribution} = 0.63 \cdot 0.94 \cdot 0.906 = 0.536,$$

where 0.906 is the percentage of the adults of voting age who are white.

Only by comparing these figures do we begin to understand how minimal was the black contribution to Maier's 1968 victory. To illustrate the matter yet another way, of the 169,885 votes won by Maier, approximately 7 percent (about 12,000 votes) were black votes in what was a landslide election. In the practical world of political calculation of contributions and rewards, all but the most minimal black demands would be out of line with what they brought to the coalition. To make heavy demands is to make oneself less attractive as a coalition partner.

Viewing black voting data from this perspective helps to reveal some of the forces at work in limiting black power in Milwaukee government. Blacks have been neither courted for the prevailing coalition nor rewarded, even to the degree to which they have contributed to the coalition's victories. A 1968 survey of black representation in policy-making positions in Milwaukee showed that blacks held only 1 of 81 appointed administrative posts in the city government and 28 of 387 positions on appointed boards and commissions.[21] Rewarding blacks in proportion to their numbers is seen as neither necessary nor appropriate.

The data on voting rates and the measures derived from them suggest some difficulties inherent in establishing cooperative interracial relationships. There are other data that bear on the nature of interracial conflict, if and when it occurs. For elites who become involved in the pursuit of interracial political conflict, the inactive members of the population may represent a potential resource. Additional participants add force to influence attempts, increase the visibility of the group, and enhance its potential voting strength. If elites are able to mobilize the respective inactive groups, interracial contests will be fought out by sides more equal than those presently constituted, since the reservoir of unmobilized citizens is larger among the black population than it is among

---

[21] Karl H. Flaming, J. John Palen, Grant Ringlien, and Corneff Taylor, "Black Powerlessness in Policy-Making Positions," *Sociological Quarterly* 13 (Winter 1972): 130.

TABLE 5.3 CORRELATIONS (GAMMA) BETWEEN TYPES OF
POLITICAL PARTICIPATION AND STATUS VARIABLES, BY RACE

| Type of political participation | Black respondents | | | | | |
	Occupation	Home ownership	Income	Organizational memberships	Education	Average coefficient
Voting	.16	.35	.35	.30	.38	.308
Verbal	.23	.40	.22	.38	.21	.288
Campaign–contact	.30	.44	.42	.47	.38	.402
Composite of types	.27	.41	.37	.44	.22	.342

| Type of political participation | White respondents | | | | | |
	Occupation	Home ownership	Income	Organizational memberships	Education	Average coefficient
Voting	.13	.15	.08	.30	.15	.162
Verbal	.26	.07	.29	.38	.39	.278
Campaign–contact	.28	.18	.26	.40	.42	.308
Composite of types	.28	.21	.25	.40	.29	.286

whites. That is, black elites would appear to have before them much larger unexploited reserves. But the crucial question to ask is whether or to what degree the unmobilized members of the two races are in fact exploitable. Are the people who score zero on the participation indices potentially mobilizable, or have the two racial populations been mobilized to their limits? To judge the nature of the potential that the unmobilized citizens hold for elites in search of larger active constituencies, we must establish some crude probabilities of the likelihood that they *can* be mobilized.

The inactives are not, of course, simply a random selection of citizens. They tend disproportionately to come from lower-status groups. The chances of mobilizing low-status people are much less than those for middle- or high-status people, but these chances seem to differ slightly by race.

Table 5.3 shows that conventional political activity is positively related to social status. This is, of course, a standard finding in social science research. Much less a matter of routine expectation are the slight racial differences that emerge here: *Status is somewhat more strongly related to participation among blacks than among whites.* This is especially the case where voting is concerned, and only slightly less so for campaign participation.

One way to understand the significance of this finding is to note that, while the proportion of lower-class people of both races in the inactive category is notably large, *it is slightly larger among blacks,* suggesting that insofar as low social status is an obstacle to mobilization, black inactives as a group are likely to be especially resistant.

Efforts to mobilize low-status whites have indeed been more successful than similar efforts with low-status blacks, as the following illustrations show:

1. In terms of *occupation*: 51 percent of the black sample were unskilled;

69 percent of these were participants in politics;[22] 34 percent of the white sample were unskilled; 79 percent of these were participants in politics.

2. In terms of *income*: 16 percent of the black sample annually earned $3000 or less; 56 percent of these engaged in some degree of political activity; 8 percent of the white sample annually earned $3000 or less; 80 percent of these engaged in some degree of political activity.

3. In terms of *organizational membership*: 43 percent of the black sample belonged to no organization; 66 percent of these were participants in politics at some level; 31 percent of the whites belonged to no organization; of these, 79 percent were participants in politics at some level.

4. In terms of *education*: 26 percent of the blacks had eighth-grade education or less; 67 percent of these were participants; 21 percent of the whites had eighth-grade education or less; 83 percent of these were participants.

5. The percentages of the entire black and white samples that scored at least 1 on the composite or summary index were 78 percent and 88 percent, respectively.

One may summarize by saying that the probability of activating people of lower class is less than that of activating people of higher class. And since the inactives are disproportionately of lower-class status (they are inactive to some extent *by virtue* of their status), fresh efforts to mobilize them will likely meet with limited success. *It is evident, however, that those elites interested in mobilizing lower-class whites have been somewhat more successful than those elites interested in activating lower-class blacks for similar enterprises.* This suggests two possible lines of analysis, with differing implications for our evaluation of the nature of the potential resource that the inactives represent.

One possibility involves the assumption that the black and the white lower classes are equally apathetic or politically unaware. The explanation for their differential rate of mobilization lies in the differences in the skills and resources of their respective elites, insofar as those elites have sought to activate members of their own racial communities. That is, certain elites have been more successful in penetrating white lower-class apathy because those elites have been able to bring more experience and greater resources to bear in their effort. There is some evidence on comparative elite resources in Milwaukee to support this view.

The case of David Walther, a political novice, illustrates the point. But academic observers of Milwaukee politics also point out that the appearance of black elites on the political scene of that city is relatively recent. When this survey was conducted, blacks had had only a scant decade in which to gain leadership skills and positions, and their location in the structure of power was marginal compared to that of whites, who dominated the political and governmental machinery in disproportionate numbers. Even within the black com-

---

[22] A "participant" here is one who has scored at least 1 on the composite participation index.

munity, scarce resources were employed as much in internecine competition for leadership as they were for mass mobilization.[23]

This sort of perspective suggests that if elites who depend on a white power base have been able to mobilize the white lower classes, so too is it likely that black elites will be able to mobilize the black lower classes in time. From this point of view, the inactive black lower classes represent an untapped resource, the equivalent of which in the white community is much smaller, *having already been exploited to some degree.* Blacks may hope eventually to gain more activists, relative to the number whites may gain. The lesson blacks draw here is that the mobilization of some segment of the inactive lower classes simply awaits the development of black leadership and the consolidation of elite resources.

But this conclusion does not exhaust the possible evaluations of the nature of the potential resource that the respective inactive groups offer racial elites. Apathy may not be the only barrier to mobilization. If it is not, then acquisition by elites of the skills required to breach mass apathy probably will not achieve mobilization of the inactives. An alternative or additional explanation for the nonparticipation of the inactives is that they reject certain basic assumptions upon which conventional politics is based—a reflection of a general alienation, born of deprivation. Their inactivity may be a more or less considered stance, and, to the extent that this is so, efforts to mobilize them will be less likely to succeed.

To test this possibility, we may establish the receptivity of the black and white inactives, respectively, to some of the norms that lie behind conventional politics. If black and white inactives and actives are equally receptive, then the apathy–elite skills argument is valid. However, to the extent that the inactives of either race are not receptive, we must conclude that elite efforts to mobilize the unreceptive nonparticipants for conventional activity would be less fruitful.

The index of political integration offers an appropriate measure of receptivity to certain norms underlying conventional politics. Running the integration index (Table 3.10) against the composite participation index (Table 5.1), we found that the correlation (r) for blacks was .21, that for whites .03. Receptivity, then, did not vary according to activity within the white sample. White inactives were just as receptive to conventional mobilization as were white actives. Within the black sample, however, inactives were somewhat less likely than actives to embrace the integrative norms. The white inactives, therefore, offer elites a resource of greater potential. The black inactive group, although larger proportionally, would be more difficult to mobilize.

To summarize, inactive blacks were relatively hostile to integrative norms and presumably would not be especially receptive to efforts to mobilize them for conventional politics. Inactive whites would be more receptive to such efforts. Thus, while the black inactive group was somewhat larger than its counterpart

[23] Henry J. Schmandt, John C. Goldbach, and Charles Vogel, *Milwaukee: A Contemporary Profile* (New York: Praeger, 1971), pp. 111-112.

group among whites, it may be far more difficult for elites to mobilize black inactives for conventional activities. It would appear that the boundaries of the active black population are stretched close to their limits. For elites interested in mobilizing whites, however, the inactives still offer some potential constituents, a situation that holds out the possibility of strengthening an already strong position vis-à-vis blacks, should interracial conflict in conventional politics occur.[24]

National and Local Orientation

The summary participation indices employed above are based on related types of political activity; they make no distinction among political acts according to whether they are directed toward national or local ends. Because our intention is to focus on local participation, two further indices were developed: an index of local participation and an index of national participation. The indices were derived from the same basic set of questions that make up the summary indices. Some questions can tap activities that took place at several times and in different political settings. For example, some people worked both in presidential and in aldermanic election campaigns. When a respondent reported that he had engaged in the same type of activity in the two different settings, he was awarded one point for local involvement and one point for national (regardless of the number of campaigns he had worked in at either level).

Comparing the races on these orientation indices reveals no inconsistencies with previous findings (Table 5.4). On both indices, whites were more likely than blacks to score high. Whites were more active, in other words, in both local and national politics. Greater numbers of both races were active to some degree in national politics than in local politics. In all cases, however, the disparities in participation between the races were relatively low.

The socioeconomic correlates of active local and national participation differ slightly for the two races (Table 5.5). For whites, the standard status indicators of occupation, income, and education are related to national participation, but home ownership is not. However, home ownership is the best predictor among the independent variables of a high score on the local participation index, while the other status measures are generally much less important for this index than they are as correlates of national participation. Among whites, then, property ownership, rather than strictly class indicators, is the most important common denominator among local political activists. The ethic of home ownership apparently transcends class and impels people into local politics.

---

[24] It is possible that factors that we cannot anticipate or control for, such as the emergence of an attractive black mayoral candidate, would succeed in fully activating black inactives. As a general rule, however, it appears that the white inactives offer more potential for mobilization.

**TABLE 5.4 DISTRIBUTION OF RESPONDENTS' SCORES ON
NATIONAL AND LOCAL INDICES OF POLITICAL PARTICIPATION,
BY RACE**

Score	Black respondents		White respondents	
	%	N	%	N
National participation index (range 0–5)[a]				
0	27	66	14	47
1	24	59	25	84
2	26	63	33	109
3	20	50	19	62
4	3	8	8	25
5	0	0	1	4
Total	*100*	*246*	*100*	*331*
Local participation index (range 0–4)[b]				
0	36	89	29	95
1	37	92	29	95
2	21	51	33	109
3	5	13	8	27
4	*	1	2	5
Total	*99*	*246*	*101*	*331*

[a]Differences are significant at .001 level (χ^2 = 21.86).
[b]Differences are significant at .003 level (χ^2 = 16.68).
*Indicates less than 1 percent.

For blacks, home ownership is an equally strong predictor of black local
participation, but income is even more strongly related.[25] Other status indicators are also more significantly associated with local participation for blacks than
they are for whites. These figures suggest that the races contribute slightly
different types of activists to the ranks at the local level. White local activists
were predominantly homeowners but not drawn especially from any particular
class; black local activists were also homeowners, but were disproportionately
drawn from the wealthier classes. While both sets of local activists are unrepresentative in some sense of the racial populations from which they were drawn,
and unrepresentative in slightly different ways, there is no good reason to argue
that these differences are potential sources of interracial political conflict.

Racial Cohesion in Electoral Politics: Voting Patterns in Milwaukee

The cohesion of a group and its chances of influencing outcomes in politics
tend to vary in the same direction. The most elementary form of group cohe-

[25] Among blacks, home ownership and income were more strongly related (r = .31) than
they were among whites (r = .16). This may reflect the fact that whites have generally found
it easier to obtain mortgages than blacks, regardless of their incomes, and that the range of
housing options on the market is more varied for whites.

TABLE 5.5 CORRELATIONS (GAMMA) BETWEEN STATUS
VARIABLES AND NATIONAL AND LOCAL POLITICAL PARTICIPATION,
BY RACE

Status variable	Black respondents		White respondents	
	National participation	Local participation	National participation	Local participation
Occupation	.28	.23	.31	.17
Income	.31	.47	.25	.25
Education	.19	.25	.39	.13
Home ownership	.47	.38	.09	.38

sion—and the most simple to measure—shows up in the voting decisions of a
group's members. Black cohesion in national elections is well established; loyalty
to the Democratic party is now virtually unanimous. Milwaukee blacks in the
sample gave 99 percent of their votes to Hubert Humphrey in 1968—a figure
that exceeded only slightly the 92 percent that blacks gave the Democrats nationwide.[26] Whites in the sample split their votes in nearly equal proportions
between Nixon (44 percent) and Humphrey (47 percent), while nearly 7 percent
voted for George Wallace.

In local elections in Milwaukee during the 1960s, however, it appears that the
pattern of black cohesion and white division was reversed to some degree. Reliable data on the precise racial breakdown of the vote are unavailable; thus it was
necessary to use indicators based on the division of the vote in wards designated
by informed observers as being predominantly black and predominantly white.

In 1960, Henry Maier won his first term, defeating Henry Reuss, the congressman from Wisconsin's Fifth District. Maier took 58 percent of the vote. Two of
the three wards in which Maier polled fewest votes were wards with heavy black
concentrations. One of these was the old Second Ward, represented by Vel
Phillips, the sole black on the Common Council. The other later became part of
her ward, after boundaries were redrawn in 1963. The 1960 contest revolved
largely around how to proceed with urban renewal and industrial development in
the city, with prime emphasis by both candidates on the revitalization of the
downtown business area. Racial issues did not emerge in the campaign.

In 1964, Maier won against Arthur Else, a professor of economics at the
University of Wisconsin–Milwaukee whom Maier had appointed to be his administrative secretary in 1960. Maier again amassed 58 percent of the vote. Although
Else had publicly suggested that a city open-housing ordinance might not be
legal (he thought the problem might be solved through voluntary action), he
managed to win Vel Phillips's ward, the only one that Maier lost. Else had done
nothing to court the black vote. Again racial issues were peripheral to the contest, which was fought, as in 1960, over the progress of urban renewal.

[26] Axelrod, "Where the Votes Come from," p. 14.

By 1968, things had changed in the city. The confrontation of the races had assumed large proportions, giving rise to the first outspoken champion of black rights and power in a Milwaukee mayoral campaign, in the person of David Walther. While Maier won every one of the nineteen wards in his landslide victory, his poorest showings were in the the Inner Core wards. Walther came within fifty-five votes of winning the black Sixth Ward. The First Ward, which sent Orville Pitts to become the second black on the Common Council, gave Maier 62 percent of its vote, a fact that becomes remarkable only when compared to the 86 percent Maier won across the city. The Seventh Ward, still heavily white but clearly in racial transition, gave Maier 73 percent. These were the narrowest margins of victory for Maier in all of the nineteen wards.

The data are not very illuminating on the question of why Maier won the black vote in 1968, despite his established unpopularity among much of the black population. More important for our purposes, however, is that the patterns of voting by the two races across the decade do show different levels of cohesion. While both races generally supported Maier heavily, whites did so much more than blacks. An analysis of the voting returns shows blacks to have been ambivalent partners in the Maier coalition *compared to whites*. To that extent, blacks must have been viewed by Maier as less dependable allies than the white ethnics and working people upon whom he was able to rely fully.

Individual Contacts with Public Officials

One aspect of conventional political participation, citizen contacts with public officials, does not fit neatly into the matrix of campaign and electoral activities. It is worthy of separate examination here not simply because it differs somewhat in character from other conventional political acts but also because it aids us in assessing the relative visibility of groups in the society.[27]

Personally initiated contact with public officials is one of the primary means by which individual citizens make known to government their policy preferences or grievances. Citizen contact with people in government is an important dimension of the structure of political representation; contact is in effect a demand for representation, in the sense that the contacter seeks official action in response to his concerns.[28] The Milwaukee data show that there exist systematic differences between the races in the use of this opportunity for representation and the purposes to which it is put.

[27] This section is based in part on Peter K. Eisinger, "The Pattern of Citizen Contacts with Urban Officials," in *People and Politics in Urban Society*, ed. Harlan Hahn (Beverly Hills, Cal.: Sage, 1972), pp. 43-69.

[28] Hanna Pitkin defines representation as "acting in the interest of the represented, in a manner responsive to them." *The Concept of Representation* (Berkeley, Cal.: University of California Press, 1967), p. 209.

Citizen contact refers to those communications to public officials initiated by individual citizens acting in their capacity as private citizens and not as group spokesmen. These communications may take a variety of forms, as we shall see. To determine the extent and purposes of contact, respondents were asked if, "within the last couple of years," they had personally written a letter, sent a telegram, or spoken to any of a number of different types of public officials on a list that was handed to them. The range of these officials included the president of the United States, the mayor of Milwaukee, and "any person at all who works for the city of Milwaukee." If any contact had been made, interviewers determined the exact identity of the target and the purpose of the communication. Although we are primarily interested in those contacts that were made with urban officials, these patterns of contact are best understood in relation to the whole body of contacts directed toward public officials at all levels of government.

When Almond and Verba published their massive study of political attitudes in five nations a decade ago, Americans appeared supremely confident when it came to assessing their individual capacities for influencing political affairs. Most people in the American sample reported not only that they would, as individuals, seek to bring influence to bear on public officials if circumstances warranted it but also that they thought they stood a high chance of being successful.[29] But Milwaukeeans in 1970 were not so confident. Whereas Almond and Verba found that 65 percent of their nationwide sample thought they could successfully influence local government, only 20 percent of Milwaukee's blacks and 37 percent of its whites agreed with the following statement: "If a group of people have a problem here in Milwaukee, it's pretty easy to get somebody in the city government to listen to them." Only 46 percent of the blacks, but 72 percent of the whites, said they would feel free to talk to someone in the government about getting something done for their neighborhood.

These sentiments were reflected in behavior. Among the white sample, 109 respondents (33 percent) had made a total of 261 contacts, or 2.4 contacts per contacter. Only 11 percent of the black sample (N = 28) had made contacts, and their total number of such communications came to 33, or slightly better than one contact per black contacter.[30]

As with any form of conventional political self-assertion, the data reveal that contacting public officials is associated with socioeconomic status. For both races, the relationship is strongest between contact and education. For blacks, the gamma coefficient is .65; for whites, .40. In short, the opinions, complaints,

[29] Almond and Verba, *Civic Culture*, p. 188.

[30] Verba and Nie provide remarkably close confirmation for the racial breakdown and frequencies in these data. Using similarly worded questions, they found that 33 percent of the whites in their nationwide sample, polled in 1967, reported having initiated contact with public officials or other members of the civic elite. Only 14 percent of the black sample reported having done so. *Participation in America*, p. 166.

TABLE 5.6 TYPES OF INDIVIDUAL POLITICAL CONTACTS
MADE BY RESPONDENTS, BY RACE

	Contacts made by black respondents				Contacts made by white respondents			
	All levels of government[a]		City government only[b]		All levels of government[a]		City government only[b]	
Type of contact	%	N	%	N	%	N	%	N
Request	85	28	93	14	42	110	66	62
Expression of opinion	15	5	7	1	52	137	28	26
Uncodable	0	0	0	0	5	14	6	6
Total	*100*	*33*	*100*	*15*	*99*	*261*	*100*	*94*

[a]Differences are significant at .001 level ($\chi^2 = 21.61$).

[b]Differences are significant at .10 level ($\chi^2 = 4.65$).

and requests of the relatively well-off were communicated disproportionately to public officials through the process of individually initiated contacts. Most striking of all, the contacters were overwhelmingly white.[31]

The races also tended to use the avenue of contact for slightly different purposes. While the number of black contacters and contacts was small, several consistent patterns nevertheless seem clear. Contacts were classified into one of two broad categories: expressions of opinion or requests. Expressions of opinion include messages to public officials urging a particular course of action and comments communicating support or opposition to action already taken. Urging the president to end the Asian war or opposing his continuation of bombing are examples. Requests include complaints about perceived injustice or failures that government may rectify and demands for services or help to which individuals believe they are entitled. An example of the former is the complaint that one has been mistreated by the police. A request for help or service does not involve the sense that one has suffered injustice: Requests for information concerning zoning laws or the suggestion that a traffic light be placed at a busy intersection are common examples. One other type of request is the communication to a public official asking him to "do something" about a particular problem. This is an extremely ambiguous type of contact; it is not only difficult to know precisely what the contacter wants but also what sort of response would satisfy him.

As Table 5.6 shows, black contacts were almost exclusively requests, especially in regard to city government. Whites, however, divided their contacts more evenly between expressions of opinion and requests. As a result, much of the public opinion to which government officials were exposed was almost totally void of communications generated by individual blacks.

The significance of these messages should not be underestimated. Despite the

[31] Verba and Nie write that "the disparity between the races in frequency of contacting is perhaps the sharpest racial distinction we have found in our data." Ibid., p. 164.

TABLE 5.7   TARGETS OF INDIVIDUAL POLITICAL CONTACTS
MADE BY RESPONDENTS, BY RACE

	Contacts made by black respondents		Contacts made by white respondents	
Target	%	N	%	N
Mayor	13	2	7	7
Alderman	73	11	56	52
City bureaucrats	13	2	37	34
Don't know	0	0	1	1
Total	*99*	*15*	*101*	*94*

Note: Differences are significant at .20 level (χ^2 = 3.28).

admittedly unrepresentative quality of such contacts, public officials (congress-men, for example) seem to rely heavily on them. Raymond Bauer, Ithiel de Sola Pool, and Lewis A. Dexter write: "To our surprise, we found many congressmen looking to mail and personal contacts as sources of information on vital is-sues. . . . Visitors and telephone callers . . . are listened to as indicators of feeling back home."[32]

To the extent that public officials make or modify their decisions on the basis of their understanding of public opinion, it would appear that they do so with-out input by individual blacks. This does not mean that black interests, especial-ly on matters particularly important on racial grounds, are not put before public officials. There are, of course, a variety of predominantly black interest groups and organizations. But black individuals apparently fail to supplement or rein-force organizational initiatives by means of personal contacts. And, insofar as public officials separate those opinion messages generated by organizations and those that originate with individuals, blacks do not appear to compete with whites in the latter category.

The contacters within each race also differed in the targets among govern-ment officials whom they chose to contact. While most people tended to contact elected officials, over one-third of the white contacts were directed at bureau-crats and administrators of public agencies. Apparently, blacks virtually ignore the bureaucracies when they send complaints or demands for assistance (see Table 5.7).

Those patterns of individual contacts that have to do with the frequency and

[32] Raymond Bauer, Ithiel de Sola Pool, and Lewis A. Dexter, *American Business and Public Policy* (New York: Atherton, 1963), pp. 434, 436. R. Friedman, B. Klein, and J. H. Romani found that high-level federal bureaucrats look to letters of complaint and clients' grievances for information about public attitudes. "Administrative Agencies and the Publics They Serve," *Public Administration Review* 26 (September 1966): 196. David Olson dis-covered that citizen grievance letters received by the governor of Wisconsin were treated as an indication of agency performance and used by the state chief executive as leverage in his dealings with the agency in question. "Citizen Grievance Letters as a Gubernatorial Control Device in Wisconsin," *Journal of Politics* 31 (August 1969): 741-755.

rate of communications, their general purpose, and their targets make it clear that whites, acting in their individual capacities, dominate the communication channels from the unorganized public to government officials. By doing so, they not only enhance the public visibility of their interests but also do much to determine the general structure of public opinion. Once again, this is not to say that black interests or the concerns expressed by black citizens are not represented in local government. But black individuals play little role in the haphazard process by which the public helps to form the official's view of citizen opinion, while white individuals play a comparatively larger role. Blacks, then, have failed to exploit this means of gaining attention, and the result has been to leave the field almost exclusively to whites.

Racial patterns of contact also suggest or hint at an implicit difference in preferred styles of political assertion. While whites are generally confident *as individuals* that their voice is important to public decisionmakers, blacks are not. Yet, we know that issues of importance to blacks *as a group* are often the subject of communications to public officials generated by black-oriented interest groups.[33] Thus, blacks as a social category are not entirely invisible. But, given the absence of individual black contacts, the implication is that blacks are most confident in pressing their claims in organized groups. To the extent that this marks a stylistic preference, it may very well be a preference born of a realistic estimate of the situation. Group strength may be the only way to provide the force and impetus necessary for the demands to be taken seriously. Whites, by contrast, are relatively sure that they will be taken seriously as individuals.

Conclusions

Interracial comparisons of rates of participation in conventional political activities suggest that, in a city like Milwaukee, whites are not likely to seek out blacks in any vigorous way when nonpartisan local electoral coalitions are being constructed; blacks are not desirable political partners. The data also indicate that interracial conflicts fought by the use of conventional strategies are likely to be won quickly and overwhelmingly by whites. Group strength in political conflict is a function, in part, of visibility, cohesion, and the receptivity of potential followers to mobilization efforts. Where a minority group possesses high visibility and cohesion and is able to count upon mobilizing both its normally active and its inactive constituencies, then any conflict between that group and the

---

[33] Schmandt, Goldbach, and Vogel, *Milwaukee*, pp. 151-155. This is not to say that whites *prefer* individual contacts to group-generated contacts. Many issues of importance primarily to whites (though not specifically racial issues), such as business and commercial concerns, are the subjects of organized group communication.

majority is likely to be bitter and protracted, despite the minority status of one of the parties to the conflict. Intensity and stability can do much to make up for lack of size. But blacks as a group do not exhibit either of these characteristics, while whites do. Thus, whites in Milwaukee occupy an overpowering position in relation to blacks, not simply because of their majority status but also because the black minority is poorly organized for conventional political efforts.

Much of this poor showing in conventional politics undoubtedly stems from the sense of futility that a minority group must often feel in its dealings with the majority, but this frustration is obviously a point on a vicious circle. Lack of cohesion and poor mobilization lead to failure, failure leads to frustration, and frustration leads to withdrawal. In general, we may conclude that the white masses in Milwaukee heavily embrace the conventional style. While overall levels of black participation are only slightly lower than those of whites, they are lower especially in areas where their potential for influence is greatest, namely in voting, campaigning, and contacting officials. The impact on the political system of the area in which blacks score best—verbal participation—is not at all clear. In any event, its impact cannot be as high as that of the more formal activities.

Black elites interested in developing influence through conventional channels face a discouraging scene. Given the rates of participation and the structure of mass attitudes, neither the present nor the immediate future holds much promise of reward. Leaders may expect to do well in electoral politics only at the ward level and in wards where blacks constitute the majority. On a citywide basis they have little to offer white candidates and hence little claim to inclusion in the coalitions that form to contest mayoral elections and elections to other city posts.[34] It is undoubtedly for these reasons that the Milwaukee black community has been sympathetic, both in action and in attitude, to protest modes of participation, which appear to offer more immediate results as well as the satisfactions of the drama of open conflict. For those interested in the political mobilization of the black community, the opportunities offered by protest appear comparatively richer, as we shall see in the next chapter.

[34] Flaming et al. found that of sixty-six at-large elected officials in the city in 1968, only one was black. "Black Powerlessness in Policy-Making Positions," p. 130.

Protest in Milwaukee

6

During the past decade, an extraordinarily wide variety of Americans have chosen at one time or another to take politics into the streets. The diversity of those who have employed protest tactics is striking: Urban and rural blacks, college and high school students, farmers, veterans, white homeowners, the parents of schoolchildren, the peace constituency, construction workers, religious groups, ethnic minorities, and conservative organizations have all recently engaged in widely publicized protests of one form or another.[1] Milwaukee was profoundly affected by these developments in street-level politics during the 1960s, and its citizens appear to have taken part in protest activities more vigorously than the people of most other cities across the nation.

Scholarship on protest has given rise to the view that protest is essentially extraordinary in character,[2] and that those who use it must do so because they

This chapter originally appeared, in slightly different form, as "Racial Differences in Protest Participation," by Peter K. Eisinger, in *American Political Science Review*, Vol. 68(June 1974), pp. 592-606, and is reprinted by permission of the publisher, the American Political Science Association.

[1] Jerome Skolnick, *The Politics of Protest* (New York: Ballantine, 1969), p. 22.

[2] Lester Milbrath has written, for example, that protest demonstrations are "by definition, extraordinary rather than normal." *Political Participation* (Chicago: Rand McNally, 1965), p. 27. And Michael Lewis argues that one of the common defining threads that characterize various sorts of demonstrative political manifestations is their proclivity to go "beyond the constraints of the institutionalized political process." "The Negro Protest in Urban America (1968)," in *Protest, Reform, and Revolt*, ed. Joseph Gusfield (New York: John Wiley, 1970), p. 151.

lack the resources to employ more conventional means of bringing demands to bear on the political system. In this chapter, I shall challenge this view and begin to restate some of the generalizations built upon it. I contend that, if we examine the attitudes toward protest, the social characteristics of protesters, and the uses and organization of protest among blacks and whites separately, we find racial variations important enough to suggest substantial modifications in the standard interpretation of the role and nature of this form of political expression. Protest among blacks was found in the present research to be carried out primarily by adult members of the middle and working classes and to represent an integral and normal feature of the black adaptation to urban politics. Protest among whites, in contrast, is an extraordinary form of participation at all levels of politics for a small, predominantly upper-middle-class segment of the white community. One of the chief ironies of this more complex view of the role of protest in domestic politics, as we shall see, is that the routine nature of protest and its institutionalization in the black community, a strength in the short run, is eventually bound to strip the technique of much of its force as a means for blacks to make political demands. In pursuing this analysis, we will find that the data challenge and clarify some common assumptions about the relationship of participation in protest to the possession of social resources.

Attitudes toward Protest as a Political Tactic

Protest may be defined as a form of collective political expression, disruptive in nature, designed to provide its users both with access to decisionmakers and with bargaining leverage in negotiations with them.[3] While protest relies for its dynamics on a balance of threat and moral appeal,[4] it falls short of and may be distinguished from outright political violence.[5]

Protest as a Function of Race

Most surveys that have sought to tap attitudes toward protest have revealed predominantly hostile sentiments, as we saw in the previous chapter, leading to the view that protest is a form of political nonconformity. As an instrument for assessing society's attitudes toward protest, such surveys are suggestive, but they have two major shortcomings. One is that investigators generally have failed to

[3] James Q. Wilson was one of the first to characterize protest as a bargaining process in these terms. "The Strategy of Protest: Problems of Negro Civic Action," *Journal of Conflict Resolution* 3 (September 1961): 291.

[4] See the discussion of this point in Ralph Turner, "The Public Perception of Protest," *American Sociological Review* 34 (December 1969): 820.

[5] Peter K. Eisinger, "The Conditions of Protest Behavior in American Cities," *American Political Science Review* 67 (March 1973): 13-14; see also H. L. Nieburg, "The Threat of Violence and Social Change," *American Political Science Review* 56 (December 1962): 872.

introduce controls for race into their reports or their study design. Either marginal totals are presented for racially undifferentiated samples or the surveys themselves have been conducted only among whites. A second shortcoming involves the phrasing of questions; respondents are asked about their feelings toward *antiwar* picketing, *civil rights* demonstrations, *student* protest, and the *black* protest movement. The resulting negative attitudes may simultaneously reflect hostility toward any or all of the following: a particular *mode* of political expression (protest), presumed positions on certain broad substantive *issues* (civil rights, the war in Southeast Asia), certain distinct protesting *groups* in society (blacks, students).

The advantage of the Milwaukee survey is that it asked both blacks and whites questions about protest itself, without reference to the issues that might give rise to protest or the groups that use it—although, to be sure, we still cannot be absolutely certain that respondents did not supply their own substantive associations with protest in answering the questions. Sharp racial differences emerged in the assessment of protest as a tactic. Favorable attitudes toward protest were widespread in the black community, and these feelings transcended the boundary dividing those who actually had taken part in protest from those who had not.[6] Black protesters evidently participate in demonstrative politics in the aura of subcommunity approval and confidence. While the attitudes of the black subcommunity reinforce, perhaps even stimulate, individual decisions to engage in protest, those of the white community are largely antipathetic to such participation.

A majority of the blacks in the sample were convinced that the motivations behind protest participation were largely instrumental in nature. When respondents were asked in the survey why they supposed that "people protest and demonstrate so much these days," 56 percent of the blacks explained that protest was essentially a device to gain certain ends—to gain the attention of or access to decisionmakers or to win demands (Table 6.1). Only 8 percent attributed protest participation to such negative motives as imitation ("It's the thing to do") or meaningless troublemaking. By contrast, 38 percent of the white

---

[6] This finding seems consistent with the observations concerning widespread black support, or at least sympathy, for black rioters. Matthew Holden has written in this regard: "In addition to people accustomed to violating the law or being in trouble with the police—whose participation in riots could be easily predicted—there was a substantial reservoir of more respectable Black people who were at least *sentimentally* friendly to violence. [White observers] did not perceive how many Black people—hard-working, tax-paying, and responsible—would permit themselves to 'get caught up in the situation,' let alone how many more would say 'I wouldn't do it myself, but I can understand those who do.'" *Politics of the Black "Nation"* (New York: Chandler, 1973), p. 77.

Empirical evidence to this effect surfaced first in the Watts riot studies: David O. Sears and T. M. Tomlinson found in their study of attitudes after that riot that the major opinion cleavage in interpreting the disturbances was between the races, not between black rioters and black nonrioters. "Riot Ideology in Los Angeles: A Study of Negro Attitudes," *Social Science Quarterly* 49 (December 1968): 485–503.

TABLE 6.1   TYPES OF REASONS GIVEN BY RESPONDENTS, BY
RACE, FOR PROTEST AND DEMONSTRATION BY OTHERS

	Black respondents		White respondents	
Type of reasons	%	N	%	N
Instrumental reasons: (to gain attention; to win demands)	56	138	36	119
Expressive reasons: (because they are angry; to express outrage)	20	49	15	48
Negative reasons: (imitation; troublemaking)	8	20	37	123
Other	1	2	1	2
Don't know	15	37	12	39
Total	*100*	*246*	*101*	*331*

Note: Differences are significant at .001 level (χ^2 = 63.503).

sample interpreted protest negatively, as troublemaking or imitation, while only 36 percent saw it as an instrumental tactic. To explain protest participation in terms of instrumental motivation is not necessarily to approve it, of course, but it is to concede that some people find it genuinely useful for serious purposes. Apparently, most blacks do not question the integrity of the motives of protest participants, but a substantial number of whites do so.

Not only did most blacks consider protest a useful political tool but a significant proportion of them wanted to see it used more often (Table 6.2). Forty-three percent of the black sample, compared to only 7 percent of the white respondents, replied that they would like to see more demonstrations, rather than fewer or none. As might be expected, black protesters contributed disproportionately to the black group that wanted to see more demonstrations, *but the percentage of black nonprotesters[7] who said they would like to see more demonstrations was larger than that of white protesters who held the same view.* That is, support for protest was even greater in that segment of the black community that had never taken part in protest than it was among whites who had taken part in protest.

Among protesters themselves, blacks were much more confident than whites about the impact of their particular efforts. The protest participants were asked whether each of the protests in which they had taken part had helped "to get what you wanted." In 53 percent of the instances of participation, black protesters answered in the affirmative, compared to 38 percent among whites.

[7]As I explain in greater detail later on, protesters are those who answered affirmatively when asked in the interview whether they had ever taken part in a sit-in, demonstration, mass march, or other type of protest action. The category "protester" does not include those who merely engaged in union picketing during a strike.

Black protesters receive other supportive cues from the black community, but whites engage in protest in the face of strong community opposition. For example, as Table 6.3 shows, a high number of blacks believed that, in Milwaukee, demonstrating was *better* than voting as an instrumental device. (Forty-one of the fifty-nine blacks who agreed with this proposition were *nonprotesters*.) The overwhelming proportion of the white sample expressed an unambivalently negative opinion concerning the primacy of protest. Even the white protesters themselves disagreed that demonstrations were "better" than voting.[8]

Blacks also regarded protest in general as an *effective* device to gain the attention of government; protesters and nonprotesters scarcely differed on this score. Comparatively more whites, however, doubted the efficacy of protest.

Finally, regarding protest, blacks appeared to subscribe to an attitude similar to the notion of citizen or civic duty that scholars have developed in relation to voting. We might call this attitude "protest duty." A sizable majority of whites were either ambivalent about, or opposed to, the necessity of protest participation, but most blacks believed it important to take part.

In summary, the attitudes of the black subcommunity, in contradistinction to those of the larger white community, supported protest participation and fostered expectations of its effectiveness. Favorable attitudes toward protest were not held by a splinter minority but seemed widespread among blacks, both those who had taken part in demonstrative politics and those who had not. Previous surveys, then, have given an incomplete impression. While protest may constitute an act of political nonconformity in the society at large, it enjoys major and

TABLE 6.2 PERCENTAGE AND NUMBER OF RESPONDENTS WANTING TO SEE MORE, FEWER, OR NO DEMONSTRATIONS, CONTROLLING FOR RACE AND FOR PROTEST PARTICIPATION

Preference for frequency of demonstrations	Black respondents						White respondents					
	Protesters		Nonprotesters		Total		Protesters		Nonprotesters		Total	
	%	N	%	N	%	N	%	N	%	N	%	N
More	71	37	36	69	43	106	26	9	5	14	7	23
Fewer	13	7	20	38	18	45	40	14	53	157	52	171
None	4	2	24	46	20	48	6	2	27	80	25	82
Doesn't matter	10	1	21	40	18	45	11	4	14	40	13	44
Don't know; no answer	2	1	*	1	1	2	17	6	2	5	3	11
Total	*100*	*52*	*101*	*194*	*100*	*246*	*100*	*35*	*101*	*296*	*100*	*331*

Note: Differences between black protesters and white protesters are significant at .001 level (χ^2 = 19.044). Differences between black nonprotesters and white nonprotesters are significant at .001 level (χ^2 = 92.062).

*Indicates less than 1 percent.

[8]Twenty-two of the thirty-five white protesters disagreed with the statement; only three agreed.

TABLE 6.3 RESPONSES, BY RACE, TO STATEMENTS
INDICATING ATTITUDES TOWARD PROTEST

	Black respondents		White respondents	
Response	%	N	%	N

A. *"Demonstrations are better than voting in this city because demonstrations are about the only way to get your point across."*

Agree	24	59	4	14
Agree and disagree	22	54	11	38
Disagree	47	115	82	270
Don't know	7	18	3	9
Total	*100*	*246*	*100*	*331*

B. *"Demonstrations and mass marches are one good way to get the city government to listen to you."*

Agree	69	169	23	75
Agree and disagree	19	47	20	66
Disagree	9	23	54	179
Don't know	3	7	3	11
Total	*100*	*246*	*100*	*331*

C. *"It's sometimes important to take part in demonstrations because that's one way to make your voice heard."*

Agree	73	179	29	97
Agree and disagree	13	31	19	63
Disagree	10	24	47	153
Don't know	5	12	5	16
Total	*101*	*246*	*100*	*329*

Note: Part A—Differences are significant at .001 level (χ^2 = 79.201).
Part B—Differences are significant at .001 level (χ^2 = 157.320).
Part C—Differences are significant at .001 level (χ^2 = 120.381).

widespread support among blacks as an acceptable device for political self-expression.[9] Certainly, we may conclude that the two racial communities exhibit very different levels of sympathy for the protest style.

Protest as a Function of Social Status

In order to demonstrate the sharpness of the racial difference in regard to the protest style, this analysis will proceed with an investigation of the socioeconomic correlates of protest participation in the two racial communities. Efforts to generalize about the relationship between social status and protest participation have produced a host of ambiguities. Part of the problem may be

[9] Previous surveys conducted in Milwaukee reveal substantially the same patterns of racial difference in sympathy toward protest. The Slesinger postriot survey found that 62 percent of the black sample but only 46 percent of the white sample agreed that "demonstrations are a natural form of American politics." Jonathan Slesinger, "Study of Com-

attributed to inadequate data, but the more important source of confusion stems from inconsistent, vague, and occasionally inaccurate conceptualizations of the roots of protest.

Most empirical efforts to explore the social correlates of protest participation have been based on surveys of college students. Samples have invariably been racially homogeneous or so nearly uniform that interracial comparisons cannot be made with confidence. Drawing entirely on the educated young, these selective samples ensure that even the most tentative generalizations must be extremely limited in scope. The difficulties inherent in these studies are compounded by the contradictory conclusions that are beginning to emerge. Early studies of the southern civil rights movement and of campus protest indicated that protest participants among both black and white students were more likely to come from middle-class than from lower-class families, a finding that suggested that protest participation, like voting, is likely to be associated with the individual possession of social resources.[10] One of the most recent studies of campus political activists, however, concludes that protesters are in fact sociologically no different either from nonparticipants or from conventional activists.[11]

The Milwaukee data have the advantage of being drawn from the entire adult populations of both racial communities, which renders them somewhat more reliable as a basis for the construction of general propositions about racial differences in regard to the protest style than are data based on student samples.

munity Opinions concerning the Summer 1967 Civil Disturbance in Milwaukee" (Unpublished report, Office of Applied Social Research, School of Social Welfare and Institute of Human Relations, University of Wisconsin–Milwaukee, April 1, 1968), p. 32. The Bisbing survey, conducted in 1965, showed that 52 percent of the blacks but only 16 percent of the inner-city whites believed that "demonstrations are effective in aiding the civil rights movement," a finding possibly contaminated by the reference to civil rights in the question. Bisbing Business Research, *Attitude Study among Negro and White Residents in the Milwaukee Negro Residential Areas* (Milwaukee, 1965), p. 169. Evidence from Detroit reveals the same racial split. Joel Aberbach and Jack Walker found that 63 percent of their 1971 black sample approved of protest meetings and marches as a way of showing dissatisfaction or disagreement with government policies and actions. Only 28 percent of the white sample approved of such tactics. *Race in the City* (Boston: Little, Brown, 1973), p. 204. These surveys give us some confidence that the racial patterns found in Milwaukee in 1970 are not necessarily bound by time or place.

[10] On the social backgrounds of white student protesters, see David Westby and Richard Braungart, "Class and Politics in the Family Backgrounds of Student Political Activists," *American Sociological Review* 31 (October 1966): 690-692. Seymour Martin Lipset offers a thorough summary of the literature that arrives at these findings in "The Activists: A Profile," in *Confrontation*, ed. Daniel Bell and Irving Kristol (New York: Basic Books, 1969), pp. 45-57. On black student protest participation, see Donald R. Matthews and James W. Prothro, *Negroes and the New Southern Politics* (New York: Harcourt, Brace and World, 1966), p. 418; and John M. Orbell, "Protest Participation among Southern Negro College Students," *American Political Science Review* 61 (June 1967): 446-456.

[11] James W. Clarke and Joseph Egan, "Social and Political Dimensions of Protest Activity," *Journal of Politics* 34 (May 1972): 500-523.

The major ambiguities in the discussion of the relationship between protest participation and social status, however, are found not in the empirical works cited above, but rather in the more influential theoretical literature. In speaking of the sources of protest, several writers view the tactic as a technique of the "powerless" or the "relatively powerless."[12] Powerlessness is conceived in a generally narrow sense as a function of low social status, a condition characterized largely by the absence of middle-class resources. For James Q. Wilson, blacks are a prime example of a powerless group because they lack, among other things, the resources that come with class status.[13] Michael Lipsky characterizes "relatively powerless" groups as those lacking conventional political resources, namely the various currencies of political exchange that accompany high position in the social order.[14]

The problem here is that the Milwaukee data show that *individuals* of both races who participate in protest activity in fact possess the social attributes of middle-class status. As we shall see, these findings have somewhat different implications for the two racial communities. Since the general findings are apparently at odds with the blanket conceptualization of protest as a tactic primarily of those low in the possession of social status resources,[15] they suggest the need for some attempts at reconciliation and reformulation.

It is imperative, first of all, to consider the sort of powerlessness that gives rise to protest behavior on the part of individuals as a multidimensional phenomenon, one that may include other characteristics and conditions besides low social status. Second, it is necessary to make clear that, as long as we do conceive powerlessness in social status terms, among others, such powerlessness may refer to the relative position in society of the *group* or *collectivity* from which the protesters are drawn, without necessarily implying that the individuals who actually participate in protest are themselves low in status.

Let us turn now to the data. The extent of protest participation in Milwaukee was just high enough to enable us to discern patterns with some measure of

---

[12] Wilson uses the term "powerless." Wilson, "Strategy of Protest." Michael Lipsky speaks of the "relatively powerless" in "Protest as a Political Resource," *American Political Science Review* 62 (December 1968): 1144.

[13] Wilson, "Strategy of Protest," p. 292.

[14] Lipsky, "Protest as a Political Resource," p. 1144. Lipsky does not enumerate those resources but relies on Robert Dahl's list of resources in "The Analysis of Influence in Local Communities," in *Social Science and Community Action*, ed. Charles R. Adrian (East Lansing, Mich.: Institute for Community Development and Resources, 1960), p. 32.

[15] Wilson has written, for example, that "protest actions involving such tactics as mass meetings, picketing, boycotts, and strikes rarely find enthusiastic participants among upper-income and higher status individuals." "Strategy of Protest," p. 206. Amitai Etzioni has argued that it is the "underclasses," socioeconomically speaking, that have a special affinity for protest. *Demonstration Democracy* (New York: Gordon and Breach, 1970), p. 6. That blacks as a group, regardless of the objective social status of any given black individual, may comprise a racial "underclass" is a possibility I shall consider later.

confidence. Among blacks, 21 percent (N = 52) claimed to have taken part in at least one protest, while 11 percent of the whites (N = 35) said they had done so. Protest participation was determined by answers to a series of questions inquiring whether the respondent had ever taken part in a mass march, a demonstration, a sit-in, a protest rally or protest meeting, or any other form of protest or direct action. The variety of terms employed to refer to protest is of little importance for analytical purposes. Rather, it simply reflects the numerous conventional ways of characterizing protest in current usage.

Each respondent was asked how many times he or she had participated in each type of protest. Then he or she was asked a variety of questions concerning the details of only the three most recent of each type of incident.

Black respondents reported a total of 226 instances of participation, of which we have some details on 149. Whites reported 153 instances, of which they described 97. (It is important to note that, in the later discussion on patterns in the use of protest, the unit of analysis is often an instance of participation, not a separate protest incident. In a number of cases, instances of participation by different individuals occurred in the same protest incident.) While more blacks, proportionally, took part in protest, the rate of participation by individual protesters did not differ much by race; white protesters averaged 4.5 instances of participation, while blacks averaged 4.3.

In order to examine the relationship between protest participation and status, respondents were first divided, within each racial sample, into groups of those who had participated in protest and those who had not.[16] Protesters ranked

[16] Protest participation was initially treated both as a dichotomous dummy variable (protest–no protest) and as a continuous variable (frequency of protest participation, ranging from 0 to 10 or more). Fifty-six of the eighty-seven protesters had taken part in more than one protest. The relationships between protest participation, treated as a dummy variable, and socioeconomic and demographic indicators are, for the moment, the more important ones, since the object of the analysis is to distinguish those who take part in such activity from those who never do. The relationships are uniformly slightly stronger than when protest is treated as a continuous variable. Pearson's *r* coefficients are compared in Table A, where the protest variable is treated differently.

TABLE A   SOCIOECONOMIC STATUS AND PROTEST PARTICI-
PATION AS A DICHOTOMOUS AND A CONTINUOUS VARIABLE

Status variable	Black respondents		White respondents	
	Protest–no protest (dichotomous)	Frequency of protest (continuous)	Protest–no protest (dichotomous)	Frequency of protest (continuous)
Age	−.27	−.20	−.20	−.12
Income	.06	.08	.10	.01
Education	.37	.25	.43	.35
Number of organizational memberships	.24	.16	.19	.05

TABLE 6.4 SOCIOECONOMIC DIFFERENCES BETWEEN PROTESTERS
AND NONPROTESTERS, BY RACE

Socioeconomic indicator	Black respondents			White respondents		
	Protesters	Nonprotesters	Total	Protesters	Nonprotesters	Total
Mean annual income	$6790 (N = 48)	$6300 (N = 172)	$6400 (N = 220)	$8320 (N = 34)	$7310 (N = 270)	$7400 (N = 304)
Mean number of group memberships	1.90 (N = 52)	1.02 (N = 194)	1.21 (N = 246)	2.14 (N = 35)	1.28 (N = 296)	1.37 (N = 331)
Mean years of education	11.96 (N = 52)	9.89 (N = 193)	10.30 (N = 245)	14.57 (N = 35)	10.96 (N = 294)	11.04 (N = 329)

Note: Differences between protester and nonprotester means for both races are significant at .001 level, using a two-tailed difference of means test (*t*), except for difference in black income means (not significant) and white income means (significant at .10 level).

higher than nonprotesters in terms of income, education, and number of group memberships,[17] as we see in Table 6.4.

Protesters also fell disproportionately in the higher occupational categories. For both races, protest and high occupation are positively related. The gamma coefficient for blacks is .38, for whites, .31.[18] Eighteen percent of the black protesters were professionals or businessmen, compared to 7 percent of the nonprotesters. In the white sample, 37 percent of the protesters were professionals (none fell in the business category) compared to the 12 percent of the nonprotesters who fell in either the professional or the business classification. Among whites, skilled and semi-skilled workers were underrepresented among the protesters, but among blacks they were nearly perfectly represented. Of the black protesters, 29 percent fell into these categories, compared to 30 percent in the entire sample. Only 15 percent of the white protesters fell here, compared to 30 percent of the entire white sample.

By all standard indicators of socioeconomic status, protesters within each racial group were of higher status than nonprotesters. If these data reflect accurately more universal patterns of the correlates of protest behavior, then any implication that protest is primarily a tactic of poor *individuals* is clearly wrong.

While both black and white protesters stood above the average of status indicator scores for their respective racial samples, it appears that the black protesters *did not differ as much* from the black population as a whole as white

[17] Robert Alford and Harry Scoble offer a discussion of organizational membership as a political resource in "Sources of Local Political Involvement," *American Political Science Review* 62 (December 1968): 1203.

[18] Goodman and Kruskal's gamma is a nonparametric measure of association for ordinal grouped data. Occupational categories, based on the U.S. Census classification, are ordinally ranked.

protesters differed from the white population as a whole. In this sense, it seems possible to argue that black protesters occupy a slightly different social location in their racial community than white protesters do in theirs.

White protesters possessed all the trappings of the upper middle class. They tended predominantly to be professionals (the second largest occupational category for whites was housewives, however), and they were the only group with a mean education that fell into the post-high school years. They had nearly four more years of education, and they earned substantially more money, than white nonprotesters. By these characteristics alone, white protesters stand apart from the bulk of the white population. They are unrepresentative of the mass, a minority by virtue not only of their participation in protest but also of their status.

The black protesters are not strictly representative, socioeconomically, of the black mass population, for they too are better off, but they seem, more than their white counterparts, to resemble the norm of the community of which they are a part. That is to say, the gaps in education, income, and group memberships between black protesters and black nonprotesters are smaller than those between white protesters and white nonprotesters.

One must be cautious in dealing with this difference, for it is to some degree an artifact of statistical constraints. The *range* in the white income and education data is greater than the range in the black data.[19] Nevertheless, it would be ill-advised to dismiss the difference altogether. Consider the data on education. White protesters *averaged* two and one-half years of college; white nonprotesters did not quite average completion of high school. Both black protesters and black nonprotesters, however, averaged less than a completed high school education. The difference between high school and even some college education makes a profound difference in psychology, outlook, earning potential, and opportunity. Simply by entering college, an individual differentiates himself from his fellows in the community who do not go to college, in a way far more significant than the year or two added to his educational level would indicate. The number of years of education, in other words, does not always represent a perfect additive interval measure of all the things for which education stands, especially when the step upward from high school to college is considered. In short, the black protester with his high school education is more like the average black individual than the white protester with his college years is like the average white individual.

Two other minor points support the argument that black protesters are more typical than white protesters of their respective racial communities. One is that the income difference between black protesters and black nonprotesters is not

[19] The standard deviation for black income is 87, for white income 166. For black education, the standard deviation is .99; for white, 1.83. This simply indicates that the dispersion around the mean for blacks is lower, signifying a greater probability that black protesters' means will fall closer to the sample mean.

TABLE 6.5 CORRELATIONS (PEARSON'S *r*) BETWEEN FREQUENCY
OF PROTEST AND STATUS VARIABLES FOR PROTESTERS ONLY,
BY RACE

Status variable	Black protesters	White protesters
Income	-.14	.14
Education	-.12	.08
Number of group memberships	-.13	.23

statistically significant, as we saw in Table 6.4, while the difference in white incomes is significant at a moderate level. We may be relatively sure, then, that the white protesters differ on this dimension from the white nonprotesters, but we cannot make the same assertion with confidence about blacks.

Another point involves an examination of the correlation coefficients derived from running the frequency of protest *for protesters only* against the status indicators (protest was here treated as a continuous variable, but since we had eliminated nonprotesters from the calculations, the range of protest frequency now ran from one to ten or more). The results are shown in Table 6.5. It will be recalled that protest and.high status were related positively, to some degree, for both races, whether protest was treated as a dichotomous or a continuous variable. When nonprotesters are eliminated, however, we discover that for black protesters the frequency with which an individual took part in protest *decreases* slightly as status indicator scores increase. But, for whites, protest frequency and status vary together positively.

These coefficients are extremely small, but they suggest that, once an individual makes the decision to protest, his subsequent patterns of protest participation will differ, depending on his race. *The more that whites protest, the more likely it is that they are socioeconomically differentiated from the norm—that is, from the mean scores on the various status indicators. Black protest is most frequent, however, among those who stand just above the socioeconomic norm.* As blacks advance up the status hierarchy, becoming increasingly differentiated from the black socioeconomic average, they are less likely to protest with great frequency. Thus, if frequency of protest can be thought to indicate the degree of commitment to protest or seriousness of intent, then the most committed or serious black protesters are more likely than occasional black protesters to resemble socioeconomically their fellows in the community who do not protest. To this extent at least, protest attracts a more "normal" constituency among blacks than it does among whites.

Other data suggest that black protesters not only resemble the socioeconomic norm in the black community but also are drawn disproportionately from its more integrated, stable elements. Black protesters appear to be more likely than black nonprotesters to own or to be in the process of buying their homes.

TABLE 6.6 PERCENTAGE AND NUMBER OF RESPONDENTS
OWNING, BUYING, OR RENTING HOMES, CONTROLLING FOR
RACE AND FOR PROTEST PARTICIPATION

Residential status	Black respondents						White respondents					
	Protesters		Nonprotesters		Total		Protesters		Nonprotesters		Total	
	%	N	%	N	%	N	%	N	%	N	%	N
Own	12	6	8	16	9	22	20	7	32	96	31	103
Buying	35	18	24	46	26	64	17	6	17	49	17	55
Rent	52	27	68	131	64	158	57	20	49	144	50	164
Other	2	1	*	1	1	2	6	2	2	6	2	8
Total	101	52	100	194	100	246	100	35	100	295	100	330

*Indicates less than 1 percent.

Among whites, however, the pattern is reversed; protesters appear more likely
that nonprotesters to be renters (Table 6.6).

Black protesters and nonprotesters also tend to resemble one another in terms
of the average length of time they had lived in the city. The average for the
former is 13.6 years, for the latter, 15.0 years. White protesters had lived in the
city an average of 11.4 years compared to the white nonprotester average of
24.2 years.[20] While these figures are to some degree a function of age,[21] they
nevertheless add to the evidence that black protesters seem to be more centrally
located or integrated members of their racial community than white protesters
are of theirs.

The discovery that individual protest participation cannot be explained by
the lack of conventional resources on the part of the protesters themselves does
not necessarily require that we abandon the notion that protest is a political tool
of the powerless, *as long as we understand powerlessness as a function of other
factors besides low status.*

Powerlessness may, for example, be a function not so much of individual
poverty as of lack of group legitimacy. To lack legitimacy is to be distrusted,
ignored, or dismissed by those in power. Legitimacy implies that decisionmakers
will accede willingly to petitions for a hearing and will take seriously substantive
demands. Middle-class people have traditionally had legitimacy in American politics, but status is no guarantee of legitimacy. Race, age, and ideology are other,
often more important, factors that enter into a community's judgment about the
legitimacy of citizen political groups. When legitimacy is withheld, members of
penalized groups are not readily admitted to positions of power in political
parties or electoral organizations; they are not appointed to administrative posts;

[20] Black protesters had lived in their neighborhoods an average of 5.4 years, compared to
4.5 for black nonprotesters. For whites the figures were 6.5 and 11.3, respectively.

[21] Pearson's *r* coefficients for the relationship between length of residence and age were
.53 for blacks and .74 for whites.

their advice is not actively or routinely sought by decisionmakers. Since protest is a means of gaining access to councils of power by groups that have been denied legitimacy,[22] protest may be conceived as a strategy employed by those who are relatively powerless in terms of the legitimacy they command.

The resort to protest may also be a signal of impatience, regardless of whether or not a group has status *or* legitimacy. For the impatient, protest is a particularly useful interim tool between periods of electoral activity, designed to force consideration of certain controversial issues by an often unwieldly political system. But even in polities in which such issues are raised and discussed, action may be deemed slow or inadequate. Groups that do not control the governmental apparatus capable of hastening the consideration or the fulfilling of demands are likely to feel impatient and powerless. It goes without saying that blacks fall into this category. From this perspective, it is not difficult to understand why blacks have persisted in their use of protest despite the fact that the political system has at times finally been responsive. To be impatient about the *pace* of change and at the same time unable to affect that pace with a high degree of certainty is also to be powerless.

Finally, we may retain the original equation of powerlessness with the lack of conventional resources as a source of protest in one sense: Protest may occur *on behalf of those groups that are disadvantaged socioeconomically*. Protest in this particular context is a means by which certain better-off members of the community can *represent* their disadvantaged fellows or their disadvantaged group in the political arena and dramatize their or its concerns.

To summarize, we have seen that both black and white protesters possess more resources than those who do not take part in protest. In this respect the protesters of the two races resemble each other. But we have also seen that black protesters appear to resemble the average member of their racial community much more than white protesters do theirs. This discovery has led to the construction of a tentative argument about the different social location of protesters in their respective racial communities.

The Uses and Organization of Protest among Blacks and Whites

Up to this point we have examined data that indicate that in Milwaukee *(1)* black attitudes are broadly congenial to protest as a tactic while white attitudes are generally hostile; *(2)* black protesters, while socioeconomically somewhat

[22] A study of protest incidents in forty-three American cities indicates that protest is a more effective tool for gaining access to public officials than it is for gaining substantive demands. Protesters met with their target to present their demands in 58 percent of the 120 cases of protest, but they gained concessions in only 15 percent of the protests. Eisinger, "Conditions of Protest," p. 17.

better off than the norm in their community, are still more likely to resemble black nonprotesters than white protesters (also better off) are to resemble white nonprotesters; and *(3)* black protesters seem to exhibit more stable attachments to the community relative to nonprotesters than do white protesters. All of these findings suggest that the protest style is seen as a relatively normal form of political participation among blacks and that protest participants are integrated members of the black community. Protest among whites, however, is clearly an act of nonconformity in the broader white community, and white protesters represent a minority not only by virtue of their small numbers[23] but also by their marked deviance from the average measures of social status and community attachment. Further data, on the uses to which protest is put and the means by which it is organized, confirm and complement these findings.

First of all, protest in the black community is used almost exclusively in the local arena. Although blacks occasionally participate in protests aimed at institutions of the federal government or at nongovernmental targets, in Milwaukee their protest has been directed predominantly against municipal agencies. (Not only is most black protest aimed at city government, but, nationally, most protests against city government are carried out by blacks.)[24]

Whether or not this pattern reflects a greater interest among blacks in local government as opposed to government at other levels is difficult to say, but it does suggest a different level of focus. White protest participation was more evenly distributed among the various targets, as Table 6.7 indicates. White protesters also appear to be more physically mobile than black protesters. Forty percent of the instances of protest participation cited by whites involved leaving the city of Milwaukee; only 11 percent of those mentioned by blacks did.

In Table 6.7, instances of protest participation reported by respondents are divided according to the nature of the target and the particular area of concern that prompted the protest. State government is notably absent from the table, a reflection, undoubtedly, of its relatively low salience for the general public.[25]

Those who took part in protests against the federal government and its representatives were largely antiwar demonstrators, participants in a movement in which blacks, by all accounts, were not vigorously active.

A breakdown of the data on protest against local government targets shows that most Milwaukee blacks were moved to take part in protest through the campaign led by the Reverend James Groppi for a local open-housing ordinance. These marches took place almost daily over a period from August 1967 through March 1968. This ready availability of an outlet and focus for protest undoubtedly exaggerated or increased the concern for open housing in relation to

[23] It is appropriate to recall here that only 11 percent of the white sample had previously taken part in protest, while 21 percent of the black sample had done so.

[24] Eisinger, "Conditions of Protest," pp. 16–17.

[25] See, for example, M. Kent Jennings and Harmon Zeigler, "The Salience of American State Politics," *American Political Science Review* 64 (June 1970): 523–535.

TABLE 6.7 TARGETS OF PROTEST ACTIVITY ENGAGED IN BY RESPONDENTS, BY RACE

Target of protest and area of concern	Black respondents — Number of respondents who had participated	Totals %	Totals N	White respondents — Number of respondents who had participated	Totals %	Totals N
Federal government		3	4		24	23
Antiwar protest	2			15		
Demonstrations to escalate the war in Vietnam	0			7		
Presidential candidates	2			1		
Local government		68	101		20	19
Welfare	9			1		
Schools	12			5		
Police	8			0		
Jobs	8			3		
Housing	64			10		
Universities		*	1		10	10
Martin Luther King memorial marches		5	8		4	4
Private institutions		0			3	3
Protest seeking "civil rights" or "equality" (target unspecified)		17	10		32	31
Other		7	10		7	7
Total		100	149		100	97

*Indicates less than 1 percent.

other local issues. Nevertheless, even if the Groppi protesters are excluded, most blacks who took part in protest still directed their energies against local govern- mental institutions and agencies.

After housing, issues having to do with public education stimulated the most protest participation among blacks. This finding accords closely with data on aggregate patterns of protest incidents in American cities. A survey of protests against local government targets in forty-three large cities found that the public education system was the major target of protesters.[26]

A variety of issues have stimulated protest against the Milwaukee school system. The principal one has been the issue of de facto segregation, a problem first brought to public light in 1963 by Lloyd Barbee, an attorney who was at that time chairman of the Wisconsin Conference of the branches of the NAACP and who served as a state assemblyman for more than a decade. Barbee was instrumental in organizing a one-day school boycott by black children in May 1964 to dramatize segregation and to protest the reluctance of the school board to confront the issue. The boycott itself was a success: Between 11,000 and 15,000 of the city's 24,000 black students stayed out of school.

In the face of the school board's continued refusal to deal with de facto segregation, Barbee prepared to go to court. The coalition he had helped to form between the NAACP and the local CORE chapter, called Milwaukee United School Integration Committee (MUSIC), went on to pursue other school issues. In May and June of 1965, the coalition organized adult demonstrations and picketing to protest the intact bussing policy, whereby black children bussed from overcrowded schools were kept in all-black classrooms. Barbee himself was arrested during these demonstrations. So was Father Groppi—the first of his many arrests.

In October 1965, Barbee organized a second boycott. Although it lasted longer (three and one-half days), it was less successful numerically than the earlier boycott. Other school-related protests occurred in 1968, most of them in the form of minor boycotts and picketing by students over demands for black studies and "soul food."

The focus of black protesters on local government probably is explained best by the greater black dependence on municipal services. For blacks, much more than for whites, the level and nature of the local public commitment to housing, police, schools, and welfare substantially determine the quality of daily life. Hence, the perceived failures, oversights, and transgressions of municipal govern- ment agencies are less easy to ignore; most blacks have no way of substituting private resources for inadequate public ones, in order to secure the decent amen- ities of urban living. Whatever the explanation, the patterns of participation indicate that, for blacks, protest is a tactic of major importance on the local scene, an integral part of their pursuit of urban politics. For whites, it plays a

---

[26] Eisinger, "Conditions of Protest," p. 17.

more peripheral role in local politics. Indeed, many whites who take part in protest directed at local targets do so on behalf of primarily black causes, judging from the proportion of instances of white participation in the Groppi marches.

Although the races appear to use protest for substantially different purposes, in one way their protest experience is very similar. For most people of both races, individual protest participation is not a function of organizational membership. Only 27 percent of the black protesters and 20 percent of the white protesters said they belonged to an organization that had taken part in some type of protest. The types of such organizations and the membership of protesters in them are shown in Table 6.8.

Despite the lack of formal group affiliation among the protesters, most protests in which blacks took part were carried out by stable, ongoing organizations—principally the NAACP Youth Council, NAACP, CORE, and the Milwaukee chapter of the National Welfare Rights Organization—rather than by ad hoc groups created for a single protest campaign. The Youth Council was named, in 75 out of 149 instances of participation, as the organization responsible for initiating the protest in which the respondent took part. The Youth Council, under Groppi's "advisorship," not only managed the long open-housing campaign but also was responsible for extensive picketing to protest against the membership of white public officials in the segregated Eagles Club and for several other minor demonstrations. An additional 31 instances of black participation were inspired by other civil rights and welfare rights organizations.

In contrast, white protesters were mobilized less frequently by ongoing organizations. Out of a total of 97 instances of white participation, only 11 were prompted by Groppi, 6 by civil rights groups, and 7 by peace groups. However, 20 instances appeared to be stimulated by ad hoc student groups, and 13 by individual clergymen. Another 10 occurred in protests organized by ad hoc neighborhood organizations formed to press one particular grievance, primarily opposition to open housing.

These findings are suggestive on several counts. For both races, the major

TABLE 6.8 PROTESTER RESPONDENTS WHO BELONGED TO
GROUPS RESPONSIBLE FOR STIMULATING INSTANCES OF PROTEST,
BY TYPE OF GROUP AND BY RACE

Type of protest organization	Black Protesters		White Protesters	
	%	N	%	N
Ongoing, stable organization	72	107	26	25
Ad hoc organization	11	17	46	45
Undetermined	17	25	28	27
Total	*100*	*149*	*100*	*97*

portion of the potential protest constituency does not lie within the confines of organizational membership lists. While we can be certain that many protest leaders or organizers know their potential constituency, we can be equally sure that many do not. The task of mobilizing unattached or unaffiliated individuals for protest can now be seen to assume major proportions. Communication with potential participants is made more difficult by the absence of organizational ties and networks linking those individuals. Protest constituencies must often be assembled anew each time a protest occurs.

The two races, however, seem to confront this problem differently. At least in Milwaukee, blacks more than whites seem to have institutionalized the organization of protest, hence, they are potentially more efficient in performing the mobilization task. But we have no way of knowing at present whether or not this is peculiar to the city of Milwaukee.

Institutionalization occurs because most protests are organized by ongoing groups. These groups supply a ready leadership cadre as well as auxiliary workers, and they have other resources at hand, such as office space and mimeograph machines. In addition, they have institutional experience, which may be drawn upon over and over to provide guidelines and lessons for dealing with new situations. In effect, the black organizations that mobilize protesters on a semi-regular basis as one of their several functions are analogous in certain respects to local political party organizations, and may in some sense be surrogates for them. After all, party organizations are essentially collections of leaders and workers, one of whose tasks is to seek out, identify, and mobilize potential voters among the populace.

The protest into which whites are drawn is less institutionalized, in the sense that its organization is carried out most often by ad hoc groups created for the immediate purpose at hand. The task of mobilization is made all the more difficult by the fact that white groups on each occasion must organize anew; establish leaders, create communication networks, seek workers and resources, and set out without prior institutional experience to identify likely partisans of a particular cause.

The patterns of the uses of protest and the ways in which it is organized substantiate and enlarge upon the earlier findings based on protester characteristics. All of the evidence presented indicates that protest is a tactic that blacks have singularly adapted to the pursuit of urban politics, a tactic, moreover, that represents an integral and widely accepted part of the institutionalized political life of the black community.

Protest for whites involves a more eclectic focus, for their efforts are not confined to the local political arena. In any given political setting, white protest is a relatively rarer phenomenon, carried out by a small, socioeconomically privileged segment of the population. White protest is, then, extraordinary, non-institutionalized, and deviant from the norms of the broader community.

Some Conclusions

While one might argue that even the most casual observers have known for a long time that blacks support and use protest,[27] the data presented above specify and describe for the first time the nature and scope of that support and also suggest its *integral*, as opposed to its *extraordinary*, role in the black community. This sort of specification and modification of commonly held interpretations is useful in itself. The data and analysis offered here, however, also throw light upon some other problems, including the nature of the relationship between socioeconomic status and protest participation, and the implications of the institutionalization of protest among blacks.

Social Status and Protest Participation

If we examine protest participation as a function of individual social characteristics, it is clear (at least in Milwaukee) that protesters themselves cannot be called "poor." They rank higher on every measure of social status than do their nonprotester fellows in their respective racial communities. To what extent can we accept, then, the alternative interpretation that protesters are at least drawn from "poor" groups, that is, in the words of Lipsky, those groups that are powerless by virtue of their lack of conventional resources?

This interpretation is of little use in understanding the roots of white protest, because white protesters cannot be viewed as advantaged members of a group that is, as a whole, socioeconomically disadvantaged. There are at least two other interpretations, both of them more satisfying logically and empirically. On the one hand, we might view white protest as an expression by members of groups that lack power, either because they lack legitimacy or because their members do not occupy positions of authority and power. At least one-fourth of the instances of protest cited by whites were connected with the peace movement or were organized by college students. These represent subgroups that, although high in social status, do not command universal legitimacy and whose inability to gain their ends is very much a function of the fact that their members do not occupy positions of formal power. On the other hand, we may see white protest as a means of representing or supporting disadvantaged groups to which the white protesters themselves do not belong. This interpretation can help to explain why approximately one-half of the instances of white protest took place on behalf of black groups and black causes. Viewing protest as a means of supporting or representing other groups, whose powerlessness may or may not be a function of their lack of conventional socioeconomic resources, scarcely permits one to call white protest a tactic of the poor.

[27] Gary Marx published data documenting black *support* for protest as early as 1967. *Protest and Prejudice* (New York: Harper and Row, 1967), pp. 15-17.

In the case of black protest, it is at first glance intuitively acceptable to view protest as a tactic of the relatively powerless, whose condition is a function of their low status in the socioeconomic hierarchy. That is to say, we know that blacks as a racial group are socioeconomically disadvantaged in relation to whites and thus are relatively powerless. Yet, within that disadvantaged group, those who are most likely to take part in protest are of higher status. The problem with interpreting black protest is that it is not clear that the *powerlessness* of blacks is any *more* a function of their collective relative poverty than it is of their lack of legitimacy (a function simply of being black or of adherence to racially threatening ideologies) or of their lack of formal power in political institutions. In short, the precise relationship between the lack of conventional socioeconomic resources on the part of any given group and the tendency of that group's members to take part in protest is not at all clear. Previous formulations of protest as a tactic of the powerless (defined as a function of the lack of conventional resources), the underprivileged classes, or the poor require further specification and clarification and in many cases may be plainly erroneous.

The Institutionalization of Protest in the Black Community

It is a standard observation that the institutionalization of a process leads to its routinization—a reduction of its initial novelty, excitement, and impact. Protest among Milwaukee blacks is relatively institutionalized in relation to that among whites. If it is not yet routine, then it faces the danger of becoming so. After more than a decade of experience, the value of mass protest persists only so long as protest is organized more or less spontaneously for the issue at hand. Long protest campaigns and long-lived, stable protest organizations are not likely to maintain their status as frightening, forceful, galvanizing devices. To lose the capacity to shock and thereby gain media attention is to lose a means of communicating with what Lipsky has called "third party reference publics," who serve as potential allies.[28]

In such a situation the protest organizer will be under pressure to escalate his tactics, in order to break the routine and reestablish the credibility of his passion. Escalation ultimately leads to the necessity to consider violence, a step that most practitioners of protest do not wish to take. So they are caught in a dilemma, the resolution of which is not at all clear. In any event, the routinization of protest implies that the more it is used the less effective it will be. This means that black urban communities that have relied upon protest as an important means of wielding influence in the city may strip themselves of power by their own efforts to gain it through protest. To weaken oneself despite the

[28] Lipsky, "Protest as a Political Resource," pp. 1145–1146.

intensification or persistence of one's own struggle is perhaps both the irony and the true meaning of powerlessness.

We may nevertheless conclude that in the short run the patterns of protest participation and the regard in which such tactics are held make it evident that those who wish to achieve political prominence in the black community have fertile opportunities for mobilization and reputation building through the organization of such manifestations. Protest offers a quick and dramatic means to recognition and an inexpensive way to mobilize masses. Elite efforts in this direction enjoy wide support in the black community.

The possibilities for coalition of blacks and whites in protest efforts are by no means forbidding, although the small minority of whites who engage in protest have tended to spread their efforts across a wide range of issues, many of which have not been of interest to blacks.

Conclusions and Implications

7

The structure of political conflict in American cities is shaped by a multitude of factors. Group commitments, loyalties, and interests are defined in a variety of ways, and the cleavages that are central to the politics of any given conflict may differ from issue to issue. This is not to say that all cleavages are equally strong; some recur with great frequency, and some mark truly profound and enduring divisions in the society. This book has been concerned with one of the most important and pervasive cleavages in domestic urban politics, namely, that of race.

The analysis presented here has been carried out by the strategy of comparing the mass populations of the two races in Milwaukee on several dimensions of behavior and belief. We have found that in some areas the races tend to diverge sharply, while in others the extent of convergence is high. We have also discovered that within the mass populations of the two races there are segments that share belief and behavior patterns across racial lines, although these segments often constitute markedly different proportions of their respective racial populations.

What has stimulated this enterprise has been the need to understand the context of interracial politics. The point has not been to predict the likelihood of interracial cooperation or conflict, but rather, to make some statements about the shape of mass-generated pressures and their probable impact on interracial political relationships. We have proceeded by attempting to make clear what we might call the paths of greatest and least resistance for elites in the respective racial communities, as they struggle to bring their followings into political relationships of conflict or cooperation across racial lines.

This has involved a theoretical attempt to make explicit the role of mass populations in shaping elite opportunities and in establishing the costs that elites must face in pursuing various types of interracial relationships. What has emerged is a kind of map of mass behavior and belief, whose tracings suggest *(1)* that conditions affecting the rise and persistence of elites vary within the two racial communities, *(2)* that certain forms of interracial coalitions are probably more easily forged than others, and *(3)* that elites are generally under mass pressure to pursue interracial conflict in certain distinctive ways.

The results of this study do not establish specific probabilities that elites will follow these paths of least resistance or that they will act in accordance with these mass pressures. Nor can we estimate the extent to which these mass patterns are themselves shaped by elite manipulation. It is sufficient to know that such pressures and opportunities exist and that they take particular forms. From what we know about the nature of elite dependence on mass followings, it follows that elites who *persistently* behave as if these pressures did not exist are not likely to maintain their status as leaders and spokesmen over time. To this extent, we can see that, as long as elites and aspirants to elite positions take the potential costs of their strategies into account, the patterns of mass behavior and belief are likely to shape significantly the nature of interracial political relationships.

A Summary of the Prevailing Patterns

The general strategy of the analysis has been to compare mass-level samples of the two racial communities, treating them as relatively undifferentiated aggregates on a variety of attitudinal and behavioral dimensions. While it has become evident that neither racial group exhibits a monolithic structure of thought or action, the strategy of such comparisons does not simply represent a convenient means of procedure; it has substantive validity as well. Not only do the races come into conflict on occasion *as racial communities*, but the prevailing or modal tendencies within these communities establish the major outlines of the context of costs and opportunities that the elites of each race confront. Although I propose to dissect the two communities later in order to make some finer comparisons, it is appropriate at this point to present a summary of the broad patterns that we have found.

The overriding difference between the contexts that elites confront in the two racial communities is the marked racial divergence in commitment to the various integrative norms. Examining once again the racial distribution of scores on the summary integration index proposed in Chapter 3 (Table 3.10), we find that one-half of the black sample scored low, compared to only 11 percent of the white sample; 37 percent of the whites scored high, compared to 7 percent of the blacks.

While such a pattern is suggestive about the likely quality of interracial political cooperation or competition, we cannot begin on this basis to derive even the crudest estimates of the extent to which conflict is built into the structure of interracial confrontation. For this, we needed to discover whether the races differ substantially on what many have argued is a central underlying issue for modern urban dwellers—one that subsumes other more immediate issues. This issue is the problem of developing or resurrecting "community." We hypothesized that, if the two racial groups defined community in different ways, showed differing levels of concern over its presumed loss, or exhibited markedly different ways or levels of interest in reconstituting community, then we could argue that most of the issues that touch on the interests of the two racial groups can be interpreted in light of their differing requirements regarding the quest for community. This would result in a situation in which conflict was, in effect, built into racial encounters, regardless of the nature of the issue at hand. The divergence in dealing with the problem of community, as an underlying or first-order issue, would color approaches to and perceptions of all other issues. We found, however, that this did not appear to be the case in Milwaukee; neither race exhibited more than a minimal level of concern over community. The whole theory of loss of community and the quest to which that sense of loss is thought to give rise is unsupported by the Milwaukee data.

We did find, however, that the races had different priorities in regard to more concrete issue areas. This suggested that conflict—or cooperation—would tend to arise around the interests involved in the immediate issue at hand and not because of any built-in or underlying differences in social and political outlook.

Finally, we explored patterns of participation in conventional and protest politics. We found that whites are more active conventional participants. They dominate the channels of access and the field of view of public officials, not only by their sheer numbers but by their activity and cohesion in local politics. On the other hand, we found that blacks are substantially more active in protest politics.

These, then, are the prevailing patterns. Given the whole structure of my argument, we can derive from these patterns a set of implications for the quality of interracial politics in Milwaukee and for elites who operate in the respective racial communities. Since these implications derive strictly from the logic of the data in light of my theoretical argument, they must be viewed as tentative in nature. Therefore I shall present these implications as propositions to convey their hypothetical character.

Proposition 1 Prevailing mass pressures in the black and white communities are such as to make it likely that interracial political relationships, whether cooperative or conflictual, will be relatively unstable.

Instability, as I have conceived it, is a function of the failure of parties in a political relationship to agree on the basic ground rules and assumptions that regulate political interchange. These rules and assumptions regulate the political arena, in the sense that limits are set on the permissible modes of competition, conventions are established for the purpose of ending conflicts, and the behavior of the parties to a relationship falls within a predictable range. Where groups do not agree on these integrative norms and commitments, the relationships they establish will be marked by uncertainty, suspicion, and tentativeness. This is so even when one group professes a commitment to the norms—a point we shall take up in more detail momentarily. Elites who seek to combine or aggregate the resources of these various groups under such conditions will find, in all likelihood, that respective levels of commitment to such an aggregation are low and easily withdrawn.

More important, perhaps, under conditions of mutual suspicion and uncertainty elites may not even try to aggregate the resources of different groups. The situation after the 1967 riot is illustrative.[1] Mayor Maier's response to the disorders was to develop a program of thirty-nine reforms and initiatives—of which only seven fell within the city's jurisdictional capacities[2]—in consultation with the moderate black Interdenominational Ministerial Alliance and another group of people, primarily small businessmen, whom Maier's office selected as "grass-roots" spokesmen for the black community. Maier refused to invite to the deliberations a newly formed coalition of fifteen black organizations called Common View, which claimed to be more representative of the black community than the ministers and selected spokesmen. This group, which included a number of militant organizations but also the Milwaukee Urban League, formulated its own program of twenty-four points—nearly all of which fell within the city's capacities. Maier perceived this as a hostile challenge, rather than an opportunity. At first he refused even to meet with Common View. When he finally did, the meeting was acrimonious,[3] and the mayor and Common View were never able to engage in fruitful debate or to pool their efforts and resources. Whether or not Common View was *more* representative of the black community than the two groups Maier chose to talk with is beside the point here. What is important is that the organization represented the viewpoint and offered the resources of a considerable segment of the black community, and those resources were not exploited by a political leader in a position to do so.

The prevailing pressures that are likely to contribute to unstable interracial political relationships mean that cooperative ventures will take the form of some sort of *accommodation*, a situation, described in Chapter 1, in which the parties

---

[1] David J. Olson, "Racial Violence and City Politics: The Political Response to Civil Disorders in Three American Cities" (Ph.D. dissertation, University of Wisconsin, Madison, Wisconsin, 1971), pp. 167-218.

[2] Ibid., p. 179.

[3] Ibid., p. 182.

to a coalition represent potential liabilities to one another. Competition between the races will most likely tend to take the form of what was described as
divergent conflict, a condition characterized by high levels of suspicion, antagonism, and the absence of readily apparent bases for compromise.

These prevailing pressures naturally have implications for elites who seek to
lead or speak for the two racial communities, which leads us to a second
proposition.

Proposition 2 Under the pressures of an unstable relationship, both black and
white elites are likely to choose the role of hard-liner rather than that of negotiator. Although both sets of elites are likely to perceive compromise as a danger-
ous threat to their respective interests, the negotiator role may be less risky for
whites than for elites who seek to lead in the black community.

This implies that elites who lead racial groups in cooperative or competitive
enterprises across racial lines are more likely to take rigid, rather than flexible,
positions in regard to their own interests and vis-à-vis the demands of the other
race. Elites who arise in the black community find much support for this rigid
posture in the attitudes among blacks toward compromise. But, even though
white attitudes are supportive of the norms of integration in the abstract, white
elites who enter into political relationships with apparently intransigent black
elites are likely to take unyielding positions themselves. Maier's refusal to yield
on the open-housing issue in the face of Father Groppi's demonstrations and
rhetoric is a case in point. So, too, is the case of the school board, which refused
to recognize or consider the problem of de facto segregation in the face of Lloyd
Barbee's boycott campaign.

The greater risk for the negotiator in the black community is a consequence
of the widespread absence among blacks of positive commitment to bargaining
norms and of a general lack of faith in the fairness of government as an arbiter.
Compromise with potential coalition partners, competitors, or government decisionmakers is likely to be perceived as a form of betrayal of black interests.
Hence, for a black leader who wishes to rise to power and maintain his legitimacy, the safest course—though not necessarily the most productive in terms of
the acquisition of collective goals—may be to adopt rigid postures to demonstrate the leader's absolute commitment to the integrity of the interests for
which he speaks.

Proposition 3 For elites in both racial communities, pressures to adopt dramatic
public styles of leadership probably will be great—a factor that inhibits successful negotiation.

The same factors that support the presentation of rigid positions also support
the development of a flamboyant public style. This involves dramatic and uni-
lateral seizures of initiative, the laying of one's cards on the table in public, and
public announcements binding oneself to a certain position. These may be ex-

cellent negotiating tactics under some conditions, but such a style also may inhibit negotiation. Dramatic public politics has the value of demonstrating to followers that nothing is going on behind the scenes in the way of compromising stated positions—an especially important consideration for leaders in the black community, given its particular structure of attitudes. But a public announcement has the effect of binding a leader before his constituents.[4] To maintain the faith built on such a demonstration, the leader must in fact avoid compromising negotiations. To this extent, the dramatic style makes accommodation by either side extremely difficult.

Where elites are committed to a strategy of dramatic moves and countermoves, quiet efforts by others to avoid, mute, or resolve conflicts are not always appreciated. To some extent, such efforts are perceived as attempts to undercut or circumvent dramatically established positions. For example, Maier's response to the 1967 riot was dramatic. He quickly called on the governor to order out the National Guard, and he imposed a tight curfew on the city. As Maier and others around the country viewed it, this was a tough and firm response. When a state official named Joseph Fagan, a man with a reputation for establishing quiet lines of communication between the state and residents of the Inner Core, sought unilaterally to issue letters of recognition to civil rights workers to allow them to cross police lines to aid in calming the rioters, Maier denounced him as a "curbstone commissar" and threatened to investigate the possibility of legal action against him.[5]

In other instances—in the school boycotts, for example—black leaders were asked to halt protest demonstrations in exchange for admittedly vague promises of negotiation. Such demonstrations proceeded routinely, however. In general, then, the situation is conducive to the display of flamboyant, even demagogic, impulses or to a leadership based on personality and charisma, rather than one built on the less dramatic skills of the technician and the compromiser.

Proposition 4 The structure of beliefs and attitudes generally militates against the rise and survival of "statesmen" in the city.

By "statesmen" I mean those who seek to be leaders of "all" the people, by self-consciously seeking to transcend the boundaries separating constituencies (in this case racial constituencies). Even where people of both races share a common goal, they are often likely to be separated by profoundly differing views regarding the necessity of commitment to bargaining norms and regarding the neutrality of the political system. A leader cannot easily represent both groups over time, for he must ultimately confirm the suspicions of those who do not trust the system or betray those who do. Thus, the situation favors the persistence of racial elites committed to the representation of racially particularistic interests.

[4]On this point see Thomas Schelling, *The Strategy of Conflict* (New York: Oxford University Press, 1963), pp. 23 ff.

[5]Frank Aukofer, *City with a Chance* (Milwaukee: Bruce, 1968), p. 16.

Opportunities for those who would rise above the partisan divisions of race to assume statesmanlike leadership roles are clearly minimal.

Up to this point, we have concentrated heavily on the implications, for inter-racial political relationships and for elites, of mass divergence on integrative norms. A second major element of the patterns of belief and behavior that affects elite opportunities, and thus affects race relations, concerns the rates and styles of political behavior. The races do not differ as sharply here as they do in attitudes important for integration, but the differences that exist help to structure elite opportunities within the two racial communities in somewhat different ways.

Let us begin by breaking down the two racial samples on the political partici-pation dimension. First, we may divide the respondents according to whether they are relatively active or relatively inactive participants in conventional poli-tics, by using the simple composite index of conventional participation discussed in Chapter 5 (Table 5.1). Scores on this index were derived by awarding one point for participation in each of nine areas, including voting, campaign work, and so on. Those who scored four or fewer points were deemed relatively in-active; those who scored five or more were classified as relatively active. Each of these two groups was further divided according to whether the respondent had ever taken part in protest activities.[6] Thus, we get four types of political be-havior:

	High conventional participation score (5-9)	Low conventional participation score (0-4)
Protest	Type I	Type II
No protest	Type III	Type IV

A brief examination of the socioeconomic characteristics of these four types shows some interesting differences among them. The Type I group (high con-ventional, activity–protest participation) ranks highest within each racial sample on all the status indicators (see Tables 7.1 and 7.2). Both blacks and whites in this group were drawn disproportionately from the professional occupations and the moderately well-to-do income class. They were the only people who aver-aged more than two group memberships, and their average education was above high school.

For a substantial number of people who have taken part in protest, especially among whites, protest appears to complement other forms of political activity. Indeed, it would seem, in the main, to represent simply an additional weapon in

[6] Conventional activity and protest were positively related for both races when protest–no protest was run against high–low scores on the conventional participation index. Gamma coefficients were .33 and .65 for blacks and whites respectively.

TABLE 7.1 STATUS OF RESPONDENTS AND PROTEST
EXPERIENCE, CONTROLLING FOR LEVEL OF CONVENTIONAL
POLITICAL ACTIVITY, BY RACE

Status variable	Type I High conventional activity–protest participation	Type II Low conventional activity–protest participation	Type III High conventional activity–no protest participation	Type IV Low conventional activity–no protest participation
Black respondents				
Mean annual income	$7830 (N = 23)	$5880 (N = 26)	$7720 (N = 60)	$5520 (N = 111)
Mean years of education	12.08 (N = 25)	11.82 (N = 27)	10.49 (N = 65)	9.57 (N = 127)
Mean number of group memberships	2.48 (N = 25)	1.32 (N = 27)	1.76 (N = 65)	.65 (N = 128)
White respondents				
Mean annual income	$8550 (N = 29)	$7000 (N = 5)	$8140 (N = 116)	$6690 (N = 154)
Mean years of education	14.60 (N = 30)	14.40 (N = 5)	11.60 (N = 129)	10.45 (N = 165)
Mean number of group memberships	2.27 (N = 30)	1.60 (N = 5)	1.49 (N = 129)	.87 (N = 167)

the arsenal of an extremely small, politically active segment of the middle class. Amitai Etzioni has written: "Each social group may be said to find a comparative advantage in one political tool or another; those disadvantaged in the use of more conventional techniques find in demonstrations a tool that operates to their relative advantage."[7] This argument implies that groups will choose one or the other mode of political action, and that those who choose protest will be relatively disadvantaged in terms of the sorts of resources that ensure the successful use of conventional strategies. While this may be true to some extent in the black community, the data presented here indicate, rather, that many of those who use one form of political expression also use others, and that these people are overwhelmingly drawn from the higher-status segments of the society.

The status characteristics of the Type II respondents (low conventional activity–protest participation) are somewhat different from those of the Type I

[7]Amitai Etzioni, *Demonstration Democracy* (New York: Gordon and Breach, 1970), p. 19.

TABLE 7.2 OCCUPATION OF RESPONDENTS AND PROTEST
EXPERIENCE, CONTROLLING FOR LEVEL OF CONVENTIONAL
POLITICAL ACTIVITY, BY RACE

Occupation	Type I High conventional activity–protest participation		Type II Low conventional activity–protest participation		Type III High conventional activity–no protest participation		Type IV Low conventional activity–no protest participation		Proportion of racial sample	
	%	N	%	N	%	N	%	N	%	N
Black respondents										
Professional	24	6	0	0	3	2	1	1	4	9
Managerial	8	2	4	1	5	3	5	6	5	12
Clerical	12	3	25	7	9	6	8	10	11	26
Skilled	0	0	4	1	5	3	4	5	4	9
Semi-skilled	32	8	21	6	32	21	23	30	26	65
Service, housewives	24	6	46	13	46	30	59	76	51	125
Total	100	25	100	28	100	65	100	128	101	246
White respondents										
Professional	43	13	0	0	8	10	2	4	8	27
Managerial	0	0	0	0	10	13	4	7	6	20
Clerical	17	5	20	1	25	32	18	30	21	68
Skilled	7	2	0	0	9	12	10	17	9	31
Semi-skilled	7	2	20	1	22	29	23	39	21	71
Service, housewives	27	8	60	3	26	33	42	70	34	114
Total	101	30	100	5	100	129	99	167	99	331

155

group. Their incomes were low, resembling those of the relatively inactive Type IV respondents. Their education was high, however, and the number of their group memberships was comparable. Few of them were college students at the time of the survey, which casts doubt on one possible explanation for the conjunction of low incomes and high education. Only five out of the twenty-seven in the black Type II group and two out of the five in the white Type II group were in college in 1970.

What perhaps is most notable here is the fact that very few of the white protesters but over one-half of the black protesters fall into the Type II category. One explanation is that most whites, whether they had engaged in protest or not, seemed committed to conventional politics and believed in the efficacy of such activities. But a significant number of blacks, including approximately one-half of the Type II protesters, either were unsure of their commitment or had no faith in the conventional electoral process at all.[8]

While the two racial populations had nearly equal proportions of political activists who had taken part both in protest and in conventional political efforts (Type I), as we can see in Table 7.3, the black community had a significantly higher number of Type II respondents. The inactive segment of the white community was smaller than that of the black population, but, as we saw in Chapter 5, its socioeconomic makeup and the nature of its members' beliefs suggest that it would offer white elites a more fertile field for mobilization efforts than the black inactive group would offer elites who work in the black community. Finally, among nonprotesters, a larger proportion of whites than blacks were active in conventional politics, either at an extremely active level (Type III) or in a modest way (Type IV, as shown in the breakdown for that group).

Several logical propositions concerning elite opportunities can be derived from these patterns.

Proposition 5 Opportunities for the development of stable, enduring protest leadership are much greater in the black than in the white community.

This is not simply a function of the general community support for protest, which we examined in Chapter 6; it is also a consequence of the relatively large pool of citizens who are prepared to take part in protest. In addition, most protesters have taken part in such activity several times, indicating that the pool of participants exists over time and not simply at one moment.

Proposition 6 Black elite electoral activity in Milwaukee is likely to be confined, in the foreseeable future, to ward-based contests in predominantly black wards.

[8]For example, 86 percent of all the white protesters disagreed with the statement "Voting is no use in this city, because the government will do what it wants no matter how you vote," compared to 62 percent of the black protesters; and 82 percent of the white protesters disagreed with the statement "A good many local elections aren't important enough to bother with," compared to 49 percent of the black protesters.

TABLE 7.3 DISTRIBUTION, BY RACE, OF LEVEL OF
CONVENTIONAL ACTIVITY COMBINED WITH PARTICIPATION
IN PROTEST

	Type I High conventional activity–protest participation		Type II Low conventional activity–protest participation		Type III High conventional activity–no protest participation		Type IV Low conventional activity–no protest participation		Total
Respondents	%	N	%	N	%	N	%	N	N
Black	10	25	11	28	27	65	52	128	246
White	9	30	2	5	39	129	50	167	331

Type IV breakdown

	Moderate scorers (participation score = 1-4)		Inactives (participation score = 0)		Total	
Respondents	%	N	%	N	%	
Black	30	74	22	54	52	
White	38	128	12	39	50	

157

Proposition 7   Since opportunities for black elites in Milwaukee to seek citywide influence or office through electoral activity are not good, they are likely to seek leadership positions and expend leadership resources in other areas, such as interest groups and public agencies concerned especially with problems relating particularly to blacks.

Both of the above propositions derive from the facts that *(1)* blacks are a small minority in the city and hence a small part of the city's electorate, *(2)* their rate of electoral participation is modest relative to that of whites, and *(3)* the opportunities for conventional mobilization already seem to be stretched virtually to their limits in the black population.

Since the possibilities for increasing the number of black conventional participants is relatively low, black elites will be reluctant to expend scarce leadership resources for such basic conventional efforts as voter registration. Those interested in electoral activity are more likely to concentrate on the organization in black wards of followings composed of those who have already demonstrated an interest in conventional politics. Black elites, then, are not likely to play major roles in electoral politics at the municipal level in Milwaukee and cannot be expected to gain the rewards that accompany such efforts.

An examination of black representation in positions of power in Milwaukee, conducted in 1968 by Karl H. Flaming and others, lend support to these propositions. Of the sixty-six officials elected in the city at large, only one was black at that time.[9] In 1974, there were no blacks among the at-large group of elected officials; and there were still only two black aldermen, both still from the black wards of the Inner Core.

While black politicians have won citywide elections in other cities whose black populations are comparable in size to Milwaukee's (Los Angeles, for example, elected Thomas Bradley mayor although its black population was only 18 percent), this has not happened in Milwaukee. Indeed, there are no black figures waiting in the wings with the potential following necessary for a serious mayoral candidate. Two blacks have entered recent mayoral primaries (Frank Stribling in 1968, Lucille Berrien in 1972), but they did not make significant showings. Neither made the runoff election; neither carried the all-black wards. Berrien, for example, received only about 25 percent of the vote in the First and Sixth wards and only 8 percent of the vote in the entire city. It seems typical of black electoral politics in Milwaukee that neither candidate had a prior reputation in the political arena. They were unable to amass resources, and neither had an organizational base. City-level electoral politics for blacks in Milwaukee scarcely appears promising at present.

Opportunities for civic influence for blacks in Milwaukee have lain primarily in such welfare and service organizations as the Urban League and the Social

---

[9]Karl H. Flaming, J. John Palen, Grant Ringlien, and Corneff Taylor, "Black Powerlessness in Policy-Making Positions," *Sociological Quarterly* 13 (Winter 1972): 130.

Development Commission. The Flaming study found that, in 1968, 125 (26.5 percent) of the 472 top positions in the city's service organizations were staffed by blacks. Black power, however, tended to be concentrated in those organizations concerned particularly with the problems of minorities.[10]

Although Maier was able to retain the support of some moderate and conservative black churchmen and small businessmen, it is not apparent that those supporters reaped the rewards one might expect. According to journalists responsible for covering city hall, Maier in 1974 still had made no major overtures to the black community as such or to any segment of it, had proposed no new programs designed to deal with minority problems, and had made few significant black appointments. In short, there are and have been few obvious rewards for blacks who stake their resources in electoral contests at the citywide level, either on the side of the winning coalition or in opposition.

We shall have more to say about elite opportunities and the various types of participants, but let us turn first to the third area in the patterns of mass belief and behavior, namely, the degree of racial agreement on political goals.

While we found that neither racial group seems particularly concerned about the quality of the political community as a community or interested in ways to establish a community of shared norms, the races do accord slightly different priorities to various discrete problems that they believe face the city. Blacks appear more concerned over housing and unemployment, while whites are worried about their heavy tax burden. In short, the races appear to be in agreement about what is *not* ailing the city, but this essentially negative convergence is no basis on which to build a cooperative political effort. On the other hand, the range of discrete problems that members of the two races cite is large, and the priorities differ only slightly. At best, we can say that persistent, stable pressures for either interracial conflict or cooperation do not appear from this examination to be built into the structure of attitudes. The basic sorts of political relationships (conflict or cooperation) that the races establish with one another will depend on situational factors at any given moment.

The problems that members of the two races see facing them and their city and the goals implicit in these perceptions nevertheless have several possible implications for the context of leadership.

Proposition 8 Neither black nor white elites will find much sentiment in Milwaukee favoring the establishment of control-sharing institutions; hence, the elites cannot expect to rise to local prominence or organize and consolidate a local power base through such devices.

This is especially problematic for black elites. The control-sharing movement has been viewed since the inception of the federal antipoverty community action program as a means for the development of leadership in black communities as

[10] Ibid., p. 132.

well as a device for mobilization. Since there is little sign in Milwaukee of mass response to this issue, it seems unlikely that black elites will pursue control-sharing vigorously. Finding little encouragement here, they are likely to turn to other ways of building mass followings. In the absence of control-sharing institutions, the number and type of institutional settings for the discovery and training of indigenous leaders is greatly limited.

Proposition 9   White elites will find great encouragement for the adoption of a fiscally conservative stance, while black elites will find support for urging increased spending.

White concern over the tax burden is symptomatic of the times. Not only in Milwaukee but in the nation as a whole, there are strong signs that the white population is pressing for a period of fiscal retrenchment. Blacks are still likely to advocate program expansion and innovation, but the number of white allies upon whom they will be able to count probably is going to be small during the middle years of the decade of the 1970s.

Varieties of Elite Opportunity

The strategy of comparing the two racial communities on these dimensions of belief and behavior has the advantage of providing a picture of the general configuration of the respective contexts in which elites operate. But what such a strategy tends to obscure is the variety of minor opportunities that energetic elites might hope to exploit. That is to say, there is no single path within either racial community along which elites *must* travel in order to achieve positions of leadership and survive. Some paths, of course, are much easier to follow than others, and these offer more certain rewards. The relatively easy paths to leadership are those that are shaped by the well-established and dominant patterns of mass belief and behavior. Here, the opportunities seem best for gaining a large mass following, while the risks of popular repudiation seem minimal.

However, not all elites and aspirants to elite positions are prepared to follow the dominant trends, and many are not comfortable speaking the rhetoric of prevailing sentiment. Some of these, of course, may never find any mass support in their quest for leadership; but many may search out, mobilize, and depend upon pockets of opportunity in the mass public.

These pockets of opportunity will be found in those groups in the population whose patterns of behavior and belief, to a greater or lesser degree, are not congruent with the prevailing tendencies of their racial group. How large these pockets must be to provide a base to support a leader cannot be estimated, but, depending on the nature of the leader's ambitions, we can safely say that they probably can be very small.

These pockets may be composed of citizens whose behavior and beliefs are directly antithetical to those of the great majority. In such a case it is unlikely that leaders thrown up or supported by this segment will have legitimacy in the eyes of those citizens whose behavior and beliefs accord with more central tendencies. Except in a few extraordinary cases, such leaders will not wield significant power in a community or take part in its public decision making. More likely, such leaders will be limited to the pursuit of strategies designed primarily to gain attention—a course that will generally restrict their role to that of the gadfly.

In other cases, these pockets of opportunity may provide different but not antithetical bases of support for leaders. The majority members of the population tolerate or even support certain patterns that do not conform to the dominant ones, even though they do not themselves actually take part in them. Protest behavior in the black community is an apt example of such a case. Protest participation is not a dominant pattern, but, while different from the views of the larger part of the black community, it is not antithetical to them. Those who gain leadership status on the basis of this type of support may, in some cases, have a chance for more general leadership.

Our data are not detailed enough to isolate all the pockets that probably exist, but some undoubtedly may be identified by cross-tabulating the integration score categories (high, medium, low) with the typology of political activists. It should be understood that the resulting table does not show ideological or policy differences within or among these population segments, but it does show where racial elites may expect to derive strategic opportunities.

The percentages entered in each half of Table 7.4 represent proportions of each total racial sample. We may distinguish at least four types of population segments in each racial group, which seem to offer somewhat different, although in some cases overlapping, opportunities for elite mobilization initiatives and leadership. These segments differ markedly in the proportions of their respective total racial populations that they represent, making clear that the structure of opportunities facing elites and elite aspirants of the two races is different. In addition, we can see that the proportional breakdown has implications for the nature of interracial political relationships. The relative sizes and proportions of these population segments, represented by the areas enclosed in boxes in Table 7.4, are shown in Table 7.5.

On the basis of this table, it is possible to derive several propositions relating to the nature of elite opportunities, the structure of leadership in the respective racial communities, and the most advantageous strategies for joint racial political efforts.

Proposition 10 White elites have one clearly marked path to positions of leadership—conventional electoral activity—and in general may be expected not to deviate from it.

This is a proposition so obvious in character that it scarcely requires com-

TABLE 7.4 DISTRIBUTION OF RESPONDENTS, BY RACE, ACCORDING TO CATEGORY OF SCORE ON POLITICAL INTEGRATION INDEX AND LEVEL OF CONVENTIONAL ACTIVITY COMBINED WITH PARTICIPATION IN PROTEST

Integration-score categories	Type I High conventional activity–protest participation		Type II Low conventional activity–protest participation		Type III High conventional activity–no protest participation		Type IV Low conventional activity–no protest participation		Total	
	%	N	%	N	%	N	%	N	%	N
Black respondents										
High	*	1	1	3	3	7	2	5		
Medium	6	14	3	7	11	28	23	57		
Low	4	10	7	18	12	30	27	66	99	246
White respondents										
High	2	7	*	1	20	67	14	46		
Medium	7	22	1	3	18	58	27	90		
Low	*	1	*	1	1	4	9	31	99	331

Note: Percentages for both racial samples total less than 100 due to rounding errors.
* Indicates less than 1 percent.

TABLE 7.5 DISTRIBUTION OF MAJOR POCKETS OF
OPPORTUNITY AS INDICATED BY MASS PARTICIPATION AND
INTEGRATION PATTERNS, BY RACE

Boxed totals from	Black respondents		White respondents	
Table 7.4	%	N	%	N
1. Moderately integrated hybrid activists (Type I respondents with high and medium integration scores)	6	15	9	29
2. Alienated protesters (Type II respondents with high and medium integration scores)	10	25	1	4
3. Integrated conventional activists (Type III respondents with high and medium integration scores)	14	35	38	125
4. Moderately integrated conventional mobilizable pool (Type IV respondents with high and medium integration scores)	25	62	41	136

ment. White elites have not only a large pool of citizens who are extremely active in conventional politics and highly committed to integrative norms but also an even larger pool of occasional activists and nonactivists who are firmly committed to the norms that form the basis of standard conventional bargaining political strategies.

Proposition 11 In contrast to white elites, those who aspire to achieve and maintain leadership status in the black community have no clearly dominant path to follow in order to mobilize followings.

The pattern of mass behavior and belief in the black population is a highly fragmented one. While it is true that more black activists appear committed to pure conventional strategies than to any other sort of political expression, the numbers are comparatively small. We scarcely should be surprised, in retrospect, at the failure of mayoral aspirants like Stribling, Berrien, and Walther. While they all failed, *it is quite possible that they mobilized whatever support was actually mobilizable.* In addition, black elites run a high risk in pursuing electoral coalition strategies, to the extent that they attract activists with an extremely low commitment to integrative norms. This can shake the stability of any interracial coalition. It can also endanger the tenure of the leader himself, for he will be hard pressed to meet the expectations of both the integrated and the alienated activists.

Because there is no obviously distinguishable dominant configuration of behavior and belief, blacks are faced with a number of pockets of extremely modest opportunity. This fragmentation of the black population clearly has implications for the structure of leadership in the black community, to which we shall turn momentarily.

Proposition 12 The major pocket of opportunity for white elites who do not follow prevailing trends lies in the pursuit of hybrid strategies in which both protest and conventional activities are employed.

Members of the population segment that presents this opportunity are relatively firmly committed to integrative norms, a fact suggesting that elites who pursue bargaining strategies will not lose control of their following during negotiating sessions. If a large number in this group were not so committed, the chances, for example, of the transformation of a peaceful protest effort into a violent one might undercut elite negotiations. Furthermore, the ability of members of this group to take part in both protest and conventional activity provides a high degree of flexibility for elites in planning or executing political campaigns.

I would suggest that such elites are probably best exemplified in Milwaukee by the numerous members of the liberal white Catholic clergy, who have taken major roles in a variety of controversies involving minority and poverty issues. Their rhetoric has seldom been violent, unlike that of Father Groppi, who is not a typical representative. All of them have shown a thorough commitment to racial integration, and many have brought some of their white parishioners into their campaigns. The Reverend Matthew Gottschalk, who was active in the MUSIC boycotts, and the Reverend Dismas Becker and the Reverend Thomas Mahaney, who took part in National Welfare Rights Organization protest and petition efforts, are good examples.

Proposition 13 Black elites also have a pocket of opportunity in the integrated hybrid activists, but it is smaller relative to other pockets than the same segment is in the white population.

Proposition 14 A more significant pocket of opportunity for elites in the black community is the low conventional participation-protest group. These people represent a major resource for a certain class of black elites whose interest in conventional politics is minimal, if present at all.

Ten percent of the black sample fall in this relatively alienated low conventional participation-protest category (Table 7.5). Its members appear to have little apparent interest in conventional politics, little faith in the neutrality of the political system, and a low commitment to the norms of accommodation. For these reasons, they are unlikely to embrace leaders who advocate both protest and conventional strategies. This group, then, offers a highly distinctive base of support for militantly antisystem elites. Similarly inclined white elites have no parallel base of any significant proportions in the white community.

Proposition 15 The leadership pool in the black community is likely to be characterized by a sharper division of labor than that in the white community, at least insofar as ideological differences are held constant.

Most white leaders will be committed to conventional electoral strategies, since they can expect to attract the greatest mass support by these means. Even those white elites who seek to tap the other major pocket of opportunity in the white community, the hybrid activists, confront a constituency committed to integrative norms. This is bound to be a constraint on strategic choices. In addition, those white leaders of the hybrid segment must deal with a population that is extremely active in conventional politics as well as in protest. Thus, such elites are pressed to develop the skills necessary to organize conventional campaigns as well as protests. Black elites, however, confront a population that is fragmented by virtue of its diversity of normative beliefs and behavior preferences. Those who seek to tap the protest constituency are not likely to develop or seek to exercise more conventional skills, nor are they strategically so constrained by the high integrative commitments of their constituents.

The higher level of fragmentation of both the black citizenry and the black leadership suggests that *from the strategic viewpoint* the potential for active community cohesion in politics is lower among blacks than among whites. Such a statement ignores the possible divisive effects on both communities of ideological differences or the possible cohesive effects of racial identification, which can transcend disagreements on strategic preferences, at least temporarily. Nevertheless, to the extent that constituencies exist whose preferences for political strategies are distinctive rather than hybrid, elites will develop specialized skills to tap these preferences. The lack of elite versatility may make united community efforts more difficult to organize and sustain.

Conflict and Cooperation between the Races

Consider, first, the rise of a significant number of elites whose best strategy for survival, all things being equal, is to adopt rigid postures, a flamboyant style, a perspective shaped by racial interests, a commitment to liberal fiscal policies, and a set of political strategies governed by the fact that there are little hope and few resources for gaining major office or influence through conventional electoral activity. This is a composite profile of the elite characteristics that the central patterns of mass belief and behavior and the situational context favor in the black community in Milwaukee.

Consider, in addition, the probable response of white elites to black leaders who exhibit these characteristics. The behavior of white elites is not likely to differ much from that of the elites they confront, although their basic set of strategic choices is more promising.

Given these two considerations, we may conclude that *in general* the political relationships that blacks and whites establish—relationships either of conflict or of cooperation—will be deeply marked by mutual distrust and suspicion. The black and white masses do not share a commitment to the various normative mechanisms that facilitate conflict resolution or foster the accommodating predispositions necessary to hold together stable coalitions. Black elites are likely to be fiercely protective of their followers' interests, a stance that can easily discourage coalition building.

We have seen, to be sure, that there exist in the black community very small pockets of integrated activists upon whom elites might rely in forging stable relationships of conflict or cooperation with whites. But we may conclude that, to the extent that leaders in the black community hope to establish themselves as spokesmen for that community as a whole, they are likely to feel constrained by the central tendencies.

In other words, they cannot rely simply on mobilizing a small portion of the population that represents a pocket of opportunity. Thus, to estimate the probable character of interracial relationships in politics we must look to the broad patterns of mass behavior and belief—the *general* context within which elites discover and estimate opportunities and costs. These patterns establish a mood to which the activists of different types, the moderate participants, and the nonactivists all contribute. This general mood in the black population is quite different from that among whites, as we have seen. In the last analysis, the breadth of elite ambitions must be taken into account in speculating on the strategies they choose. We may end, then, by offering one final proposition.

Proposition 16 To the extent that black elites hope to mobilize and lead the black community as a whole, they will probably elect strategies of political assertion that will have the effect of establishing unstable relationships with white groups with whom they compete or cooperate.

Conclusion

This study has attempted to show how the patterns of mass behavior and belief may favor the rise and persistence of certain types of elites over others in the respective racial communities. The nature of the elites who emerge in positions of leadership is likely, in turn, to affect the way in which groups in the two racial communities manage to engage in cooperative political efforts or to pursue conflict.

The dominant impression, with which we might close, is that elites and those who aspire to positions of leadership in the black community appear to be subject to a much more limiting set of constraints than their white counterparts. Blacks have no predominantly attractive options among the paths to leadership, for their opportunities are laid out in a highly fragmentary way. Any choice of strategy they make is bound to alienate significant segments of their potential following. Black leaders in such a situation are not likely to be especially strong. Thus, the well-established patterns of white hegemony are likely to persist and flourish.

Derivation of Conventional Political Participation Indices

Nine conventional political participation items, treated as dichotomous variables, were intercorrelated. The resulting correlation matrices are reproduced in Table A.1.

For both races, three relatively distinct clusters of items emerge. These clusters are especially evident within the black sample. The inclusion of items in each cluster was based on the patterns of intercorrelation. Examination of these patterns is an essential step in the index construction, because mere intuitive grouping is apt to lead the researcher astray. For example, one might expect that voting for president and talking to someone about that same presidential election would be more closely related to one another than voting for president and voting (at another time of year and in a nonpartisan election) for mayor. This is not the case, however. The correlation coefficient for the former pair is .13, while that for the latter pair is .99. In general, with only three exceptions in the white campaign–contact cluster, those items that are interrelated at the .20 level or above were judged to form a cluster.

TABLE A.1 CORRELATION (PEARSON'S r)MATRICES AMONG TYPES OF RESPONDENTS' CONVENTIONAL POLITICAL PARTICIPATION, BY RACE

Type of participation	Vote for president	Vote for mayor	Talk about presidential election	Talk about mayoral election	Persuade someone to vote	Contact a public official	Campaign work	Give money	Register voters
Black respondents									
Vote for president	—								
Vote for mayor	.99	—							
Talk about presidential election	.13	.12	—						
Talk about mayoral election	.15	.14	.66	—					
Persuade someone to vote	.15	.12	.57	.61	—				
Contact a public official	.08	.08	.21	.18	.24	—			
Campaign work	.03	.03	.22	.20	.21	.35	—		
Give money	-.06	-.07	.28	.21	.28	.22	.29	—	
Register voters	-.05	-.07	.22	.20	.21	.24	.34	.28	—
White respondents									
Vote for president	—								
Vote for mayor	.99	—							
Talk about presidential election	.07	.05	—						
Talk about mayoral election	-.07	-.06	.50	—					
Persuade some to vote	.04	.11	.34	.26	—				
Contact a public official	-.05	-.07	.26	.30	.21	—			
Campaign work	.08	.06	.18	.10	.28	.25	—		
Give money	-.10	-.09	.23	.21	.12	.17	.21	—	
Register voters	.03	.03	.10	.07	.15	.12	.12	.20	—

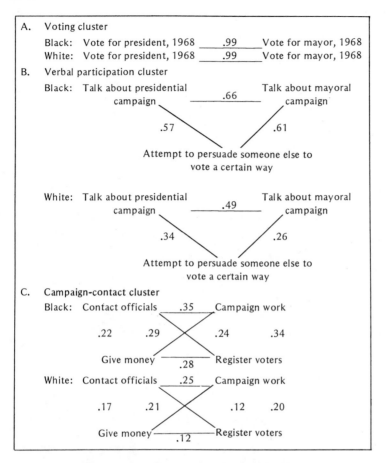

Figure A.1. Clusters of participation items.

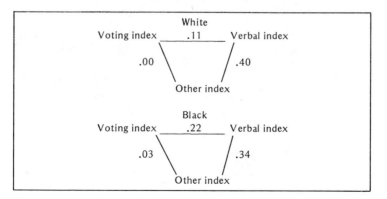

Figure A.2. Intercorrelation of the participation indices.

Questionnaire Used in the Survey

1. What do you think are some of the most important problems faced by the city of Milwaukee today? (Anything else?) _____

   _____

   _____

   _____

2. Do you think the city government is doing anything about these problems?

Yes	No	D.K.
↓	(TO Q 3)	(TO Q 3)

   2a. What kinds of things is the city government doing that you know of?

   _____

   _____

   _____

   2b. . Do you think there is anything else that the city government *should* be doing but isn't?_____

   _____

   _____

3. Which of the problems that Milwaukee faces do you think is the most important?

    _____

    _____

4. Look at this card and rank the following things in the order of importance for black people in this city. Which *one* is the most important, (the next most, etc., to least important)? (SHOW CARD 1)

    RANK _____ CARD 1 _____

    _____ better housing

    _____ jobs and job training

    _____ higher welfare payments

    _____ better police protection

    _____ political power for grass-roots people

    _____ good education

    _____ aid to help neighborhood people own their own businesses

Interviewer's Name: _____ Int. No.: _____

Date: _____ Time Started: _____

Now I'd like to ask you a few questions about voting and things like that.

5. Did you happen to vote in the presidential election in 1968 when Nixon and Humphrey and Wallace were all running or were you too young?

Yes	No	Too young
↓	↓	(TO Q 7)

    5a. Do you remember who you voted for?   5b. Which candidate did you prefer?
    (Who?)

    _____   _____

6. Do you remember if you voted in the election for mayor of Milwaukee in 1968 when Maier and Walther were running?

Yes	No
↓	(TO Q 7)

    6a. Do you recall who you voted for? (Who?)

    _____

7. In the last two years or so, do you recall ever doing any of the following things? Did you talk to anyone about the presidential election of 1968?

Yes   No

8. Did you talk to anyone about the election for mayor of Milwaukee in 1968?

Yes   No

9. Did you ever try to persuade someone to vote in a certain way for president or any other candidate?

Yes   No

10. Within the last couple of years did you personally write a letter, send a telegram, or talk to any of the following people about your opinion or about a problem?
(✓ CHECK ALL THAT APPLY AND FOR EACH CHECK RECORD ON CHART ON NEXT PAGE)

None
(TO Q 11)

_____ A. the mayor of Milwaukee

_____ B. your representative in congress

_____ C. your representative to the state legislature

_____ D. the President of the United States

_____ E. your U.S. senator

_____ F. a Milwaukee city alderman

_____ G. the governor of Wisconsin

_____ H. any person at all who works for the city of Milwaukee

_____ I. any person who is a leader in this neighborhood

_____ J. any other person in public life I might have left out that you wrote or spoke to (GET *TITLE* and *NAME* IN 10a) (SEE CHART NEXT PAGE)

(FOR EACH COMMUNICATION RECORD LETTER FROM Q10)

Record letter	10a. Who was this?	10b. What contacted about?

10a. Who was this? (RECORD ON CHART ABOVE)
10b. What did you contact (him or her) about? (RECORD ON CHART ABOVE)

11. Did you help out in an election campaign in the last couple of years?

    Yes   No
     ↓   (TO Q 12)
11a. Could you tell me whose campaign you worked in?_____

_____

12. Did you ever give any money to a political party or an individual candidate?

    Yes   No

13. Have you yourself ever run for any public office?

    Yes   No
     ↓   (TO Q 14)
13a. What did you run for? _____

14. Is there an anti-poverty community action program in this neighborhood that you know of?

    Yes   No
     ↓   (TO Q 15)
14a. Did you ever vote for any anti-poverty board members?   Yes   No

15. Have you heard of the Model Cities program here in Milwaukee?

    Yes   No
     ↓   (TO Q 16)
15a. Do you happen to know any of the things it's supposed to do? No , or (What?)

_____

15b. Do you remember if you voted for any of the people who ran for the board of the Model Cities program?

Yes   No

16. Did you ever work in a voter registration drive to get people to register to vote?

Yes   No

A lot of people participate in demonstrations and marches and picketing and things like that these days . . . .

17. Have you ever taken part in a mass march or demonstration of any kind?

Yes   No
↓   (TO Q 18)

17a. About how many would you say you've been in? _____

17b. Could you tell me what the people marching or demonstrating wanted? (Now what about the 2nd, 3rd?)

1. _____

_____

2. _____

_____

3. _____

_____

17c. Where did this march or demonstration take place?

1. _____

2. _____

3. _____

17d. Who organized this march or demonstration?

1. _____

2. _____

3. _____

17e. Did this march or demonstration help you get what you wanted?

1.   Yes   No   Explain: _____

_____

2.   <u>Yes</u> <u>No</u> Explain: _____

_____

3.   <u>Yes</u> No Explain: _____

_____

17f. Was there any violence at this march or demonstration?

1.   <u>Yes</u> <u>No</u>

2.   <u>Yes</u> <u>No</u>

3.   <u>Yes</u> <u>No</u>

17g. Were you arrested at this march or demonstration?

1.   <u>Yes</u> <u>No</u>

2.   <u>Yes</u> <u>No</u>

3.   <u>Yes</u> No

18. Have you ever taken part in picketing, like for a labor strike or to protest something?

<u>Yes</u>   <u>No</u>
↓   (TO Q 19)

18a. About how many times have you picketed? _____

18b. Could you tell me what the people picketing wanted? (How about the 2nd, 3rd?)

1. _____

_____

2. _____

_____

3. _____

_____

18c. Who were you picketing?

1. _____

2. _____

3. _____

18d. Who organized the picketing?

1. _____

2. _____

3. _____

18e. Did picketing help you get what you wanted?

1. <u>Yes</u> <u>No</u> Explain: _____

_____

2. <u>Yes</u> <u>No</u> Explain: _____

_____

3. <u>Yes</u> <u>No</u> Explain: _____

_____

18f. Was there any violence during this picketing?

1. <u>Yes</u> <u>No</u>

2. <u>Yes</u> <u>No</u>

3. <u>Yes</u> <u>No</u>

18g. Were you arrested during this picketing?

1. <u>Yes</u> <u>No</u>

2. <u>Yes</u> <u>No</u>

3. <u>Yes</u> <u>No</u>

19. Have you ever taken part in a sit-in?

<u>Yes</u>   <u>No</u>
 ↓   (TO Q 20)

19a. About how many sit-ins would you say you've taken part in? _____

19b. Could you tell me what the people sitting-in wanted? (How about the 2nd, 3rd?)

1. _____

_____

2. _____

_____

3. _____

_____

19c. Where did this sit-in take place?

1. _____

2. _____

3. _____

19d. Who organized this sit-in?

1. _____

2. _____

3. _____

19e. Did this sit-in help you get what you wanted?

1.   <u>Yes</u> <u>No</u>   Explain: _____

2.   Yes No   Explain: _____

3.   Yes No   Explain: _____

19f. Was there any violence at this sit-in?

1.   Yes <u>No</u>

2.   Yes <u>No</u>

3.   Yes <u>No</u>

19g. Were you arrested at this sit-in?

1.   Yes <u>No</u>

2.   Yes <u>No</u>

3.   Yes <u>No</u>

20. Have you ever attended a civil rights rally or meeting?

<u>Yes</u>   <u>No</u>
  ↓   (TO Q 21)

20a. About how many rallies and meetings would you say you've attended? _____

20b. Could you tell me what the people were meeting about? (How about the 2nd, 3rd?)

1. _____

_____

2. _____

_____

3. _____

20c. Where did this meeting or rally take place?

1. _____

2. _____

3. _____

20d. Who organized this meeting or rally?

1. _____

2. _____

3. _____

20e. Could you tell me who spoke at this meeting or rally? (NAME)

1. <u>Yes</u> _____ <u>No</u> <u>DK</u>
           NAME   POSITION

2. <u>Yes</u> _____ <u>No</u> <u>DK</u>
           NAME   POSITION

3. <u>Yes</u> _____ <u>No</u> <u>DK</u>
           NAME   POSITION

21. Have you ever taken part in any other type of protest or direct action that I might have missed?

       <u>Yes</u>   <u>No</u>
        ↓   (TO Q 22)

21a. Could you tell me what it was? _____

_____

_____

21b. What was the purpose of this? _____

_____

21c. Where did this take place? _____

_____

21d. Who organized this? _____

21e. Did this help you get what you wanted? <u>Yes</u> <u>No</u> Explain: _____

_____

21f. Was there any violence at this? <u>Yes</u>   <u>No</u>

21g. Were you arrested at this? <u>Yes</u>   <u>No</u>

22. You may recall that there were riots or disturbances in Milwaukee in the summer of 1967. Were you involved in any way at all in that? Just tell me "yes" or "no"—I don't have to ask about the details. <u>Yes</u>   <u>No</u>

23. Did you ever stop buying at a particular store because of a boycott organized by a civil rights group?

    <u>Yes</u>   <u>No</u>

24. Have you ever taken part in a boycott of the schools—like not sending your children to school as a protest?

    <u>Yes</u>   <u>No</u>

25. Did you ever boycott anything else?

    <u>Yes</u>   <u>No</u>
      ↓   (TO Q 26)

    25a. What? _____

26. Some black leaders in New York City a few months ago asked all black people to stay home from work on a certain day as a kind of general protest against racism. And last fall white college students also asked people to stay home from work for a day to protest the Vietnam war. Have you ever joined a protest of this type—a moratorium —in any way?

    <u>Yes</u>   <u>No</u>
      ↓   (TO Q 27)

    26a. What kind of protest was that? _____

27. Why do you suppose people protest and demonstrate so much these days?

_____

_____

28. Do you or your family rent this (house) (apartment)?

     Yes   No
      ↓   (TO Q 32)

29. Do you think the landlord takes very good, fairly good, or poor care of this property?

     Very good   Fairly good   Poor

30. Do you think the rent is fair? Yes   No

31. Have you ever taken part in a rent strike? Yes   No

32. Is there a neighborhood, block, or tenants' association around here that you know of?

     Yes   No
      ↓   (TO Q 33)

    32a. What is the name? _____

    32b. Are you a member? Yes   No

    32c. What kinds of things does the association do? _____

_____

33. Do you think people have a right to hold a rent strike if the landlord won't fix up his building properly? That is, not pay their rent until he fixes things up.   Yes   No

34. Do you belong to any organization or group that took part in any demonstration in Milwaukee?   Yes   No

35. What would you say about demonstrations or marches over the last few years in Milwaukee, have they helped black people a great deal, helped a little, hurt a little, or hurt a great deal?

     Helped a great deal   Helped a little   Hurt a little

                Hurt a great deal   DK

36. Would you like to see more demonstrations or fewer demonstrations or do you think it doesn't matter one way or the other?

           More   Fewer   None   Doesn't matter

37. Some people say that no good can ever come from riots like those that happened in Detroit and Newark a few years ago. Other people say that such riots do some good. Which comes closest to the way you feel?

           No good   Some good   DK

38. Generally speaking, do you think of yourself as a Republican, a Democrat, an Independent, or what?

> Republican   Democrat   Independent   Other: _____
>   ↓   ↓   ↓   ↓

38a. Would you call yourself a strong   38b. Do you think of yourself as closer to
(Rep) (Dem) or not very strong   the Republican or Democratic party?
(Rep) (Dem)?

> Strong   Not very strong   Republican   Democratic

39. A lot of people get so angry about certain things that they think that violence is the only way to get the government to do something. Have you ever felt this way?

> Yes   No

Now I'd like to read several statements to you and I'd like to know how you feel about each one. Do you strongly agree, agree, both agree and disagree, disagree, or strongly disagree? (SHOW CARD 2 AND RECORD LETTER)

CARD 2

A.	Strongly agree	C.	Agree and	D.	Disagree
B.	Agree		disagree	E.	Strongly disagree
				X.	Don't know

40. People in the government in this city don't care much what the average person thinks. (LETTER, CARD 2)

CARD 2

A.	Strongly agree	C.	Agree and	D.	Disagree
B.	Agree		disagree	E.	Strongly disagree
				X.	Don't know

41. If a group of people have a problem here in Milwaukee, it's pretty easy to get somebody in the city government to listen to them.

_____ (LETTER, CARD 2)

42. A good many local elections aren't important enough to bother with. _____

43. Most of the people running the government in Milwaukee are honest. _____

44. Politics is so complicated that the average person can hardly understand it. _____

45. Demonstrations are better than voting in this city because demonstrations are about the only way to get your point across. _____

46. Compromise is a good thing; everybody gets a little bit of what he wants. _____

47. Voting is the only way the average person can influence government in this city.____

48. The only way to get quality education for our children is to let professional educators run the whole school system. _____

49. Demonstrations and mass marches are one good way to get the city government to listen to you. _____

50. Voting is no use in this city, because the government will do what it wants no matter how you vote. _____

51. It's sometimes important to take part in demonstrations because that's one way to make your voice heard. _____

52. Would you say that black people in Milwaukee have a harder or an easier time than white people getting what they want from the city government or would you say it's about the same?

    <u>Harder</u>   <u>Easier</u>   <u>Same</u>   <u>DK</u>

53. When you think about the "government," what comes to mind? _____

    _____

    53a. Anything else? _____

    _____

    _____

54. When you think about the government in Milwaukee, what comes to mind?

    _____

    _____

    54a. Anything else? _____

    _____

55. What do you think are the three most important things the city government does for people in Milwaukee? _____

    _____

56. Can you think of anything that the government in this city should be doing that it's not?   <u>Yes</u>   <u>No</u>
              ↓

    56a. What? _____

57. Would you say in general that the government in Milwaukee does an excellent job, a good job, a fair job, or a bad job?

    <u>Excellent</u>   <u>Good</u>   <u>Fair</u>   <u>Bad</u>

58. Let's say a group in your neighborhood wanted to get a traffic light on the corner. What would you do about getting this done? Would you call someone or go see someone? Who? (Name and position.)

    _____

    _____

IF CALL OR SEE SOMEONE

58a. What if (he) (they) refused to do anything? What would you do then?

_____

_____

59. We hear a lot these days about "community control," like for example, community control of the schools. What do the words "community control" mean to you?

_____

_____

_____

_____

60. Are you in favor of any type of community control?

      Yes   No
       ↓   (TO Q 61)

60a. What kinds of things should the local community control?_____

_____

_____

61. Suppose a group of people around here wanted to get the government of Milwaukee to do something for this neighborhood. Would you feel free to go talk to someone in the government about it?

      Yes   No
       ↓   (TO Q 62)

61a. Who would you go to first? _____

62. Is there anyone in this community you can name who is not in the government who could help get something done for this neighborhood?

      Yes   No
       ↓   (TO Q 63)

62a. Who? (ASCERTAIN ROLE OR POSITION OF PERSON NAMED).

_____   _____
            NAME   POSITION

Now I'd like to read some more statements to see how you feel. (SHOW CARD 2, AND RECORD LETTER)

CARD 2

A.	Strongly agree	C.	Agree and	D.	Disagree
B.	Agree		disagree	E.	Strongly disagree
				X.	Don't know

63. Demonstrations just hurt your cause; people shouldn't use direct action methods.

_____ (LETTER, CARD 2)

64. The government of Milwaukee is usually pretty fair to the average person. _____ _

65. White people usually get what they want from city government. _____

66. A group has to compromise too often to get what it wants from government.

_____

67. Demonstrations in this city are no use; the government just refuses to listen anyway.

_____

68. Black people shouldn't have to make compromises when they make demands because they've waited so long to be treated fairly. _____

69. Now suppose a group in your community thought that the police didn't patrol the neighborhood often enough at night. What could you do about getting better police protection? _____

_____

70. Have you heard of the Organization of Organizations (Triple O) here in Milwaukee?

<u>Yes</u>   <u>No</u>
 ↓   (TO Q 71)

70a. Do you happen to know what kinds of things it does?

<u>Yes</u>   <u>No</u>
 ↓   (TO Q 71)
EXPLAIN: _____

_____

70b. Do you think this is a good way to fight poverty?   <u>Yes</u>   <u>No</u>

71. Some federal government programs, like the poverty program, call for local "citizen participation." What do the words "citizen participation" mean to you?

_____

_____

72. Have you heard of the decentralized school system in New York City?   <u>Yes</u>   <u>No</u>

73. Do you think decentralized schools would be a good thing for Milwaukee?

<u>Yes</u>   <u>No</u>
 ↓   ↓
73a. Why do you say that?   _____

_____

74. Which of these statements would you agree with most:

　　　＿＿＿＿＿＿   A.   The people in the local community know better than the people
　　　　　　　　　　　in the city government what is best for them.

　　　＿＿＿＿＿＿   B.   The people we elect to the city government know best what is
　　　　　　　　　　　good for the local communities.

74a. Why do you say that?   ＿＿＿＿＿＿＿＿＿＿＿＿＿＿＿＿＿＿＿＿＿＿＿＿

＿＿＿＿＿＿＿＿＿＿＿＿＿＿＿＿＿＿＿＿＿＿＿＿＿＿＿＿＿＿＿＿＿＿＿＿

＿＿＿＿＿＿＿＿＿＿＿＿＿＿＿＿＿＿＿＿＿＿＿＿＿＿＿＿＿＿＿＿＿＿＿＿

75. Who do you think should have the main control over the schools in this neighborhood: the parents, the central school board, or the teachers and principals? (CHECK
EACH MENTIONED)

Parents	School Board	Teachers/Principals	All	Other
			SPECIFY: ＿＿＿＿

76. Let's just suppose that the parents could control the schools and you got elected to
the local school board. What kinds of changes would you make?

＿＿＿＿＿＿＿＿＿＿＿＿＿＿＿＿＿＿＿＿＿＿＿＿＿＿＿＿＿＿＿＿＿＿＿＿

＿＿＿＿＿＿＿＿＿＿＿＿＿＿＿＿＿＿＿＿＿＿＿＿＿＿＿＿＿＿＿＿＿＿＿＿

＿＿＿＿＿＿＿＿＿＿＿＿＿＿＿＿＿＿＿＿＿＿＿＿＿＿＿＿＿＿＿＿＿＿＿＿

77. Do you think the police treat people fairly in this neighborhood?

Yes	Depends	No
(TO Q 78)	↓	↓

77a. Could you explain?   ＿＿＿＿＿＿＿＿＿＿＿＿＿＿＿＿＿＿＿＿＿＿

＿＿＿＿＿＿＿＿＿＿＿＿＿＿＿＿＿＿＿＿＿＿＿＿＿＿＿＿＿＿＿＿＿＿＿＿

77b. What do you think would make them act more fairly?   ＿＿＿＿＿＿＿＿＿＿

＿＿＿＿＿＿＿＿＿＿＿＿＿＿＿＿＿＿＿＿＿＿＿＿＿＿＿＿＿＿＿＿＿＿＿＿

＿＿＿＿＿＿＿＿＿＿＿＿＿＿＿＿＿＿＿＿＿＿＿＿＿＿＿＿＿＿＿＿＿＿＿＿

78. Would you say that the schools do a very good job now, a fair job, or a poor job
teaching children?

Very good	Fair	Poor

79. Do you think that parents who don't know anything about education and teaching
should be allowed to have a voice in running the schools in this community?

Yes	No	DK

80. Do you think it would be a good idea if we had just black policemen in black neighborhoods and just white policemen in white neighborhoods?

           <u>Yes</u>   <u>No</u>   <u>Depends</u>

81. Why do you say that? _____

_____

82. Do you think it would be a good idea if each neighborhood elected a board of local residents to watch over the police in their precinct and handle citizen complaints about the police?

           <u>Yes</u>   <u>No</u>   <u>Depends</u>

83. Why do you say that? _____

_____

_____

84. Would you agree or disagree with this statement: It's much better for the city government to decide what's best for everyone rather than letting individual neighborhoods do their own deciding?

           <u>Agree</u>   <u>Disagree</u>   <u>Depends</u>   <u>DK</u>

85. Would you say that people in local neighborhoods need a lot of help, a little help, or no help from the city government in running their poverty programs and Model Cities programs?

           <u>Lot</u>   <u>Little</u>   <u>None</u>

Now I'd like to ask you a few questions about some city officials and politicians.

86. Do you happen to recall the name of the mayor of Milwaukee or is this something you don't pay much attention to?

_____ , or <u>DK</u>

                        NAME

87. What about the name of the city alderman from around here, or is that something you aren't too interested in?

_____ , or <u>DK</u>

                        NAME

88. Would you happen to remember the name of your representative to congress from this district?

_____ , or <u>DK</u>

                        NAME

89. I have a list here of the names of several people. Some of them work in the city government and some are city politicians. Now most people wouldn't recognize very many of these names but I'd like to see how many you're familiar with. (SHOW CARD 3) (CHECK WHICH NAMES R RECOGNIZES)

✓		CARD 3	89a.

NONE
(TO Q 90)

	A.	Richard Gousha	_____
_____	B.	Harold Brier	_____
_____	C.	Henry Maier	_____
_____	D.	Robert Jendusa	_____
_____	E.	Joseph Baldwin	_____
_____	F.	Richard Perrin	_____
_____	G.	Frank Schleichert	_____
_____	H.	John Lungren	_____
_____	I.	Lawrence Gram, Jr.	_____

89a. Do you happen to know what _____ does? (RECORD ABOVE)

These final questions will help us to interpret the results of the study.

90. How long have you lived in this neighborhood? _____

91. How long have you lived in Milwaukee? All life, or _____
                                   (GO TO Q 94)

92. Would you tell me where you were born? _____

93. Were you brought up on a farm, a small town, small city, suburb, or large city?

        Farm   Small town   Small city   Suburb   Large city

94. What is your present age? _____

95. Are you employed now, looking for work, or what?

    Employed   Looking Retired Housewife Other: _____
      ↓   ↓   ↓ (TO Q 96) ↓

95a. What job are you now working at? 95b. What kind of job did you have on
     BE SPECIFIC   the last regular job you had?
                             (BE SPECIFIC)

_____   _____

_____   _____

96. Did you ever have a job working for the city of Milwaukee?

    Yes   No
    ↓   (TO Q 97)

96a. Have you ever gone on strike from your city job?

      Yes   No
      ↓   (TO Q 96c)

96b. What was the purpose of the strike? _____

96c. Have you ever taken part in a work slowdown while working for the city?

    Yes   No

97. Do you own or are you buying this home or what?

    Own   Buying   Rent   Other: _____

98. Will you please look at this card (SHOW CARD 4) and tell me which figure comes closest to your total family income for 1969 before taxes that is. Just tell me the letter next to the figure that fits you best.

CARD 4

A. Under $1,000	E. $4,000-$4,999	I. $8,000-$8,999
B. $1,000-$1,999	F. $5,000-$5,999	J. $9,000-$9,999
C. $2,000-$2,999	G. $6,000-$6,999	K. $10,000-$14,999
D. $3,000-$3,999	H. $7,000-$7,999	L. $15,000-$19,999
		M. $20,000 or over

99. Some people belong to organizations or clubs—like church groups, or unions or lodges or civil rights groups. Can you tell me if you belong to anything of this sort? (SHOW CARD 5)

CARD 5

✓

NONE
(TO Q 100)

_____ Any parent-teacher group

_____ Church-connected groups (Usher's Club, Ladies Aid, etc.)

_____ Fraternal lodge or auxiliary

_____ Neighborhood clubs; Community Center (including the YMCA, YWCA)

_____ Card clubs or social clubs

_____ Groups of people of the same nationality

_____ Labor unions

_____ Veterans' association

_____ Service club (Rotary, Lions, etc.)

_____ Professional or business groups

_____ Civic organizations (participation in charity drives, Red Cross, etc.)

_____ Sports team

_____ Participation in political activities, a political club or party

_____ Civil rights groups (NAACP, CORE, etc.)

_____ Other organizations (Describe) _____

100. What was the highest grade of school or year of college that you completed?

_____ (GRADE OF SCHOOL), or_____(YEAR OF COLLEGE)

(IF R BLACK, SKIP, GO TO Q 102)

101. What is the original nationality of your family on your *father's* side? (IF "AMERI-CAN," ASK: What country did his family come from originally?)

_____

102. Where was your father born? _____

City   State   Country

(IF R BLACK, SKIP, GO TO Q 104)

103. What is the original nationality of your family on your *mother's* side? (IF "AMERI-CAN," ASK: What country did her family come from originally?)

_____

104. Where was your mother born? _____
                                              City   State   Country

105. Finally, would you look at this card (SHOW CARD 6) and tell me whether you or
anyone in your immediate family are currently receiving any of the following? Just
tell me the letter.

✓	CARD 6

<u>None</u>

_____ A.   ADC, or AFDC

_____ B.   Government surplus food

_____ C.   Government food stamps

_____ D.   Social security

_____ E.   Unemployment compensation

TERMINATE INTERVIEW

INTERVIEWER'S SUPPLEMENT

A1.   Time interview ended: _____

A2.   Make sure the data on contacts you have made at this housing unit, including the
present contact, has been supplied in full on bottom of Cover Sheet.

A3.   (IF R REFUSED TO GIVE TOTAL FAMILY INCOME) Estimated Total Family
Income for 1969:
            $ _____

A4.   R's race is: <u>White</u>   <u>Negro</u>   Other:_____

A5.   R's sex is: <u>Male</u>   <u>Female</u>

A6.   Other persons present at interview were: <u>None</u>   <u>Children under 6</u>

        <u>Older children</u>   <u>Spouse</u>   <u>Other relatives</u>   <u>Other adults</u>
                        (CHECK MORE THAN ONE BOX IF NECESSARY)

A7.   This housing unit is in a *structure* that contains: <u>One HU only</u>

        <u>2-9 HU's</u>   <u>10 or more
                                    apartments</u>   <u>Rooming
                                                                house</u>   Other: _____

THUMBNAIL SKETCH

_____

_____

_____

_____

_____

_____

Index

A

Aberbach, Joel, 9, 94n, 96, 131n
Access to decisionmakers, 57
Access to officials, 65–66
Accommodation, 150–151
  necessary conditions for, 23–24
  variants of, 24–26
Activists, 21
Administrative decentralization, 96
Age
  and attitudes toward violence, 68–69
  and integrative commitment, 68, 70–71
  related to protest participation, 133
Ake, Claude, 54–55
Alford, Robert, 68n, 134n
Alienation
  of inactive population, 115
  of minority groups, 124
Allis Chalmers, 49
Almond, Gabriel, 106
Anomaly, 40–41
Antiwar protest, 107
Apathy, 14, 115
Atlanta, Ga., 2, 6

B

Banfield, Edward, 1, 7, 77
Barbee, Lloyd, 141, 151
Bauer, Raymond, 122
Becker, Dismas, 164
Behavior patterns, 19
Behavior problems, 80–83
Berrien, Lucille, 158, 163
Bisbing Business Research, 97n, 131n
Black elected officials, 7n
Black elites
  breadth of ambitions of, 166
  composite profile of, 165
  division of labor among, 165
  effects of mass attitudes on, 166
  fiscal expansionism of, 160
  likelihood of unity among, 29
  as likely to be elected only in black wards,
    156
  as likely to concentrate on nonelectoral
    activities, 158
  mass constraints on, 167
  no clear path to leadership for, 163
  opportunities for, 164

organizations that foster, 10
recent appearance of, in Milwaukee,
114–115
Black mayors, 2, 6, 7n, 8
Black political community, 5–6
cohesion of, 8–9
in Detroit, 9
ideological heterogeneity of, 7–8
Black population
growth of urban, 1
political fragmentation of, 165, 167
Blacks in urban politics, 6–7, 19
Black student protests, 141
Black–white coalitions, 102–104
Boredom, 99
Boston, Mass., 80
black officeholders in, 49
black population of, 42
black protest in, 81
crime rate of, compared to Milwaukee, 81
incidence of protest in, 48
segregation in, 42
socioeconomic characteristics of, 44
Bradley, Thomas, 158
Brier, Harold, 46, 97
Broad coalition, 23, 103
Byrd dynasty, 6

C

Campaign–contact cluster, 171
Campaign–contact index, 108–109
Campaigning, 124
Campbell, Angus, 107
Carmichael, Stokely, 7
Catholic church, 86
Catholic Herald Citizen, 25
Chicago, Ill., 6, 19, 42
Citizen participation, 58, 71
levels of conceptualization of, 89
survey question about, 87
understanding of, in Milwaukee, 89
Citizens Association of Wisconsin, 102
Citizens for Closed Housing. *See* Milwaukee
Citizens Civic Voice
Civil disorders. *See* Political violence
Civil rights demonstrations, 14, 107
Civil rights movement, 23, 131

Clark, Kenneth, 35
Class conflict, 8
Clausen, Aage, 39
Cleveland, O., 2, 8
Coalitions
attractiveness of blacks as partners in,
110–111, 123–124
based on pooled resources, 103
formula for relative contribution to, 112
Cohesion, 104–105, 123
racial differences in, in Milwaukee, 119
as shown by voting patterns, 117–118
Colonial analogy, 7
Commitment to integrative norms. *See*
Integrative commitment
Common Council, 46, 47, 52, 54, 85, 118,
119
Common View, 150
Communitarian perspective, 90–93
Community, 149
failure of, 77
as focus of this study, 22
lack of concern for, 98, 159
lack of importance of, as a problem in
Milwaukee, 82
as local control-sharing, 83–98
as neighborhood political identity, 78
quest for, 76
as shared norms, 78–83
Community Action, 85, 87
Community control, 83–98
attitudes toward, in Milwaukee, 93
development of the ideology of, 78
familiarity with, in Milwaukee, 84
levels of conceptualization of, 88
rejection of, and the communitarian
perspective, 92
survey questions about, 87
Compromise
attitudes toward, 67
black rejection of, 67n
made unlikely by dramatic style, 152
may be biased, 58
may be considered fair or unfair, 57
as necessary for conflict resolution, 53–54
as necessary to political integration, 57
norm of, 25
unpopularity of, in black community, 151
Conference of U.S. Mayors, 1972, 40

Conflict, 17–19, 27–28
  consensus on norms about resolution of,
    62–71
  as dependent on group strength, 104–105
  potential for, 18
  related to mass convergence or divergence,
    20–21
  types of, 18
  whites likely to win in, 123
Congress of Racial Equality (CORE),
    141–142
Contacts with officials, 104, 106, 119–124
Control-sharing, 92
  absence of mass support for, 97, 159
  attitudes toward, in Milwaukee, 93
  black elites not likely to pursue, 160
  black support for, 92
  as a concept, 87
  definition of, 83n–84n
  as an elite demand, 98–99
  freedom of elites to define, 99
  likelihood that elites will abandon, 99–100
  as a poorly articulated focus of the search
    for community, 90
  and type of political activity, 91n–92n
  understanding of, in Milwaukee, 86–87
Conventional efficacy, 71–73
Conventional participation, 119
  combined with protest in hybrid strategies,
    164
  related to protest participation, 153, 157,
    162
  related to status, 153
Conventional political activity
  as focus of study, 22
  as path to leadership for white elites,
    161–163
  white domination of, 149
Conventional political acts, 106
Conventional problems, 80–83, 100
Conventional style. *See* Political styles
Convergent cooperation
  necessary conditions for, 22–23
  variants of, 23
Cooperation, 17–19, 27
  related to mass convergence or divergence,
    20–21
  and similarity of goals, 18
  types of, 18

Council on Urban Life, 86, 97
Cross-sectional surveys, 37–40
Crump machine, 6

D

Dahl, Robert, 12
Dahrendorf, Ralf, 17–18
Daley, Richard, 45, 47
Dawson machine, 19
Dayton, O., 2
Decentralization, 83n
De facto segregation, 141
Democratic party, 118
Depression, the, 42
Detroit, Mich., 2, 9, 64, 131n
  satisfaction with police in, 96
  school decentralization in, 24n, 94n
  trust in government in, 61
Deutsch, Karl, 55
De Visé, Pierre, 43
Dexter, Lewis A., 122
Divergent conflict, 151
  necessary conditions for, 26–27
  variants of, 27–28
Downs, Anthony, 3
Downsian model, 3
Dramatic style of leadership, 151–152
Dymally, Mervyn, 61n

E

Eagles Club, 49
Economic survival, 83
Edelman, Murray, 12
Education
  and attitudes toward violence, 68–69
  and belief in political efficacy, 72
  and the communitarian perspective, 90–91
  and contacts with officials, 120–121
  and familiarity with control-sharing
    programs, 86–87
  and integrative commitment, 68, 70–71
  and participation in riots, 69n
  and perception of conventional urban
    problems, 82
  protest about, in Milwaukee, 141

of protesters, 136
related to national and local participation, 116–118
related to political participation, 113–114
related to protest participation, 133–135, 154
of Type I respondents, 153
of Type II respondents, 156
Electoral effort, formula for, 111
Elites
as constrained by unstable situations, 54
and control-sharing, 90, 99
conventional issues as a path to power for, 100
definition of, 3
dependence of, on masses, 4, 12–13, 29, 148
existence of, in racial communities, 10
functions of, for masses, 12
interrelationship of masses and, 11–17
mass constraint of, 14
mass pressures on, 19
mass support for, 13–14
opportunities for, 148–165
problems for, 73–74
rationality of, 3
selection and legitimation of, 13
Else, Arthur, 118
Equity, 62, 66
Etzioni, Amitai, 132n, 154

F

Fagan, Joseph, 152
Federation of Independent Community Schools, 86
Fein, Edith, 36
Fiscal conservatism, 160
Flaming, Karl H., 124n, 158, 159
Friedman, R., 122n

G

Gallup poll, 81
Gamson, William, 16–17, 111n
Gary, Ind., 2, 8
Gibson, Kenneth, 40n
Gittel, Marilyn, 94
Givens, John, 102

Goals
complimentary, identical, or incompatible, 75
degree of racial agreement on, 159
dissimilarity of, and potential for conflict, 18
and divergent conflict, 26–27
as an element of mass pressure on elites, 19
indicated by underlying preferences, 76
indicators of, 21–22
and institutionalized competition, 26
similarity of, required for cooperation, 18
Goodman and Kruskal's gamma, 134n
Gottschalk, Matthew, 164
Government, attitudes toward, 56, 59–62
Grand Rapids, Mich., 2
Groppi, James, 25–26, 43, 46, 48, 51–52, 101, 139, 141, 142, 151, 164
Group legitimacy, 137–138
Group memberships
and perception of conventional urban problems, 82
related to protest participation, 154
of Type II respondents, 156
Group powerlessness, 137–138
Groups, definition of, 3–4
Group strength, 104–105, 123–124
Gurr, Ted Robert, 56n

H

Hamilton, Charles, 7
Harlem, N.Y., 35, 64n
Harrington, Michael, 1
Harris poll, 107
Hartman, Elizabeth, 31n
Harwell, Larry, 84–85
Hatcher, Richard, 8
Hevesi, Alan, 94
History of blacks in urban politics, 6
Hoan, Daniel, 45
Holden, Matthew, 5, 8, 9, 127n
Home ownership
and the communitarian perspective, 91
and integrative commitment, 68, 70–71
and perception of conventional urban problems, 82
related to national and local participation, 116–118

related to political participation, 113
related to protest participation, 136–137
Housing, 81, 83
Humphrey, Hubert, 118
Hybrid coalitions, 103

I

Inactive population
  alienation of the, 115
  black, 108–109
  and conventional norms, 115
  low status of the, 113–114
  potential for mobilizing the, 112–113,
    114, 116
  as an untapped resource, 105, 115
Income
  and the communitarian perspective, 90–91
  and perception of conventional urban
    problems, 82
  of protesters, 136
  related to national and local participation,
    116–118
  related to political participation, 113–114
  related to protest participation, 133–135,
    154
  of Type I respondents, 153
  of Type II respondents, 156
Increased spending, 160
Indianapolis, Ind.
  black officeholders in, 49
  black population of, 42
  no riot in, 48
  segregation in, 42–43
  socioeconomic characteristics of, 44
Indices of conventional political participation.
  See Political participation indices
Individual efficacy, 71–73
Instability, 149–151, 166
Institutionalized competition, 26–27
Institutionalized pathology, 35
Integrative attitudes, 19, 21–22
Integrative commitment, 58
  and accommodation, 24
  and divergent conflict, 26–27
  implications of, for elites, 53–54
  and institutionalized competition, 26
  racial differences in, 63–71, 148–149
  related to age, 70–71

related to education, 70–71
related to home ownership, 70–71
related to status, 68–69
Integrative elements, measurement of, 59–71
Integrative norms, 55, 58, 150
Interdenominational Ministerial Alliance,
  150
Interracial conflict, 112
Interracial political relationships, 4–5,
  20–28, 166
Interviews, 33, 36–37
Isaacson, H. Lawrence, 31n

J

Jurgell, Cynthia M., 31n
Juvenile delinquency, 78

K

Kansas City, Mo., 6
Kerner Commission, 48, 69n, 97
Kish technique, 33
Klein, B., 122n

L

Letter-writing campaigns, 15
Lewis, Michael, 125n
Liebow, Elliot, 37
Lindsay, John, 99
Lipsky, Michael, 13, 25, 144, 145
Local participation index. *See* Political
  participation index
Longitudinal surveys, 38
Low-status population, 113–114
Los Angeles, Cal., 2, 158

M

Mahaney, Thomas, 164
Maier, Henry, 151
  and black voting patterns, 111–112,
    118–119
  few blacks appointed by, 159
  and the Model Cities controversy, 85
  1968 campaign of, 101–102

and the 1967 riot, 150, 152
and the open-housing campaign, 51–52
powerful position of, 47
profile of, 45–47
relationship of, with blacks, 46
Marquette University, 86
Marx, Gary, 14, 64n, 144n
Massell, Sam, 6
Masses
    apathy of, as a constraint on elites, 14
    behavior and belief patterns of, 17–19
    elements of pressures on elites by, 19
    elite dependence on, 12–13
    influence of, on elite opportunities, 148,
        166
    influence of, on interracial politics, 147
    interracial convergence and divergence of,
        19–21
    interrelationship of elites and, 11–17
    trust of, for elites, 16–17
    without leaders, 11
Mass initiatives, 15
Mass preferences, importance of, 2, 4
Matthews, Donald R., 7, 109
Mayoral elections
    black voting patterns in, 8
    in Milwaukee, 101–102, 111–112,
        118–119
Memphis, Tenn., 6
    black officeholders in, 49
    black population of, 42
    political violence in, 48
    segregation in, 42–43
    socioeconomic characteristics of, 44
Menominee River valley, 43
Milbrath, Lester, 125n
Milwaukee, Wis.
    black elected officials in, 124n, 158
    black officeholders in, 49
    black officials in service organizations in,
        159
    black percentage of electorate in, 111
    black population of, 42
    blacks in appointed posts in, 112
    dispute over Model Cities program in, 85
    economy of, 43–44
    emergence of a black political community
        in, 48
    history of black community in, 42–43
    likelihood of stable interracial politics in,
        73
    long mayoral terms in, 45
    mayoral elections in, 101–102, 111–112,
        118–119
    open-housing campaign in, 25–26, 43, 46,
        48, 51–52, 54, 63, 74, 101–102,
        139–142
    opinions about government in, 60–61
    overpowering position of whites in, 124
    Police and Fire Commission, 97–98
    problems identified by residents of, 80–83
    profile of, 41–49
    profile of black leaders in, 165
    protest in, 48–49, 125–146
    quality of life in, 45
    racial composition of, 41–42
    racial confrontation in, 119
    racial divergence on normative
        commitment in, 63–71
    ratio of black officeholders to black
        population in, 47
    riot of 1967 in, 46, 48, 64, 152
    as a sample city, 49–50
    school boycotts in, 46, 48
    school decentralization in, 86
    segregation in, 42–43
    small-town atmosphere of, 41
    socioeconomic characteristics of, 43–45
    structure of power in, 47
    voting patterns in, by race, 118–119
Milwaukee Citizens Civic Voice, 51, 54, 102
Milwaukee County Property Owners
        Association, 102
Milwaukee Courier, 102
Milwaukee Organization of Organizations
        (Triple O), 84, 85, 86, 101
Milwaukee United School Integration
        Committee (MUSIC), 48, 141, 164
Milwaukee Urban League, 150
Model Cities, 85, 86, 87, 92, 98
Moynihan, Daniel P., 77, 78

N

National Association for the Advancement
        of Colored People (NAACP), 141, 142
National Association for the Advancement
        of Colored People (NAACP) Youth
        Council, 51–52, 54, 142
National participation index. *See* Political
        participation index

National Welfare Rights Organization, 48,
142, 164
Newark, N.J., 2, 9, 40n, 64
New Orleans, La., 6, 48
black officeholders in, 49
black population of, 42
no riot in, 48
segregation in, 42
socioeconomic characteristics of, 44
New York, N.Y., 6, 85–86, 99
Nie, Norman, 8, 92, 120n, 121n
Nisbet, Robert, 77–78
Nixon, Richard, 118
Normative divergence, 54

O

Oakland, Cal., 27
Occupation
and the communitarian perspective, 91
and familiarity with control-sharing
programs, 86–87
and perception of conventional urban
problems, 82
related to national and local participation,
116–118
related to political participation, 113–114
related to protest participation, 134–135,
155
of Type I respondents, 153
Officials, contact with. *See* Contact with
officials
Olsen, Marvin, 107
Olson, David, 64n, 122n
Open housing, Milwaukee campaign for. *See*
Milwaukee
Openness of political system, 65–66
Organizational memberships
related to political participation, 113–114
related to protest participation, 133–136
Oversampling, 34

P

Parallel pluralistic competition, 26
Parenti, Michael, 9
Participation clusters, 108
Peaceful politics
commitment to, 56–57

commitment to, by race, 64–65
white rejection of, 74
Pendergast machine, 6
Phillips, Vel, 52, 118
Phoenix, Ariz.
black officeholders in, 49
black population of, 42
segregation in, 42
socioeconomic characteristics of, 44
Pitkin, Hanna, 119n
Pitts, Orville, 119
Pockets of opportunity, 160–161, 163–164,
166
Polarized conflict, 28
Police, 96–98
Police and Fire Commission (Milwaukee),
97–98
Political activity, 91n
Political campaigns, 15
Political community, 54–55
Political groups, 11
Political efficacy, 58, 71–74
Political integration
definition of, 53
elements of, 55–58
how to determine, 22
lack of, in Milwaukee open-housing
controversy, 52
measurement of elements of, 59–71
relevance of, to American urban politics,
53
requires agreement on formal mechanisms
for conflict resolution, 57–58
requires belief that the system is open, 57
and support for the political system, 16
Political integration index, 70–71, 115,
148–149, 162, 163
Political mobilization, 113–115
Political participation indices, 108–117, 153
derivation of, 169–171
intercorrelation of, 171
local, 116–118
national, 116–118
Political styles, 15–16, 103
advantages of using attitudes to
distinguish, 108
attitudes toward, 105–107
distinguished by degree of social approval,
105
effects of, on types of cooperation or
conflict, 18
as elements of mass pressures on elites, 19

elusiveness of, as a concept, 106
indicators of, 21–22
and pragmatic coalition, 24
racial differences in, 153
and strong coalition and broad coalition, 23
and stylized pluralistic competition, 26
and tacit coalition, 25–26
Political violence, 48, 65
attitudes toward, and age, 68–70
attitudes toward, and status, 68–70
commitment to avoid, 56–57
destructiveness of, 56n
racial differences in attitudes toward, 63–65
Pollution, 83
Pool, Ithiel de Sola, 122
Powerlessness, 132, 137–138, 144–146
Pragmatic conflict, 27
Premise 1, 2
Premise 2, 3
Premise 3, 3
Premise 4, 3
Premise 5, 3
Pretest, 33
Professional educators, 94–96
Proposition 1, 149
Proposition 2, 151
Proposition 3, 151
Proposition 4, 152
Proposition 5, 156
Proposition 6, 156
Proposition 7, 158
Proposition 8, 159
Proposition 9, 160
Proposition 10, 161
Proposition 11, 163
Proposition 12, 164
Proposition 13, 164
Proposition 14, 164
Proposition 15, 165
Proposition 16, 166
Protest
and analogy to tacit coalition, 25n
attitudes toward, 126–139
as a bargaining process, 126
black activity in, 149
black institutionalization of, 143, 145–146
black support for, 15, 124, 127–129, 144n
as a civic duty, 129
definition of, 126

effectiveness of, 129, 138n
as focus of study, 22
as a function of race, 126–130
in hybrid strategies, 164
incidence of, in cities, 48
integral role of, in black community, 126, 144
as a manifestation of black identity, 23
as an opportunity for black elites, 146
organization of, 138–146
as a possible distraction from substantive issues, 27
possibility of interracial coalition in, 146
racial differences in attitudes toward, 127–130, 138–139
reasons for, 128
stable leadership of, in black community, 156
surveys of attitudes toward, 126–127
targets of, 140
at the University of Wisconsin-Madison, 33
use of, 138–146
white opposition to, 15, 33, 128–129
Protest duty, 129
Protest efficacy, 71–74
Protesters
definition of, 128n
degree of difference of, from their racial communities, 134–136, 139
as opportunities for black elites, 164
racial representation in Type II, 156
social characteristics of Type I, 153–154
social characteristics of Type II, 154–156
status of, 131–138, 144
Protest organizations, 142–143
Protest participation
on behalf of disadvantaged groups, 138, 144
as a complement to other political activity, 153
and impatience, 138
local focus of black, 139–141
racial differences in, 136
racial rates of, 133
related to conventional participation, 153–154, 157, 162
related to group legitimacy, 138
related to home ownership, 136–137
related to number of years lived in the city, 137

related to occupation, 155
related to powerlessness, 138, 144-145
related to status, 130-138, 144-145,
153-154
survey questions about, 133
weaknesses of earlier studies of, 131-132
Protest style. *See* Political styles
Prothro, James W., 7, 109
Pruitt-Igoe projects, 37

R

Race of interviewer, 36
Race riots, black support for, 127n
Racial conflict
based on specific issues, 98
about conventional issues, 100
Racial elites, existence of, 10
Racial tension, 81
perceived as a problem in Milwaukee, 83
Racial voting blocs, 26
Rainwater, Lee, 37
Raleigh, N.C., 2
Rates of political participation, 103-104
racial differences in, 109-110
Receptivity to political mobilization,
104-105, 123
Rent strikes, 15
Representation, 119
Residential mobility, 35
Residential segregation index, 42-43
Reuss, Henry, 45, 118
Richmond, Va., 6
Romani, J. H., 122n
Rustin, Bayard, 8

S

Saint Louis, Mo.
black officeholders in, 49
black population of, 42
political violence in, 48
segregation in, 42-43
socioeconomic characteristics of, 43-44
Sample population, 32-34
Sample surveys, 31-37
San Antonio, Tex.
black officeholders in, 49
black population of, 42

no riot in, 48
segregation in, 42-43
socioeconomic characteristics of, 44
San Diego, Cal.
black officeholders in, 49
black population of, 42
political violence in, 48
segregation in, 42
socioeconomic characteristics of, 44
San Francisco, Cal.
black officeholders in, 49
black population of, 42
incidence of protest in, 48
segregation in, 42
socioeconomic characteristics of, 44
Schattschneider, E. E., 18
Schelling, Thomas, 25
Schmandt, Henry, 49
School decentralization, 85-87, 98
attitudes toward, in Milwaukee, 93,
95-96
rationale for, 94
Schools
administrative decentralization of, 96
perceived as a problem in Milwaukee, 83
Scoble, Harry, 68n, 134n
Seale, Bobby, 27
Sears, David O., 127n
Single-city surveys, 40-41
Slesinger, Jonathan, 62n, 64, 97n,
130n-131n
Social Development Commission, 158-159
Social distance problem, 36
Social resources, 131-132
Sola Pool, Ithiel de, 122
South Side Neighborhood Association, 102
Stability, 28, 75
Statesmen, 152-153
Status
related to contacts with officials, 120-
121
related to familiarity with control-sharing,
86-87
related to political participation, 113-114
Stokes, Carl, 8
Stokes, Donald, 61
Stribling, Frank, 158, 163
Strong coalition, 23
Structure of opportunities, 14-17
Stylized pluralistic competition, 26
Student protest, attitudes toward, 107

Student protesters, 131
Survey response rate, 33

T

Tacit coalition, 103
Taeuber, Alma, 43
Taeuber, Karl, 43
Taft, Seth, 8
Tally's Corner, 37
Tammany Hall, 6
Taxes, 81
  perceived as a problem in Milwaukee, 83
Thompson, Daniel, 6
Tomlinson, T. M., 127n
Triple O. *See* Milwaukee Organization of
    Organizations
Trust in government, 55–56
  measurement of, 59–62
  racial differences in, 61–62
Typology of political relationships, 21–29
  uses of, 28–29

U

Underclasses, 132n
Undersampling, 34
Unemployment, 81, 83
U.S. Department of Housing and Urban
    Development (HUD), 85
University of Michigan Survey Research
    Center, 39, 61, 81, 96, 110n
University of Wisconsin–Madison, 33
University of Wisconsin–Milwaukee, 86
University of Wisconsin Survey Research
    Laboratory, 33
Urban black population, 1
Urban crisis, 76–80, 82
Urban Data Service, 85
Urban Institute, 45
Urban League, 150, 158

Urban Observatory, 96n
Urban renewal, 118

V

Verba, Sidney, 8, 92, 106, 120n, 121n
Verbal index, 108, 109
Verbal participation, 124
Verbal participation cluster, 171
Visibility, 104–105, 123
  and contacts with officials, 119, 123
Voter registration, 14
Voting, 57–58, 104, 106, 124
  attitudes toward, 69
  belief in efficacy of, 72
  interracial agreement on, 68
  protest as better or worse than, 129
  racial levels of, 110
  racial patterns of, 118
  related to social resources, 131
Voting cluster, 171
Voting index, 108–109

W

Walker, Jack, 9, 94n, 96, 131n
Wallace, George, 118
Walther, David, 101–102, 114–115, 119, 163
Walton, Hanes, 6
Warren, Roland, 7
Watts, Cal., 127n
White elites
  clear path to leadership for, 161, 163
  fiscal conservatism of, 160
  hybrid activists as opportunities for, 164
Wilson, James Q., 1, 6, 77, 78, 79, 80, 81,
    126n

Z

Zeidler, Frank, 45

A 6
B 7
C 8
D 9
E 0
F 1
G 2
H 3
I 4
J 5

Lewis and Clark College - Watzek Library

JS1112 .E57   wmain
Eisinger, Peter K./Patterns of interraci

3 5209 00302 1371